CALVIN'S C

Stephen Edmondson articulates a coherent Christology from Calvin's commentaries and his *Institutes*. He argues that, through the medium of Scripture's history, Calvin, the biblical humanist, renders a Christology that seeks to capture both the breadth of God's multifaceted grace enacted in history, and the hearts of God's people formed by history. What emerges is a picture of Christ as the Mediator of God's covenant through his threefold office of priest, king and prophet. With Christ's work as the pivot on which Calvin's Christology turns, Christ's person becomes the goal to which it drives: for Christ mediates our union with God only through union with himself. This is the first significant volume to explore Calvin's Christology in several decades. It clarifies an important but perplexing subject in Calvin studies through its focus on Christ's work in history and allows Calvin a voice in the current theological conversation about Christology.

STEPHEN EDMONDSON is Assistant Professor of Church History, Virginia Theological Seminary.

£ 25

CALVIN'S CHRISTOLOGY

STEPHEN EDMONDSON

Virginia Theological Seminary

PUBLISHED BY THE PRESS SYNDICATE OF THE UNIVERSITY OF CAMBRIDGE
The Pitt Building, Trumpington Street, Cambridge, United Kingdom

CAMBRIDGE UNIVERSITY PRESS
The Edinburgh Building, Cambridge, CB2 2RU, UK
40 West 20th Street, New York, NY 10011–4211, USA
477 Williamstown Road, Port Melbourne, VIC 3207, Australia
Ruiz de Alarcón 13, 28014 Madrid, Spain
Dock House, The Waterfront, Cape Town 8001, South Africa

http://www.cambridge.org

First published 2004

Printed in the United Kingdom at the University Press, Cambridge

Typeface Adobe Garamond 11/12.5 pt.   *System* LATEX 2ε   [TB]

A catalogue record for this book is available from the British Library

Library of Congress Cataloguing in Publication data
Edmondson, Stephen.
Calvin's Christology / Stephen Edmondson.
p.   cm.
Includes bibliographical references and index
ISBN 0 521 83371 X (hardback) – ISBN 0 521 54154 9 (paperback)
1. Jesus Christ – Person and offices.   2. Calvin, Jean, 1509–1564.   1. Title.
BT203.E36   2004
232′.092 – dc22   2003055898

ISBN 0 521 83371 X
ISBN 0 521 54154 9

To my Mother and Father

Contents

vii

Preface

If I do not at once begin by stating my reasons for the plan I have
adopted in the composition of this Work, it will undoubtedly incur the
censures of many . . . [S]ome . . . will think that I have inconsiderately
and therefore unnecessarily altered the order which the Holy Spirit
himself has prescribed to us. Now, there cannot be a doubt that what
was dictated to Moses was excellent in itself, and perfectly adapted for
the instruction of the people; but what he delivered in Four Books, it
has been my endeavour so to collect and arrange, that it might seem
I was trying to improve upon it, which would be an act of audacity
akin to sacrilege . . . [But] I have no other intention than, by this
arrangement, to assist unpracticed readers, so that they might more
easily, more commodiously, and more profitably acquaint themselves
with the writings of Moses; and whosoever would benefit from my
labours should understand that I would by no means withdraw him
from the study of each separate book, but simply direct him by this
compendium to a definite object; lest he should, as often happens, be
led astray through ignorance of any regular plan.
Preface to the *Commentary on the Last Four Books of Moses*, pp. xiv–xv.

The project of this book is, to some degree, a synthetic one, as I have
gathered Calvin's diffuse discussions of the person and work of Christ and
organized them under categories that Calvin suggests. This synthetic task
is necessary in my endeavor to understand Calvin's Christology, and it
evinces the simple reality that any act of understanding is always to some
degree an act of accommodation. It is an organization of material in a
manner that makes sense to the reader so that some meaning between two
parties might be shared. It makes no sense to speak of an unaccommodated understanding of any human being, particularly of a human being
with whom we can no longer converse and whose world is separated from
ours by four hundred and fifty years. To read carefully, even in the original
language, is always already an act of translation. We can distinguish faithful accommodations that are attentive to categories and experiences with

which a writer is working from unfaithful accommodations, but we also might acknowledge, and even celebrate, the possibility of truly productive accommodations that tease out meanings from a text that are not readily apparent on a first reading.

Such accommodations are not claims to understand writers better than they understood themselves, but they do rely on the principle that all of us (or at least those of us who are self-reflective) will understand ourselves better through conversation with those who will make connections between our thoughts and feelings that we never imagined. The synthetic dimension of this project is, I believe, a faithful accommodation of Calvin's work, and it will be productive for the community of Calvin readers. Would it have been productive for Calvin? Would he, at the end of this conversation, have responded: "I never thought of it in that way"? Or would he have replied: "Well, of course, that's what I've been saying all along"? I do not know, but I am convinced that he would have recognized the thinking in this book as his own.

Simply to speak of Calvin's *Christology* is, to some degree, an act of accommodation, insofar as Calvin wrote no independent Christology and, indeed, never used the term "Christology." But to ask about Calvin's Christology is fruitful, insofar as it allows us to achieve a clarity about a topic central to Calvin's thinking, and it is faithful if it does not serve as a Trojan horse, bearing within it a twenty-first-century agenda. I have tried to avoid in this work the mistake of the twentieth-century discussion of the knowledge of God in Calvin – a discussion that was misdirected not in its question, but in its hopes, through this question, to resolve a contemporary debate.

Faithful versus unfaithful accommodation is a matter of agenda, and we must be wary of how subtly our agendas can infiltrate our understanding. It is ironic, for example, that one recent call for faithfulness in our reading of Calvin asks us to eliminate harmonization of Calvin's various expressions of his theological thinking and concern for any systematic unity of his thought or his relevance for the modern theological discussion, as these occlude access to the historical Calvin.[1] Whatever the merits of this methodology as a way of doing history (and I question whether a lack of concern for the internal or external coherence of a subject's thinking serves our understanding of that subject in any substantial way), it begins from an agenda that is distinctly modern and thus imports into our reading of Calvin a set of concerns that Calvin would little recognize.

---

[1] Richard Muller, *The Unaccommodated Calvin: Studies in the Foundation of a Theological Tradition* (New York: Oxford University Press, 2000), pp. 3–17, esp. pp. 6, 10.

Indeed, when we stand before the diversity of Calvin's theological exposition, we often find ourselves in a position similar to Calvin as he prepared to comment on the last four books of the Pentateuch. We may be convinced that he ordered his teaching in a manner "perfectly adapted for the instruction of the people," but at the same time we feel that we are called to alter this order with the intention "by this arrangement, to assist unpracticed readers, so that they might more easily, more commodiously, and more profitably acquaint themselves" with Calvin's thought. We do this neither to rip Calvin out of his context, nor to deflect our attention from each expression of Calvin's thought in its uniqueness. Rather, we hope through such work to direct readers "to a definite object; lest [they] should, as often happens, be led astray through ignorance of any regular plan." Again, this work focuses more on Calvin than on his context, not to denigrate the importance of that context, but to provide a hypothesis about the nature of Calvin's Christological thinking from which such historical work might proceed.

Acknowledgments

"Acknowledgments" is too slight a term to carry the burden of thanks that I would offer. The projects of our lives are possible, the pains we encounter in them bearable, and the joys that we harvest from them attainable only in the context of the communities of friends and family (and what is the dividing line between these two?) that surround us. This book is the labor of several years, and yet there is a lifetime of gratitude caught up in its production.

To my family, Linda, Mary, Art, Clarice, David, and, especially, my mother and father, Clarice and Bud, I owe all the resources that I brought to this work, through their support of me and, even more, through their formation of me in their love, discipline, humor, and imagination. Without a sure foundation, no house can stand, and they are my foundation.

Many thanks to those who taught me at Yale: Marilyn McCord Adams, Brevard Childs, Margaret Farley, Paul Holmer, David Kelsey, George Lindbeck, Cyril O'Regan, Katherine Tanner, Nicholas Walterstorff, and Serena Jones, in particular, who advised me through the dissertation that became this book. So many of the questions that I brought to Calvin grew out of my conversations with them. The rigor with which I pursued these questions was instilled in me by them; and the sense of theological vision that allowed me, perhaps in some small way, to see what Calvin might have seen, was rooted in the vista on God, world, and humanity to which they guided me. To fully acknowledge my debt to them, I must go beyond their contributions to this book and thank them for teaching me how to teach with dedication, passion, and humility. I only hope that I have learned a bit of this lesson.

My colleagues in the graduate program at Yale – Barbara Blodgett, Jaime Clark-Soles, Shannon and Seth Craigo-Snell, Antony Dugdale, Niles Eastman, John Geter, Amy Laura Hall, Karin Harmon, Ruthanna Hooke, Kevin Mongraine, Stephen Penna, Sarah Pinnock, Stephen Ray, Warren Smith, George Sumner, John Utz, Ann Wierda, and Anna Williams – supplied me with laughter, warmth, and stimulation, so that we made a potentially hermetic life a community. Mark Retherford was a supportive housemate, a debate partner, and a parent to our dog Abby; Kym Lucas was a gracious host in my last semester. But most particularly I must celebrate Kaudie McLean, whose theological insight, personal compassion, courage, and strength made her a welcome partner in our journey through the limbo of graduate school. She also has lent me her editorial expertise for this work, ridding it of much of its clumsiness and endowing it, I hope, with some measure of grace.

I thank the Virginia Theological Seminary for allowing me to participate in the ministry of formation of leaders for the Church. I am grateful that they have provided a space for the development as well as the conveyance of the Church's ongoing tradition. This book would not be possible had they not offered me the time and the encouragement to see it through. My colleagues here, in their generosity of spirit and their dedication to the Church's mission, have provided me with a model of what an academic community might strive to be. They have all supported me. I especially thank Kate Sonderregger and Jeff Hensley for their willingness to read and offer advice on this text along the way.

Without the Christian communities of which I have been a part – Trinity, All Saints, St. John's, Ascension, St. Cyprian's, the Middlesex Cluster, and St. Mark's – I would have been inattentive to the breadth of vision that Calvin displays. The willingness of folks within these communities to share their lives with me and to teach me life through this oblation has opened for me a richer understanding of all that Christ might do to touch us.

The staff at Cambridge University Press have been a joy to work with, both in their careful attention to quality and in the persistence of their confidence in my work. Kevin Taylor and Katharina Brett were gifted shepherds of a sometimes bewildered sheep, and the entire editorial staff have shown an expertise and professionalism that have been a delight to work with.

Finally, I thank my wife, Cyndi Hess, for her quiet calm, her gentle prodding, her willingness to challenge, and her consistent conviction. This project might never have come to completion without her presence in my life.

Battles' translation of the *Institutes* is reproduced from *Calvin: Institutes of Christian Religion*, Library of Christian Classics, ed. John T. McNeill, with kind permission of Westminster John Knox Press. The *Calvin Theological Journal* is gratefully acknowledged for their permission to print quotations from their translations of Calvin's letters to the Polish Brethren.

Introduction

Bernard's admonition is worth remembering: The name of Jesus is not only light but also food; it is also oil, without which all food of the soul is dry; it is salt, without whose seasoning whatever I set before us is insipid; finally, it is honey in the mouth, melody in the ear, rejoicing in the heart, and at the same time medicine. Every discourse in which his name is not spoken is without savor.

John Calvin, *The Institutes*

Calvin's theological writing and thinking are a variegated field, heavy laden and ready for harvest, and yet so densely planted and so thickly intertwined in its growth that it is difficult to state in any definitive manner exactly what he has sown or the pattern by which he has sown it. Thus, among the reapers, there is confusion over what we should gather and the best method for our gleaning, not to mention the matter of separating the wheat, or whatever fruits we are searching for, from the tares. There is, simply, so much there and so much that seems at tension with itself, not only in terms of its content, but also in terms of its methodological underpinnings and its authorial purpose. In the past century, we have been told that Calvin's theology is centered on the sovereignty of God, predestination, Christology, the Trinity, the knowledge of God, and faith, and that it has no center at all; that he is a theologian who systematized Reformation insights and that he is a pastor whose interest lay not in any systematic presentation of theology, but in the spiritual nurture of his wards; that his theology is structured by pedagogical and consolatory and apologetic and polemical rhetorical ends, and that it is structured by the many theologies that can be found in Scripture. Calvin is a natural theologian and a theologian to whom natural theology is anathema. He has been called a theologian of one book, his *Institutes*, while in this book he argues that it is subservient to the many books of his commentaries. He is even a man who, in his thinking and writing, manifests two personalities – he is both medieval and modern, both a schoolman and a humanist, a practitioner of dialectical thinking, which dialect is resolved through the accommodation of the Divine Orator to us very human subjects. And the remarkable thing is, this all is in some sense correct. The field is overgrown. It is no wonder that Barth was provoked to comment: "Calvin is a cataract, a primeval forest, a demonic power . . . I lack completely the means, the suction cups, even to assimilate this phenomenon, not to speak of presenting it adequately."[1]

In such a tangle, crops will go unharvested and plantings be neglected. Indeed, Calvin's complex theological ecology almost insures a consistently partial ingathering, but it would no doubt dismay Calvin to discover that his Christology – that savor-making seasoning – is too often ignored, under-utilized, or mis-taken in the cornucopia of modern Calvin scholarship. We have passed over the first fruits, he would decry. It is not that we disdain Christology or Calvin's thoughts on the matter, but readers of Calvin seem unable either to discern or to explain its content or its purpose in convincing detail. Thus, Serene Jones claims that we are often simply baffled by Calvin on this *locus*.[2]

This bafflement is most obvious in a work like Bouwsma's, where references to Christ are scant and trifling, but it is apparent in more theological readings of Calvin as well.[3] Brian Armstrong, in an excellent essay on a rhetorical strategy that helps to shape the *Institutes*, offers the strong claim that "Calvin's entire theology is conditioned by his understanding of redemption through Christ," that Calvin's chief concern, humanity's relationship with God, is accomplished in Christ and our incorporation into his body.[4] Such a gesture obviously takes Calvin's Christology seriously. Yet, within the article as a whole, Armstrong both rejects without comment any notion of Christology as the doctrinal center of the *Institutes* and skips over the specifically Christological sections of the *Institutes* when he recounts the contents of the work as a whole.[5] Armstrong appears unable to cash out his claim for the significance of Christology in Calvin's thinking.

There are more substantive recent appraisals of Calvin's Christology. Richard Muller offers what, in many ways, is a précis of the argument of this book in his brief observations about both the soteriological emphasis

[1] From Barth's letter to Eduard Thurneysen, June 8, 1922, found in T. H. L. Parker, *Calvin's Old Testament Commentaries* (Edinburgh: T. & T. Clark, 1986), cover page.
[2] Serene Jones, *Calvin and the Rhetoric of Piety* (Louisville: Westminster/John Knox, 1995), p. 44, n. 70.
[3] William Bouwsma, *John Calvin: A Sixteenth-Century Portrait* (New York: Oxford University Press, 1988).
[4] Brian Armstrong, "The Nature and Structure of Calvin's Thought According to the *Institutes*: Another Look," *John Calvin's Institutes: His Opus Magnum*, Proceedings of the Second South African Congress for Calvin Research (Potchefstroom: Potchefstroom University for Christian Higher Education, 1986), pp. 70, 61.
[5] Ibid., pp. 55, 71.

of Calvin's Christology, an emphasis manifested through the Christology's historical form in the context of the economy of salvation, and Calvin's privileging in his account of Christ's work over Christ's person.[6] However, within the scope of this earlier work, Muller is unable to flesh out more thoroughly these intimations, and, in a later work, when he takes up the structure of the *Institutes*, Christology has again fallen off the map.[7] Randall Zachman's construal of Calvin's Christology in his work on assurance in Calvin and Luther offers a portrayal that is accurate to the details and spirit of Calvin's work; perhaps this is the benefit of a dedicated exegesis of the argument of the *Institutes* in its entirety.[8] His emphasis on Christ as the fountain of every good thing through his life and work among us again sounds a theme that I develop in this work; but Zachman provides little framework that would helpfully synthesize the pieces of Calvin's Christology in their relationship to each other, and he mistakes a result of Christ's saving work as Mediator, that he is the image of the invisible Father, for the heart of this work. His difficulty is that he reads Christology from within Calvin's narrative of the human conscience rather than locating its proper narrative context within Calvin's theology, God's covenant history with God's chosen. So even here, where much of the substance of Calvin's Christology is laid to hand, there is a certain bafflement about the order and logic behind the substance.[9]

Calvin's adherence to the Reformation platform of *sola Christi* commits him to a certain Christocentrism in his theology, at least on a material if not on a formal level. His recollection of Bernard's counsel of the centrality of Jesus-talk to any reflection on God and the world serves as his earnest to make good on that commitment. If we want to make good on our

[6] Richard Muller, *Christ and the Decree* (Durham, NC: Labyrinth Press, 1986), p. 28.
[7] Muller, *The Unaccommodated Calvin: Studies in the Foundation of a Theological Tradition* (New York: Oxford University Press, 2000), pp. 118–139. Note particularly his dismissal of Battles' claim for a particular Christological sequencing within the structure of the 1559 *Institutes*; this rejection, given the lack of a counter-claim for the proper Christological sequencing of the text, serves as a rejection of any Christological dimension to the *ordo* of the work (see p. 135).
[8] Randall Zachman, *The Assurance of Faith* (Minneapolis: Fortress Press, 1993), pp. 159–187. Such a commitment can help one read Calvin's Christology substantively, but it does not assure it. You find, on the one hand, in Wendel's comprehensive study of the *Institutes* a discussion of Christology which, though misguided at places (so I will argue), is complete and substantial. On the other hand, you find in Niesel (as I will discuss shortly) a discussion of Christology within the context of the *Institutes* which entirely skips over Calvin's discussion of Christ's work – what I will argue is the very center of his Christology.
[9] Robert Peterson's treatment of Calvin on Atonement falls into this same category. In his work he explicates the diversity of images through which Calvin would highlight the fullness of Christ's saving work, but he provides no integrating principle which provides some doctrinal coherence. (Robert Peterson, *Calvin's Doctrine of the Atonement*, [Phillipsburg, New Jersey: Presbyterian and Reformed Publishing Company, 1983]).

desire to gather the full harvest of Calvin's sowing, then we must strive for an understanding of Calvin's Christology that is not merely adequate to what he says in places, or reflective of a theme echoed here or there within his entire corpus, but that captures the full-throated, robust hymn of Jesus' saving work that Calvin would sing to a Church otherwise bereft of God without the clarity of this Gospel. Hence this book on understanding Calvin's Christology.

In the following pages, I hope to offer at least an initial persuasive answer to the question of Calvin's Christology, an answer that allows those who wish to enter into conversation with this book a greater appreciation of the tenor and dynamic of Calvin's Christological discourse and of the role that this discourse plays in his theology overall.[10] My answer is persuasive to the extent that it presents a Christology accurate to Calvin, especially as it is coherent, richly funded, and forcefully centered. Therefore, this book is integrally informed by three methodological decisions that are consistent each with the others.

First, I draw my material largely from Calvin's commentaries on the Old and New Testaments as well as from the 1559 *Institutes*. This decision reflects the formal recognition, with so many Calvin scholars of late, that the *Institutes* are in many ways best understood as a complement to his copious exegetical writings, not as their compendium;[11] but it also conveys my conviction that Calvin's commitment to the interpretation of Scripture as his primary theological task bears fruit in the depth and diversity of

---

[10] I, of course, am not the first to write on Calvin's Christology, both in its details and in its relationship to his theology overall. Niesel has attempted to interpret the whole of the *Institutes* from a Christological perspective, Willis has explicated the whole of Calvin's Christology under the rubric of its relationship to the *extra-calvinisticum*, and Van Buren and Jansen have explored Calvin's notion of Christ's atoning work and Christ's threefold office, respectively, just to name a few: Wilhelm Niesel, *The Theology of John Calvin*, trans. Harold Knight (Philadelphia: The Westminster Press, 1956); David Willis, *Calvin's Catholic Christology*, Studies in Medieval and Reformation Thought, vol. 2 (Leiden: E. J. Brill, 1966); Paul Van Buren, *Christ in our Place: The Substitutionary Character of Calvin's Doctrine of Reconciliation* (Edinburgh: Oliver and Boyd, 1957); J. F. Jansen, *Calvin's Doctrine of the Work of Christ* (London: James Clark and Co., Ltd., 1956). Each of these texts is insightful with respect to Calvin's theological project, and each has contributed to the production of this book, as the body of my text will manifest. Yet I also must aver that none of them through their exposition have secured for Calvin's Christology its rightful place in any interpretation of Calvin's thought. They are incomplete, leaving important questions lingering. Thus the lack of scholarly consensus.

[11] See, for example: T. H. L. Parker, *Calvin's New Testament Commentaries* (London: SCM Press, 1971), chs. 1–2; Edward E. Dowey, Jr., "The Structure of Calvin's Thought as Influenced by the Twofold Knowledge of God," in *Calvinus Ecclesiae Genevensis Custos*, W. Neuser, ed. (Frankfurt: Peter Lang, 1984), p. 141; Elsie Anne McKie, "Exegesis, Theology, And Development," in *Probing the Reformed Tradition: Historical Studies in Honor of Edward A. Dowey, Jr.*, Brian Armstrong and Elsie Anne McKie, eds. (Louisville: Westminster/John Knox, 1989), pp. 154–172; Muller, *The Unaccommodated Calvin*, pp. 140–158.

Christological material found in his biblical commentaries.[12] I have chosen to work largely with the 1559 *Institutes* over against the earlier iterations of this text because we find the culmination of his thinking within it, especially as it is the primary beneficiary of his exegetical work on the Gospels and the books of the Old Testament.

Second, I treat the Christological picture that emerges from this consideration holistically, not developmentally. Calvin, at least from his Gospel commentaries on, works within one general Christological framework through to the end of his writings. He further defines the picture within this framework with successive works, but the overall picture is never discontinuous with what preceded it.[13] One advantage to taking his Christological thinking as a whole is that it allows me to establish a baseline Christology that might be amended or questioned by further work with Calvin, rather than leaving the reader only with fragmentary images that allow us little traction on the broader question.

Finally, I take as the center of Calvin's Christology his repeated titular definition in the 1559 *Institutes* of Christ as the Mediator and articulate the form and content of Calvin's teaching around this central focus. In the *Institutes*, Calvin not only introduces his Christology proper (II.xii–xvii) with a discussion of Christ as the Mediator, he also begins his narration of the broader story of God's saving history with God's chosen after the Fall under this same rubric, arguing that now, "no knowledge of God apart from the Mediator has had power unto salvation" (II.vi.1). Calvin repeatedly returns to this designation in his exegesis of Christ's person and work in the *Institutes*, and we also find that it pervades the Christological passages in his commentaries.

A variety of implications are entailed by Calvin's choice of this central moniker for Christ, but let me call our attention to one of them here at the start. For Calvin, a focus on Christ as the Mediator makes the doctrine of Christ's office in its relationship to Christ's work the fundamental organizing principle in his Christology. It is, to begin with, a statement about the centrality of Christ's office so that his entire discussion of the metaphysics of Christ's person is undertaken within the context of this initial statement.

---

[12] I largely neglect Calvin's sermons in this work, except for his *Sermon on the Deity of Christ*. Their tendency toward ad hoc doctrinal development and pastoral application, along with the sheer amount of material, made them less helpful for this project. A useful future endeavor would be to ask how the Christological picture that emerges here has play in Calvin's preaching.

[13] I would understand Jansen's insight that Calvin comes to grips with the prophetic dimension of Christ's threefold office only late in the game (so that in the early instantiations of the *Institutes* he begins with only a twofold office of priest and king) as an example of development within a framwork and not a reworking of the entire framework (Jansen, *The Work of Christ*).

Calvin's intention, I shall argue, is to point his reader to the culmination of his Christology, how Christ accomplished our salvation (ii.xvi), given his claim that Christology as a whole is directed to this one objective, that we seek salvation in Christ (ii.xvi.1). We fully understand this exposition of Christ's saving work only as we grasp the relationship between this work and Christ's mediatorial office. In some sense, this commitment on my part is a substantiation and expansion of Oberman's comment that in Calvin there is a shift of accent "from a natures-Christology to an offices-Christology, converging towards a Mediator-theology."[14]

The task that I have laid out is primarily analytic and descriptive in character, but to carry it out I must include a synthetic, constructive dimension as well. I would argue that the perplexity over Calvin's Christology is due, in part, to the lack of organization and incomplete expression of its form in Calvin's writings. The Christology in the *Institutes*, for example, does not communicate completely and clearly all that Calvin has to say on this matter, which is not surprising, given that Calvin's purpose for the book was not exhaustive, doctrinal exposition. My purpose, however, is such exposition. Calvin was not interested in writing a Christology, but it would be of great benefit to Calvin's modern audience to have his Christology at hand – to help us both to understand Calvin and to understand Christology. Therefore, I need to find within Calvin's writing structures that hold his many Christological notions together and that are distinctly his. Fortunately, I believe that such structures are readily evident and emerge from the methodology that I outline above.[15]

Indeed, Calvin's concern that theology be a low-level flight over the reading of Scripture and his understanding of Christ through his office as the Mediator point us toward the fundamental Christological structures that organize his thought. Principally, these are: (1) a perception that Scripture narrates, in the first place, God's history with God's people, a history that culminates in the Gospel history of Christ. Notice the emphasis on history, an emphasis for which Calvin's training as a humanist has implications. (2) An understanding that the covenant, made first with Abraham and fulfilled in Christ, is essential to this history of God with God's people. Scripture's history, then, is the covenant history, which means that Christ's office as Mediator is defined by his role as the Mediator of this covenant. This delineation of Christ's mediatorial office in its relationship to the covenant history is evident throughout Calvin's biblical commentaries, and Calvin's work on these commentaries shapes his understanding of Christ's work as

---

[14] Heiko Oberman, "The 'Extra' Dimension in the Theology of John Calvin," *Journal of Ecclesiastical History* 21:1 (Jan. 1970), 60–62.
[15] I have discussed this synthetic move more fully in the preface to this book.

the Mediator in the 1559 *Institutes*. (3) A delineation of Christ's mediatorial office within the context of the covenant history, under the threefold rubric of his work as priest, king, and prophet. The significance of this rubric to Calvin is, again, evident throughout his Old Testament commentaries, commentaries which led to the composition of his chapter on Christ's threefold office in the 1559 *Institutes*.

THE OUTLINE OF THIS BOOK

The organization of this book is determined by the methodological and material commitments that I have just described. Chapter 1 introduces more expansively the fundaments of Calvin's Christological thinking through an exploration of his controversy with Stancaro over Christ's office as Mediator. This introduction allows us a brief look at the medieval theological tradition to which Calvin is responding – a tradition that Stancaro is attempting to champion – and the manner in which Calvin contrasts his Christology with this tradition, as represented by Stancaro. Four points emerge in this chapter about Calvin's understanding of thinking about Christ: that it should have a biblical shape; that it should emphasize the fullness of Christ's office; that this fullness stands in relationship to the whole of Christ's person; and that our understanding of Christ's person and office needs to be focused on Christ's work in God's economy for our salvation.

In chapter 2, I take up the first point, the biblical shape of Calvin's Christology, and explore both the fundamental structure that Calvin sees in Scripture – the history of the covenant through which God has chosen to redeem and relate to God's Church – and the manner in which Calvin relates Christ to this structure – he is the Mediator of the covenant. This involves setting forth the general narrative of this covenant history while highlighting Christ's role within the narrative. It also takes us to the question of what it means for Calvin's Christology that it is set in the context of this historical narrative. I rely on Calvin's commentaries on the Old Testament and the four Gospels in my discernment of this relationship of Christology to covenant history, as these recommend themselves as the best sources to discover Calvin's Christological reading of Scripture; but I take the template read-off of these commentaries and apply it to Calvin's *Institutes* in the following chapters, in the belief that we find this same structure of the covenant history reflected there.[16] With this structure of the covenant

---

[16] Indeed, as I argue at the beginning of chapter 2, the imprint of these commentaries, written between the 1550 and 1559 versions of the *Institutes*, is readily visible in the first two books of the 1559 text, which have been reoriented around Christ as he is presented in the covenant history of the Old Testament and the Gospels.

history in its relationship to Christ's mediating work in place, we find the categories of Christ's threefold office as priest, king, and prophet, which form the ribs of the structure. This leads us into the rest of the book.

In chapters 3, 4, and 5, I engage in a detailed explication of Christ's threefold office, exploring Calvin's explanation of Christ's work for us as priest, king, and prophet as it is found both in his Gospel commentaries and in the *Institutes*. In the process, these chapters also develop the manner in which Christology relates to the *Institutes* as a whole and stands, in some sense, at its center. In chapter 3, I begin with Calvin's explication of Christ's priestly office and how Christ has opened the way for the Church's relationship with God through his expiation of our sins. Within this discussion, I examine Calvin's understanding of Atonement as expiation found in the *Institutes*. Noteworthy in this understanding is the manner in which Calvin interweaves the so-called objective emphasis of Anselm, in its concern for what Christ has done apart from us to set our relationship straight with God, with the so-called subjective emphasis of Abelard, in its concern for Christ's drawing us into God's waiting embrace.

In the chapter 4, I take up Calvin's explication of Christ's royal office, through which he, as the one Head, unites the many members and bestows blessings upon the fellowship that is his body. Here we find the many rubrics under which Calvin expansively defines this one office, that Christ is our brother and our Lord, the Fountain of Life and the pattern by which we live our lives. This discussion leads us past the specifically Christological sections of the *Institutes* (II.xii–xvii) into Calvin's discussion of the form and content of the Christian life (*Inst.* III) and the relationship of Christ to creation and to God's predestination of the elect.

My discussion of Christ's prophetic or teaching office in chapter 5 takes a different shape from the preceding two chapters. I not only consider the dimensions of this office as it is fulfilled by Christ, but also note that Calvin understands the work of all the Church's teachers, from the Old Testament prophets to pastors and theologians in the contemporary world, to have a part in this teaching office. Thus, we are opened to the question of how Calvin as a teacher of the Church, especially in his *Institutes*, carries out this office; and, insofar as the central purpose of this office, according to Calvin, is to set forth Christ and him crucified, I ask in what way we can find a Christocentric focus in the *Institutes*.

In chapter 6, I consider Calvin's understanding of Christ's person within the context of the understanding of his work developed in the previous chapters. I first examine how Calvin uses the term *persona* in a manner congruent with his emphasis on Christ's activity in history. I then explore the significance that Calvin places on Christ's revelation as the God–human within the covenant history before concluding with his discussion of the metaphysical reality of Christ's two natures within his one person.

Two methodological notes, apparent from this summary, can be added. First, my exploration of Calvin's Christology is not guided by a historical narrative of the theological battles in which Calvin was engaged. I note these conflicts when they impinge on Calvin's expression of the substance of his Christology, but I believe that they determined neither this substance nor its expression in any systematic way.[17] Rather, the form and the substantial content of Calvin's Christology were determined first and foremost by his reading of Scripture, especially as Scripture relates the narrative of God's covenant history with God's Church, fulfilled in Christ's Gospel.[18] It would be fruitful to examine both the manner in which theological controversy stretched or molded Calvin's expression of his Christology in a variety of texts and the manner in which Calvin used Christology as a weapon in such disputes; indeed, such a study might suggest pertinent modifications of the theses that I develop in this book. But I do not believe that any such study would invalidate the theological fundamentals of Calvin's Christology as I outline them, and to include such a study would, in the end, only make this book unwieldy in its exposition of Calvin's Christological thinking.

Second, outside of chapter 1, there is little sustained exploration of the relation of Calvin's Christology to the theological traditions that preceded him. My reasons for this decision are manifold, but they principally evolve

---

[17] So, for example, I argue in chapter 5 that Calvin's dispute with Servetus led him to devote far more space to his discussion of the distinction of Christ's two natures (which point Servetus disputed) than to his discussion of the unity of those natures (which was not a matter on which Calvin thought theological correction was required) in the *Institutes* (II.xiv). But, that he discusses the unity and distinction of Christ's two natures in his one person at this point in the *Institutes*, and the content with which he fills this discussion, are not determined by this dispute.

[18] The influence of Brevard Childs and Hans Frei is apparent in this description of my take on Calvin. The fundamentally biblical shape of Calvin's theology and the fruitful relationship between Calvin's work in the *Institutes* and commentaries was first suggested to me by Childs, and I have found this suggestion manifestly demonstrated across Calvin's writings (Brevard Childs, *Biblical Theology of the Old and New Testaments: Theological Reflection on the Christian Bible* (Minneapolis: Fortress Press, 1992), esp. pp. 47–51). More particularly, my commitment to understand Calvin's Christology in the context of Scripture's narration of God's covenant history with God's Church is obviously derivative of Frei's work on biblical narrative, especially insofar as Frei argues for Calvin as the archetype of narrative interpretation of Scripture which he champions in his *Eclipse* (Hans Frei, *The Eclipse of Biblical Narrative: A Study in Eighteenth and Nineteenth Century Hermeneutics* (New Haven: Yale University Press, 1974), see esp. pp. 18–37). I will diverge from Frei, however, in my claim that, for Calvin, the reality of the history which Scripture narrates, upon which the enactment of God's grace within that history depends, is as vital to a proper grasp of the biblical narrative as is the meaning which this narrative imparts through its realistic depiction or revelation of the character of God. Moreover, as I note in my conclusion, I understand Calvin's interest in narrative in far simpler terms than did Frei.

out of my perception of the possible and the helpful. There was not a single theological tradition that preceded Calvin but innumerable traditions, many with a depth and complexity equal to Calvin's. Thus, although it is admirable always to place Calvin in this broader context, attempts to do so often betray the traditions that they are trying to honor through explications that are inevitably superficial.[19] This book is weighty enough (in ounces if not in wisdom) as it simply attempts to manage Calvin's thought.

Moreover, I would argue that, whatever Calvin's relationship to the traditions that preceded him, we first need to understand his Christology as distinctly his Christology. Regardless of which, any particular piece of his argument is radically new, we should recognize that the manner in which he configures a teaching broadly drawn from the Church's tradition puts a definitive stamp on the teaching, making it Calvin's own. As I tell my students yearly, what makes a theology unique and powerful is, as often as not, the particular emphases within a broader consensus or a subtle nuance in expression within a shared vision that help to shape the spiritual life in one direction or another. Such emphases and nuance must first be recognized in their relation to the topography in which they are embedded before they can most fruitfully be held up for comparison with other theological landscapes. This book is as much about such emphases and nuance in Calvin's work as it is about any set of theological *nova*. Thus, after chapter 1, in which we get a broad sense of how Calvin would distinguish his Christological landscape from at least one strand of the tradition that preceded him, I focus on the specific contours of Calvin's thinking in the belief that this is the primary context in which we can hear what was Christologically significant to him. A more comparative Christological work, looking at a variety of types of Christology within the theological traditions of the medieval and Reformation periods, would be helpful; but such a work would depend

---

[19] My first chapter runs this risk, tracing the development of Christian understanding of Christ's role as Mediator across a millennium and a half. To avoid this pitfall, I define my topic narrowly (Christ's role as Mediator) and focus its purpose tightly (giving an orientation to Calvin). Muller over-extends himself when reaching for a comparison between Calvin's and Bonaventure's Christology in this same context (*Christ and the Decree*, p. 193, fn. 128). Not recognizing the differences between Bonaventure's fundamentally speculative/metaphysical Christology (see Zachary Hayes, *The Hidden Center: Spirituality and Speculative Christology in St. Bonaventure* [St. Bonaventure, NY: The Franciscan Institute, 1981]), and Calvin's more historical vision (see my chapter 2), he mistakes the similarity of their interests in Christ's role as the Medium or Mediator of history, respectively.

Susan Schreiner's *Where Shall Wisdom be Found?* (Chicago: University of Chicago Press, 1994) is a comparative approach that works beautifully, setting Calvin's interpretation of Job in the context of previous efforts by Gregory I, Maimonides, and Aquinas. Schreiner has taken a narrow topic that she can explore across a wide field. I take the opposite tack – a broad topic examined over a narrow field.

on efforts like this one, which explore the constitutive parts from which this larger quilt would be sewn.[20]

We can understand Calvin's Christology only as we grasp the peculiar shape of this doctrine that emerges out of Calvin's reading of Scripture. His teaching is shaped by his relationship to this particular source, but we must also acknowledge and explore the manner in which his teaching is shaped by his relationship with his audience. Particularly in the *Institutes*, as Serene Jones has reminded us, Calvin's authorial concern was not simply the exposition and ordering of the theological *topoi* that one finds in Scripture; rather, alongside this commitment to proper doctrinal exposition, Calvin was concerned to so structure his argument rhetorically that he might induce Christian piety in his readers.[21] Thus, one task of this book, in its attempt to listen to Calvin, is to locate and define the rhetorical purpose of Calvin's Christology in the *Institutes*. I ask, therefore, not merely who Calvin says that Christ is or what he has done, but also in what manner Calvin hopes, through his answers to these questions, to draw his readers into a fruitful relationship with Christ, inculcate in them faith in God through their relationship with Christ, and empower them by this relationship to live pious lives in the midst of a threatening world. Indeed, I also supply an answer to the question that Jones puts to those who argue for a Christocentrism in the *Institutes* (as this book does) when she asks how Calvin intended to "rivet the attention of his audience upon the person and work of Jesus Christ" through the structure and argument of his text.[22] In this sense, Jones' work uncovers in Calvin one of the agendas for my own.

We must note, however, Jones affirms that Calvin's desire to shape his readers through a rhetorically well-crafted exposition of Christian doctrine is constrained and informed by the role that Scripture plays in determining doctrinal meaning.[23] In other words, Calvin is interested both in the effective rhetorical form in which doctrine is expressed and in the authentic Christian content that this doctrine expresses. He is not a thoroughgoing functionalist. Jones' book focuses most closely on the rhetorical agenda of the *Institutes*, but in this book I begin with the Christological content that informs this rhetorical interest. In one sense, this means that I inventory and examine the Christological material through which Calvin is able to undertake his project of inculcating piety in his reader; but, in a deeper

---

[20] Zachary Hayes' exploration of Bonaventure's Christology (*The Hidden Center*) would be another such work. Indeed, it would be fascinating to look at Calvin and Bonaventure together, given the divergent directions of their Christologies alongside their similar starting points – Christ as Medium in the case of Bonaventure, Christ as Mediator in the case of Calvin.

[21] Jones, *Rhetoric of Piety*.   [22] Ibid., p. 57.   [23] Ibid., p. 199.

sense, this book discovers the manner in which the material determines Calvin's rhetoric both in its end, insofar as Calvin's pastoral undertaking in the *Institutes* is directed toward the incorporation of his readers into Christ, and in its means, insofar as the heart of Calvin's rhetoric is the representation of the grace and love of God that Christ enacts in his Gospel history. Thus, I will look not only to the manner in which Calvin's Christology is shaped by his rhetorical purpose, as content is shaped by its form of expression, but also to the manner in this Christological content demands a certain form, so that it as much shapes Calvin's rhetoric as it is shaped by it.

To conclude with a final thought on this book before it is presented to you, the reader – my project in this text is to present a coherent and persuasive picture of Calvin's Christology, to uncover its lineaments and details. I was moved to undertake this task by the convictions that what Calvin had to say about Christ was of utmost importance to Calvin, as I believe it should be to any Christian theologian, and that modern interpreters have had little sense of what Calvin finally had to say. Insofar as Calvin articulated a theology that was authentic to the principles of the Reformation, including its principle of *sola Christi*, and insofar as this theology would be powerfully effective in the Church, to his own mind, only as it was thoroughly Christologically seasoned, it seemed a disservice to allow the Christological aspect of this theology to go unrecognized or misunderstood. Therefore, I have sought to present this Christology in a manner that highlights the coherence and power of Calvin's vision expressed within it.

To this end, I have not attempted to critique Calvin's Christology in terms of its internal relationship to his theology as a whole, in its relationship to the Church's theological tradition, or in its adequacy vis-à-vis modern notions of history or modern readings of Scripture, though I shall offer a few constructive thoughts in my conclusion. Whatever the merits or demerits of Calvin's Christology may finally be – and surely there are some of both – my primary concern is to give Calvin voice on this matter, not to determine the weight this voice should be given within the Church's conversation. Obviously I express a certain endorsement of Calvin's thinking about Christ merely by applying myself to this endeavor, and, in the course of my work, I have found Calvin's understanding of Christ and his work as they are presented in Scripture to be compelling, primarily as Calvin has been able to develop a more robust picture of Christ's Gospel than many on the market today. I do believe that a theological imagination shaped by the Christological template contained in this book is opened to a richer proclamation of the Gospel; that is a fruit of Calvin's theological harvest.

But this book offers only a template to the modern preacher. It presents the Christology of a sixteenth-century French theologian making his exiled residence in Geneva, for whom monarchy was the accustomed means of government, God's wrath was just expression of God's will toward sin, and God's prophets sought to teach God's people to work within the structures of this world, not to overturn them. Calvin's world is not our world. Thus, if this template is to be helpful in shaping imaginations, those imaginations must apply themselves to reconceiving its content, where necessary, to apply it to God's dealings with us today. How is Christ effectively our brother, the fountain of our life, the reconciler of our alienation from God, or the teacher of God's way? These are the questions that Calvin's Christology asks. My task is simply to aid him in his articulation. I believe that my readers can, in turn, provide fruitful answers.

CHAPTER I

Christ as Mediator

Toward the end of his literary career, Calvin was dragged into a theological skirmish by the Protestant churches in Poland. A wandering Italian theologian, Francesco Stancaro, was teaching that Christ mediated between humanity and God only in his human nature and not in his complete person as the God–man. The theological tradition of the Church had spoken of Christ's mediation in many ways, but at the heart of all of them lay the notion that God sent Christ into the world in order for Christ to stand between God and humanity and to serve as the agent or means or instrument (and the noun one chooses depends upon one's theology of mediation) by which humanity is reunited to God. Thus, Stancaro, while acknowledging that both a divine and human nature are united in Christ's one person, argued that the divine nature, because it was shared equally and fully by the three persons of the Trinity, cannot mediate or stand between God and humanity – to say that the Son mediates between the Father and humanity in his divinity would imply that he was subordinate to the Father in his divinity, and this would be the Arian heresy. Other theologians in Poland, however, argued that Stancaro was merely renewing the Nestorian heresy by limiting Christ's mediation to his humanity apart from his divinity. The hypostatic union is apparently dissolved by Stancaro's doctrine, they claimed. The debate initiated by Stancaro was dividing the Polish churches, and so they appealed repeatedly to the great lights of the Reformation in Basel, Strasburg, Geneva, and Zurich to help them resolve it. Calvin attempted to hold himself aloof from this battle, being more concerned with the anti-Trinitarian teaching of George Blandrata in Poland at the time; but eventually he was importuned into responding twice to Stancaro's teaching in two letters to the Polish Brethren.[1]

---

[1] Joseph Tylanda does an excellent job in relating the details of this controversy and Calvin's role in it. My brief narrative is drawn from his more complete discussion, and I have also relied on his translations of Calvin's two responses to Stancaro, with one or two exceptions, noted below. See

I take up Calvin's two volleys in the Stancaro controversy in the initial chapter of this book because they provide an excellent introduction to Calvin's Christological thinking. Calvin argues for nothing radically new to his Christology in his missives to the Polish churches, but merely repeats themes that had dominated his Christological writing throughout his career.[2] The subject of the debate with Stancaro is the role of Christ's divinity in his mediation; yet, to make his case Calvin must consider the completeness of Christ's threefold mediatorial office – that Christ mediates not only as he is priest, but also as he is king and prophet – and with the relation of Christ's complete person, as the God–man, to this office. Christ's mediation in his divinity is entailed for Calvin by these other two facets of Christology. Moreover, Calvin will claim, we shall come to such a proper understanding of Christology when we allow Scripture's witness to guide our thinking about it. Christology has its sense principally within the narrative of God's economy for our salvation of which Scripture speaks. In Calvin's responses to Stancaro, then, we shall find, in summary form, the foundations upon which his Christology is built.

The Stancaro controversy stands as a useful introduction to Calvin's Christology in a second way, however, since it highlights the broader methodological significance of the last plank described above, Calvin's commitment to the guidance of Scripture. At the center of this controversy lay the question of the implications of Trinitarian doctrine for Christological formulation – how does the unity of the Son with the Father determine our understanding of the work of the Son among us? From Calvin's perspective, Stancaro has isolated the doctrine from the language of Scripture, when he should have contextualized it within that language. This allows the doctrine to dominate the text, rather than allowing the text and its concerns to open the doctrine to a richer modality of meaning. Scripture needs to guide us, Calvin argues, on the strategic as well as the tactical level; it provides the broad framework into which we need to fit doctrinal definition, not as a way of subverting doctrine, but as a way of sounding its depths. Stancaro's position is reflective of a strand of Christological argument in the tradition of the medieval West, though what was only a strand in this tradition seems to form the whole cloth for Stancaro. Considering Calvin's challenge to Stancaro, then, might begin a conversation between Calvin and this broader tradition, though that is not the subject of this book.

Joseph Tylanda, "Christ the Mediator: Calvin versus Stancaro," *Calvin Theological Journal* 7 (1972), 5–16 and "The Controversy on Christ the Mediator: Calvin's Second Reply to Stancaro," *Calvin Theological Journal* 8 (1972), 131–157.
[2] *Pace* Willis, *Calvin's Catholic Christology*, pp. 69–71.

STANCARO AND THE TRADITIONAL DOCTRINE
OF THE MEDIATOR

In 1560 the Christological controversy in Poland ran over its borders when, at the Synod of Pinczow, the Polish Protestants excommunicated Stancaro for his position on Christ's mediatorship.[3] Following this action, they wrote to Calvin and others seeking an orthodox articulation of the doctrine of the Mediator. Calvin responded in June of 1560 with his first letter to the Polish Brethren. At the end of that year, the ministers of the Polish Church along with the nobility met a second time, and on this occasion they intended to drive Stancaro out of the kingdom. Armed with Calvin's first letter and with responses from Basel, Zurich, and Strasburg as well, they quickly condemned him; but, before their decree could be executed, Jerome Ossolinski, a Polish noble, stood in Stancaro's defense. Stancaro had argued that the letters from Zurich and Geneva were forgeries, and so Ossolinski proposed that a four-month truce be called, during which time Calvin, Beza, Bullinger, and Peter Martyr could again be polled for their opinions. This suggestion was accepted after a great tumult. The result was that both sides then bombarded Calvin and the others with explanations of their position.

Thus, in December of 1560, Stancaro came to write an encyclical to Calvin and the others explaining his position; Calvin eventually rejected this explanation in his second letter to the Polish Brethren in the next year. It is apparent from Stancaro's letter that he was chiefly concerned with Arianism. Indeed, at the outset of his diatribe he derides his enemies for their twofold heresy. He writes:

These Arians teach that the Father, Son, and Holy Spirit are not one God, but three gods, in such a way that they are separate one from the other as three human persons are separate one from the other, and that these three gods have three substances, three wills, three separate operations and three separate spirits . . . Moreover, [they also teach that] the Son of God, our Lord Jesus Christ, is less than the Father in his divine nature, or according to his divinity, and likewise he was without beginning (that is, from eternity) and is and will be according to this divinity priest, pontiff, and Mediator, and according to his human nature, true victim and sacrifice.[4]

It is not clear to what he is alluding when he accuses his opponents of holding that the three persons of the Trinity are "three gods" with "three distinct substances," though perhaps he has the anti-Trinitarian teachings

---

[3] This summary is taken from Tylanda, "Christ the Mediator," pp. 132–137.

[4] *Ioannis Calvini Opera quae supersunt Omnia*, ed. Baum, Cunitz, and Reuss (Brunswick, 1863–1900) (hereafter *CO*), 18:260–261.

of Blandrata in mind; but the claim that they hold Christ to be not only victim and sacrifice in his humanity but also priest and Mediator from eternity in his divinity is at the center of his position. From Stancaro's perspective, to hold that Christ is Mediator in his divinity is to hold that he is therein less than the Father, for to be a Mediator is to be one who is between two parties. To place Christ in his divinity between the Father and humanity sets him below the Father (and above humanity); and this, for Stancaro, is the Arian heresy.

Stancaro proposes an alternative: that we must understand Christ as Mediator only in his humanity – only thus is he both priest and victim – while in his divinity he is, with the Father and the Spirit, the author of this mediatorial work.[5] Stancaro's claim is not that Christ's humanity mediates as it is divorced from his divinity; but that it does so only as it is empowered by it. The divinity of the Son, along with that of the Father and the Spirit, is the source of Christ's mediatory office – it enables his humanity, for example, to be perfectly obedient, which is an aspect of its mediation. But, he is clear, we must distinguish the actual action of mediation, which belongs to the humanity alone, from this role as source, which belongs to the divinity of the Son in concert with the Father and the Spirit.

Having set these two views before Calvin, Stancaro asks for a decision. Will Calvin side with his orthodox, Trinitarian view, or will he side with the Arians?[6] Calvin, as we shall see, will reject these as the only alternatives and argue for a position that breaks out of Stancaro's binary logic, but, before we turn to his response, it will be useful to first examine the tradition that preceded Stancaro and underwrote his belief. We shall find that after the Arian crisis Christologies, which previously had been somewhat subordinationalist in character, became preoccupied with the equality of the Son with the Father, and that this new concern dictated at least one aspect of the evolution of Christological doctrine in the West, providing the background and framework for Stancaro's position.

Mediatorial Christologies of the pre-Nicene Fathers

Christological thinking in the first three centuries of the Christian era was defined largely by a concern to understand both Christ's relationship to the Father and his earthly mission in their connection with one another. This was accomplished through a vision in which Christ's intimacy with the Father establishes him as the one through whom the Father stands in

---

[5] *CO* 18:261–262. [6] *CO* 18:262.

relationship with the world. This discussion not only concerned Christ as he was incarnate as Jesus, but also embraced (and at times focused upon) Christ in his cosmic existence as the *Logos* and Son of the Father. This emphasis on Christ's mediation of God's relationship with the world permeates the witness of the New Testament from its earliest reflections on the crucified and resurrected Jesus to the great Christological hymns in John and Colossians. The cosmic dimension of this mediation is explored under its more noetic aspect in the *Logos* theologies of the second-century Apologists. Justin, for example, argues that Christ, as the *Logos* of God, is the Reason or Mind of God, through whom the cosmos was created and ordered and by whom the Truth of God might be known by all rational beings both before and through the incarnation of the *Logos* in Jesus.[7] Justin complements this soteriological vision of Christ as the bringer of truth with brief affirmations of the centrality of Christ's cross in our liberation from sin and death.[8] But only with the next generation do we encounter a full-fledged theology of Christ's mediation.

Irenaeus, writing at the turn of the third century, begins with the assumptions of the Apologists about Christ's creative and revelatory reality as the *Logos* of God and, taking them as his warp and weft, he weaves out of the biblical text a profound vision of the incarnate Christ's mediation of the relationship of the Father to the world. Christ, through his incarnation, reveals to us in a concrete manner the Father, who is beyond our grasp; and by his incarnation and obedience, death and resurrection, he recapitulates our lives in himself and so redeems them, making possible our divinization and return to God. Irenaeus writes, "[T]hus, he took up [humanity] into himself, the invisible becoming visible, the incomprehensible being made comprehensible, the impassible becoming capable of suffering, and the Word being made [human], thus summing up all things in himself: so that, . . . , he might draw all things to himself at the proper time."[9] Christ's mediation, for Irenaeus, is defined as revelation and recapitulation, and through these acts he stands between the Father and the world, reaching out from the One to the other.

These early theologies focus primarily on the relationship established between God and the world through Christ's mediation, and with Origen a

---

[7] Justin, *First Apology*, 46, 59, 64; *Second Apology*, 6 (from *The Apostolic Fathers with Justin Martyr and Irenaeus*, The Ante-Nicene Fathers, Alexander Roberts and James Donaldson, eds. (Grand Rapids: Eerdmans, reprinted 1996), pp. 178, 182, 185, 190. See also J. N. D. Kelly, *Early Christian Doctrines* (San Francisco: Harper and Row, 1978), pp. 95–101.

[8] Justin, *Dialogue with Trypho*, 41, 111, 134. See Kelly, *Early Christian Doctrines*, pp. 168–170.

[9] Irenaeus, *Against Heresies*, III.16.6, *The Apostolic Fathers*, p. 443.

tension emerges in this approach when theology's scope is broadened to take into account the relationship of the *Logos* to the Father.[10] Origen maintains a soteriology that diverges little from the tradition as outlined above – the *Logos* who becomes incarnate in Jesus mediates our relationship with the Father through his revelation of the Father and his facilitation of our adoption as children, in turn – but he explores in great detail the relationship between the *Logos* and the Father that this language of mediation implies, arguing for the true divinity of the *Logos* or Son on the basis of his eternal relationship with the Father.[11] If God is, from eternity, Father, then there never was a time when the Father did not have the Son who is God with God, he explains,[12] but, at the same time, he will maintain that the Son's divinity is less than that of the Father's. He is not homoousios with the Father, for the Father alone is unoriginate.[13] Indeed, while it is proper to say that the Son is God, it is with a derivative deity, and so the Son is, more properly, a "secondary God."[14] Origen's theology might be seen as an attempt to reflect metaphysically on the mediatorial Christology of the early Church, but the theology that results pushes the metaphor of Christ's mediation past its breaking point in its ability to describe the relationship between the Son and the Father. The fallout to the solution of the theological dilemma raised by Origen's thinking will have significant implications for the Church's understanding of Christ's mediation.

The Arian controversy

The question that arises after Origen concerns the sense of speaking of a secondary God. Can we say that this Son is God with God while at the same time denying that he is homoousios with the Father? The catalysts on either side of the dispute agree that the answer is no. Arius and the party that forms around his position argue that the Son cannot be God but must be the first of God's creatures, while the Nicene party rallies around the homoousios.

The theological debate entailed by the Arian crisis is far more complex than I either have the time or the need to relate with any thoroughness; but one aspect of the debate is significant for our story. One way to frame

---

[10] My discussion of Origen is largely dependent on Peter Widdicombe, *The Fatherhood of God from Origen to Athanasius* (Oxford University Press, 1994), pp. 7–120.

[11] Ibid., pp. 45ff., 108ff.   [12] Ibid., pp. 78ff.   [13] Ibid., pp. 39ff., 86ff.

[14] *Origen, Contra Celsus*, 5.39 (see *Fathers of the Third Century: Tertullian, Part Fourth; Minucius Fleix; Commodian; Origen, Parts First and Second*, The Ante-Nicene Fathers, Alexander Roberts and James Donaldson, eds. (Buffalo: The Christian Literature Publishing Company, 1885), p. 561.

the question that emerges in the fourth century revolves around Christ's mediation. Given the mediatorial function attributed to Christ by earlier theologians, that it is the Word made flesh who reveals the Father to the world and returns the world to the Father, what is the relationship between the Word and the Father? When the question is put this way, then the answer will be shaped to a large degree by our understanding of the requirements of mediation. The Arians argue that because the *Logos does* mediate the relationship of the Father with the world, he is in some sense between them, and so is lower than the Father – he is subordinate to the ineffable God. Indeed, he must be, for if he were truly God with God, then he would be equally opaque to our understanding and would be able to mediate no more knowledge of the Father than could the Father in his splendid transcendence. The Trinitarian party responds, contrariwise, that the *Logos* as incarnate in Christ *can* mediate between God and the world, can reveal God to the world and unite the world to God, only as he is one with God.[15] If he is merely yet another creature, then he is on the side of creatureliness, and God in God's ineffable divinity remains isolated and the world of creatures cut off from God. For the Arians, Christ's role as Mediator means that he could not be one with the Father, whereas, for the Trinitarians, this unity is the prerequisite for mediation.[16]

This matter of the implications of the Word's mediatorship for his relationship to the Father was a formal basis of the Arian controversy; but it is also significant for our discussion to note the material issue which arose in this context, revolving around the hermeneutic by which one interprets Christological passages in Scripture. There are a number of passages in Scripture which both sides read as referring to Christ or the Word and which imply a subordination of their subject to God the Father. The Arians apply a simple hermeneutic to these passages and read them all as applying to Christ/the Word in his totality. They thereby deduce that the Word is subordinate to the Father insofar as a passage like Psalm 45:6–7 ("Thy throne, O God, is for ever and ever . . . Wherefore God, thy God, hath anointed thee with the oil of gladness above thy fellows"), when read with reference to Christ or the Word, implies such a subordination in its attribution of an anointing and an exaltation of Christ by God. Athanasius, on the

---

[15] See, for example, *Contra Arianos* (hereafter *CA*), ii.17.26 and ii.21.72 in *Select Writings and Letters of Athanasius, Bishop of Alexandria*, The Nicene and Post-Nicene Fathers, Archibald Robinson, ed. (Edinburgh: T. & T. Clark, 1987), pp. 362, 387.

[16] This is obviously an oversimplification of the debate that emerged at the time of the Arian crisis, especially as it treats the multitude of positions that were labeled "Arian" as one. Rowan Williams offers an excellent detailed and nuanced discussion of the Arian debate in his book, *Arius: Heresy and Tradition* (London: Denton, Longman, & Todd 1987). See esp. pp. 111ff. and 207ff.

other hand, argues that a Christian hermeneutic must be more nuanced – that there are texts which are predicated of the Word by nature and texts which are predicated of the Word with reference to his activity in God's economy as the Incarnate Lord. So in the above passage, the verse that implies a subordination of the Son to the Father ("Wherefore, God, thy God, hath anointed thee . . .) is of this latter, "lowly" variety and thus does not define the relationship of the Word, by nature, to the Father. There is no subordination in this natural relationship, for in fact the Word and the Father are one in nature, as the "lofty" verse ("Thy throne, O God, is for ever and ever . . .") would indicate.

A third hermeneutic is possible, one which is attached to the Antiochene Christological school, structured not by the distinction between the eternal Word and the Word as Incarnate but by the distinction between the divine and human natures in Christ. Under this approach, texts incompatible with Christ's divinity/unity with the Father ("Wherefore God, thy God, hath anointed thee . . .") are referred to his human nature, while texts which expressed or relied on this unity with God ("Thy throne, O God . . .") are referred to his divine nature.[17]

These hermeneutical options would entail significant implications for the question of Christ's mediatorship once the Nicene position had won the day. Under which rubric do texts that speak of Christ as Mediator belong? For Athanasius, though the Word's unity with the Father is necessary for the activity of mediation, the texts that refer to Christ's mediatorial activity (given the subordination implied therein) are those referring to the Word incarnate. Note, however, that these texts still apply to the divine person of the Word; the only qualification relates to the state of this person – he mediates as he is incarnate, not by nature. But for a two-nature approach, the "mediating" texts are applied to Christ's human nature, not to his divine nature. So, for example, although Origen attributed to the eternal Word the function of priesthood, this is rejected after the Arian crisis because of the subordination of the Word thereby implied. The Alexandrian writers then understand Christ's priesthood in relation to the incarnate Word, while the Antiochene fathers limit this attribution to Christ's human nature.[18] The Antiochene position is aided by a central text – "there is one Mediator between God and man, the man Jesus Christ" (1 Tim. 2:5). Although there are certain Nestorian tendencies inherent in their position, it also provides a viable option for the interpretation of Christological texts.

[17] See Greer's discussion in James Kugel and Rowan Greer, *Early Biblical Interpretation* (Philadelphia: The Westminster Press, 1986), pp. 186–188.
[18] *CA* II.14.8 (p. 352). Kugel and Greer, *Early Biblical Interpretation*, pp. 189–190.

I shall say more about this distinction as I go, but note the manner in which language about Christ's mediation is already delimited by the Arian debate. One is no longer permitted to speak of the Word's mediation from eternity. Neither hermeneutic will admit this, as each allocates mediatorial texts to Christ's incarnation, allowing them to refer either to his reality as the Word incarnate or to his human nature in its union with the divine. Trinitarian grammar is used to constrict the articulation of the boundaries of Christ's mediation.

This is ironic with respect to Athanasius, given the logic of the Nicene argument outlined above. This argument works from the fact of the incarnate Word's mediation of our relationship with the Father, but it must take great care in how it uses the terms "Mediator" and "Medium." Athanasius still honors those texts that speak of the Word as God's hand in creation (to draw on one of his metaphors), but he relegates language of mediation to his characterization of the Arian position in this discussion – belittling, in effect, the notion that God would need a Mediator to do what God could not do directly.[19] Instead, he speaks consistently of the Father working *through* or *in* the Word in the act of creation, preserving the scriptural thought while avoiding any subordinationalist implications.[20] He only attaches the term "Mediator" to the Word when he can associate it with an incarnate form (the Word incarnate either in Christ or in the words of Scripture).[21] This constriction of language in Athanasius is complemented, however, by a theological creativity in response. Athanasius finally speaks of the work of the Word in creation apart from the work of the Father (as the Word is the "first-born of all creation"). But he transforms the Arian language of subordination into the regal language of condescension – "because the Word, when at the beginning he framed the creatures, condescended to things originate, that it might be possible for them to come to be"[22] – allowing that the Word might step down to creation prior to his incarnation, but only as that movement is characterized by the loving humility that Paul captures in his Philippian hymn.

Augustine

The dynamics of Christological language entailed by the Arian crisis come into focus more clearly with Augustine, especially in his use of a two-natures hermeneutic in a decidedly non-Nestorian form. Augustine was concerned

---

[19] See, for example, *CA* ii.17.24, 27 (pp. 361, 364).   [20] *CA* ii.18.31 (pp. 364–365).
[21] Ibid.   [22] *CA* ii.21.64 (p. 383).

with the implications for theology of the Son's unity with the Father. This concern is evident in his discussion of the knowledge we have of God through God's manifest image. For Athanasius, in his writings before the Arian crisis, there is an economy in which the Son is the image of the Father, so that we could come to knowledge of the Father through him, while we were re-created after the image of the Son. The pattern was Father <–> Son <–> Humanity, with the Son in the middle position mediating both our knowledge of the Father and our re-creation into the divine likeness.[23] But Augustine found this schema problematic in its subordinationalist implications. Thus, when Genesis says that we are created after the image and likeness of God, he argues that this means in the image of the Godhead as a whole, Father, Son, and Holy Spirit, and not merely of one person in the Godhead.[24] It is, therefore, more appropriate to understand that humanity was created and re-created in the image of the Trinity (which pattern he finds in the human soul – memory, understanding, and will) rather than in the image of the Son, and we likewise come to some knowledge of God through this pattern of the Trinity within us. The pattern, then, is simplified to Trinity <–> Humanity, and the Son is removed from his mediatorial position out of a concern for the unity of the Son with the Father in the divine nature.

This same concern is reflected in Augustine's discussion of the activity of God in the economy, an activity that he argues is always the unified activity of the One God in three persons. "*Opera trinitatis ad extra indivisa sunt.*"[25] Thus, we most properly speak of the Trinity creating, the Trinity redeeming, and the Trinity sanctifying, though we can appropriate these activities to the persons of the Father, Son, and Holy Spirit, respectively.[26] Augustine's point is not that the specific passions of the incarnation – birth and death, for example – are attributable to the Trinity, but this theory does have implications for how we understand the mediation that takes place in the incarnation. If the activity of the Trinity is one, then surely it is improper to say that the Son mediates between humanity and the Father.

---

[23] Athanasius, *On the Incarnation of the Word*, chs. 11–19 (in *Christology of the Later Fathers*, The Library of Christian Classics, Edward Rochie Hardy, ed. [Philadelphia: The Westminster Press, 1954], pp. 65–73).

[24] We find Athanasius already moving away from his earlier mode of framing the relation in his later writing (*Contra Arianos*, for example).

[25] This idea of the unitive work of the Trinity is not unique to Augustine; it can also be found, for example, in Gregory of Nyssa's *Answer to Ablabius* (in *Christology of the Later Fathers*, pp. 263ff.), but, within the western tradition, it is most typically traced back to Augustine.

[26] See Catherine LaCugna, *God for Us* (HarperSanFrancisco, 1991), pp. 96–101.

These principles are all brought to bear when Augustine discusses Christ as our Mediator in the *Confessions*. There he argues that "as man, he is our Mediator; but as the Word of God, he is not an intermediary between God and man because he is equal with God, and God with God, and together with him one God."[27] To be a Mediator, Augustine has explained, one must be between the two parties in need of mediation and have something in common with each. In his human nature, Christ is mortal, as we are, and is just, as God is; and so, as human, Christ can be Mediator. But, as the quotation above indicates, Christ in his divine nature in no way comes between humanity and God, but is God, and is one with the Father. Thus, when we speak of Christ as Mediator, we speak of him properly only as human, not as divine. What has happened here is that the Trinitarian assertion of the Son's unity with the Father along with the Christological grammar of his two natures has provided principles by which Christ's mediation is understood not in relationship to his person as a whole, as the Son who reveals the Father to the world and who takes up the world into communion with the Father, but in relationship to his human nature, which mediates between humanity and God, Father, Son, and Holy Spirit. Of course, Augustine adamantly adds, Christ's human nature is able to mediate only because of its unity with the divine nature – only thus is it just – and not in any sense apart from it. But, nonetheless, it is the human nature that mediates; the divine nature, we might say, only enables this mediation. In Augustine, then, we see a position similar to that of Stancaro definitively articulated.[28]

The Mediator in medieval theology

Indeed, Augustine's discussion of how Christ is Mediator sets an agenda for continued debate among theologians in the Middle Ages.[29] A substantial number of medieval theologians follow Augustine and argue that Christ

---

[27] Augustine, *Confessions*, X.43.

[28] Muller argues that Augustine, later in his career, retracts from this position "that the name of the Mediator belongs to the human nature only," positing it instead of the Son of God "when he subordinates himself in the form of a servant and thereby becomes, officially, 'inferior to the Father'" (*Christ and the Decree*, p. 195, fn. 156). But the first text that he cites in support of this claim argues rather clearly that, as God, the Son is as equally distant from us as is the Father, but that, as human, he is Mediator, near to us as a servant, but superior to us in his sinlessness (*De peccato originali*, cap. 33). This is the argument for Christ's mediation in his humanity alone in every detail, though Muller is perhaps correct that Augustine would allow the name of Mediator to apply to the whole person of Christ – but only, it seems, through his human nature.

[29] This discussion is largely drawn from A. M. Landgraf, *Dogmengeschichte der Frühscholastik*, II.2 (Regensburg: Friedrich Pustet, 1952–56), pp. 288–327.

is Mediator only in his human nature, since Christ therein is righteous like God and mortal like humanity; but a minority voice, drawn from a pseudo-Augustinian source, Vigilius Tapsensus, argues that Christ is this Medium between God and humanity in his person as the God–man, for in this way he shares in divinity with God and humanity with human persons. For most of the early Middle Ages, these options are not considered to be exclusive of one another, and more than one theologian argues for both. In either case, at this early stage of the debate, beginning with Augustine, the notion of being a Medium is used to understand the Mediator, while the question of Christ's priesthood, introduced briefly above, does not define the discussion. Christ's mediatorship, in other words, is understood in relation to his position between God and humanity (he is the *medius* between them), sharing something with both, rather than in relation to his activity by which he brings the two alienated parties back together.

With time, several distinctions are set into place, helping to order the discussion. Lombard introduces a distinction between God's activity (Father, Son, and Holy Spirit) as our Savior through the divine power and Christ's activity as our Mediator through humility and obedience. The activity in which he engages through obedience is our atonement, by which Lombard means the expiation of our sins, and Lombard specifies that this atonement is fulfilled in Christ's human nature. This distinction between divine and human activity, which is carried over as a distinction between the operations of the divine and human natures in Christ, begins to define mediation more as his activity – what Christ does through his obedience – rather than his ontological state – who he is either in his mortality and justice or in his two natures. Bonaventure articulates this more clearly when he distinguishes between Christ as Medium, which refers to his relationship to the two extremes and which he is as the God–man, and Christ as Mediator, which refers more properly to his *officium reconciliationis* and which he fulfills in his human nature. In his argument, Bonaventure relies on a sense of Christ's reconciling activity or office as it had been defined by Anselm in the *Cur deus homo*. Christ reconciles in his humanity, through his obedience and death, but this obedience is possible and this death is worthy only as his humanity is united to his divinity in his person. Again, it is the human nature that mediates, but its mediation is possible only through the hypostatic union, in which Christ's divinity makes possible the perfect obedience of his humanity.

Thomas summarizes this development and defines Christ's mediatorship in terms of both his status as Medium and his activity as Mediator, but, in each case, he follows Augustine and relates these only to Christ in his human nature.[30] We should note that Thomas understands Christ's mediation with a certain breadth, even as he works within the tradition we have examined – he defines Christ's activity not simply by his work as priest, but also by his work as king and prophet, and he includes under Christ's priestly work his gift of the sacraments as well as his atoning obedience and death – but his focus for Christ's mediation is still fixed on his priestly office.[31] We find a similar vision for the breadth of Christ's mediation in the body of Bonaventure's theology, which evinces a robust sense of Christ's work in his understanding of Christ as the center (*medius*) of all things; but in his Sentence commentary, he nonetheless only mentions Christ's obedience and death in his discussion of Christ's mediation.

Within the western medieval context, then, there is a theological convergence on the question of Christ's mediation. Though this question defines only one strand of the discussion of Christology within this tradition, nevertheless, the Trinitarian concerns which shaped this convergence greatly influenced this larger discussion, as well. Bonaventure's theology is a perfect example of this dynamic.[32] Bonaventure's Christological vision is occupied far more with Christ's reality as the Medium or Center of all things than with his activity as Mediator, but this vision is both constrained and enriched by its relationship to the Trinitarian grammar that guides his discussion of Christ's role as Mediator. Bonaventure has no problem speaking of the incarnate Christ as the center of the world as created and redeemed, and he is also able to speak of the eternal *Logos* or Son of God as the center of the Trinity (as the person who both produces and is produced).[33] But in an earlier work, when he turns to the question of how the *Logos* is the *medius* or center of God's creative relation to the world – a relationship that raises the same subordinationalist issues as Christ's role as Mediator – he must draw back from the bold claim he would like to make and argue that he is only a *quasi medium*: he is "as if a center."[34]

This constraint can, however, prove fruitful to Bonaventure's thinking, for instead of simply withdrawing in places from the Christological focus toward which he tends, he encompasses this Christocentrism within a broader Trinitarian theology that enriches his picture. Thus, in his later work, he does speak of the Word as the image by which the world was

---

[30] Thomas Aquinas, *Summa Theologica* (hereafter *ST*), IIIa.26.2 (Blackfriars edition, Colman E. O'Neill, OP, trans., vol. 50 (New York: McGraw-Hill Book Company, 1963), pp. 210–213).

[31] Ibid.: *ST*, III.22.1.ad 3 (vol. 50, pp. 136–139); *ST* III.59.4.ad. 1.

[32] My discussion of Bonaventure is shaped by Zachary Hayes' book *The Hidden Center*. See esp. pp. 55–90 and 192–204.

[33] *Hexaemeron* (hereafter *Hex.*), 1.10–39 (v:330–335).

[34] *Commentarius in IV libros Sententiarum* (hereafter, I. *Sent.*), d.27, p. 2, a.u. q.2, resp. (1, 485) in *Opera Omnia*, vol. 5.

created, but only because he has first depicted this image inscribed on creation in its Trinitarian dimension and because he has developed a notion of the Word as the center of the Trinity who thereby bears the image of the Trinity in its fullness. Bonaventure's Christocentrism in these cases is perhaps muted by his Trinitarianism; his Christological notion of creation is enveloped by a Trinitarian construct, but through this Trinitarian construct he opens up his thinking to this rich array of theological connections that otherwise might not have been suggested.

Summary

If we return now to Stancaro's letter to Calvin, we see the continuity of his position with the tradition of the western Church before him. Stancaro's chief concern is that we should not understand Christ's mediatorial activity in a manner that threatens his unity with the Father and the Spirit in his divinity, the same concern that emerged at the time of the Arian crisis. To meet this dilemma, Stancaro adopted the two-natures approach to understanding Christological texts or statements that characterized the western discussion of Christ's role as Mediator, and argued that Christ mediates only in his human nature, while in his divine nature he shares in the unitary operation of the Trinity for salvation of the world. Moreover, we also see that Stancaro follows theologians like Thomas and Bonaventure and understands mediation in relation to Christ's reconciling work as priest between God and humanity, though his focus on Christ's priestly work appears more severe than either of his predecessors who also offered broader views of Christ's work. It seems, therefore, incorrect to agree with those who would treat Stancaro's position as either novel or heterodox within the theological context of the West.[35] Indeed, it is only on the basis of his continuity with the medieval tradition preceding him that we can make sense of his statement, after the rejection of his position by the Reformers, that "Peter Lombard is worth more than one hundred Luthers, two hundred Melancthons, three hundred Bullingers, four hundred Peter Martyrs, and five hundred Calvins, and all of them ground in a mortar and pestle would not amount to an ounce of true theology."[36] For Stancaro, the doctrine that Christ is Mediator only in his human nature, dictated by the logic of the doctrine of the Trinity, is the teaching of the Church, modern and ancient, and the Reformers reject it only at their own peril.

[35] See, for example, Tylanda, "Christ the Mediator," pp. 5, 9. I believe that Willis would also fit into this camp, though it is not entirely clear from his text. See Willis, *Catholic Christology*, pp. 67–70.
[36] From Stancaro's second treatise in response to the rejection by the ministers in Zurich, found in F. Church, *The Italian Reformers* (New York, 1932), pp. 345–356 (taken from Tylanda, "Calvin's Second Reply," p. 141).

In fact, however, it is precisely this relation of Stancaro's position to the Catholic tradition preceding him which ensured that the Reformers would reject his teaching, even as they had rejected the broader Roman stance on mediation, to their own peril, from the beginning. At the center of the debate between the Reformers and Rome is the question of the mediation of the grace and knowledge of God – though not as a question of how Christ mediates, but whether Christ alone is Mediator or whether Christ mediates along with the Church in its authoritative tradition, priesthood, and sacraments. In their cause, the Reformers take up Paul's statement in 1 Timothy 2:5 ("there is one Mediator between God and men, the man Jesus Christ."), which undergirded Stancaro's argument; but the Reformers' original interest in this passage is Paul's assertion of Christ's singularity as Mediator. To support Paul's claim, they argue that Christ alone can serve as Mediator between God and the Church, for only one who is both God and human can perform this task. Zwingli serves as an example of the Reformers' position.

Zwingli contends that, *pace* the opinion of the papists, who hold (he claims) that masses, indulgences, etc., mediate between God and humanity, Christ alone mediates because he alone brings true and lasting peace between God and humanity; but he does so only in the union of the two natures in his person as the God–human. We could not be reconciled to God "by the sole strength of Christ's human weakness," Zwingli explains, "but by the power of the divine nature which is united with human strength, so that, as human weakness is joined to God through Christ and united with him, we too may be reconciled to God through the suffering and sacrifice of Christ."[37] Christ in his humanity alone could not mediate, for one who is solely human could not offer true obedience to God; likewise, he would not mediate only in his divinity, for "the Mediator must be able to get in among the angered and the hurt."[38] So, he concludes:

> He is not Mediator as a mere human being, for we have amply demonstrated that sheer human weakness cannot make satisfaction before God, unless it be both God and Man. Since he is God, he is able to fulfill the will of God; indeed, not merely fulfill it, for God's will is none other than his own will. Since he is a human being, he can be a sacrifice which pays ransom to God on behalf of us poor sinners.[39]

---

[37] Zwingli, "Exposition and Basis of the Conclusions or (67) Articles," from Huldrych Zwingli, *Writings*, vol.1, trans. E. J. Furcha (Allison Park, PA: Pickwick Publications, 1984), p. 129.
[38] Ibid., p. 131.   [39] Ibid.

The argument that Zwingli makes here is in some sense simply a variation of Anselm's argument for the necessity of the hypostatic union for our atonement – that only one who is both God and human can reconcile us to God. His Roman opponents would have had no quarrel with that contention, for they had never claimed that Christ mediated in his humanity divorced from his divinity or that the Church in its sacerdotal system mediated in any manner except as it was an instrument of Christ. But Zwingli draws a particular conclusion from this argument – that because Christ could mediate only as the God–human, so all true mediation required such a person – which excluded all merely human mediation, including that of the priests in their performance of the mass and that of the saints in their intercessions before the throne of God. A corollary for Zwingli, then, to Christ's sole mediatorship is Christ's mediation in his person as the God–man, for it is this latter fact that ensures the uniqueness of all of his activity.

But does Zwingli's argument actually defeat the traditional position that Christ mediates only in his humanity? Zwingli claims that Christ must be both God and human to mediate between humanity and God because only through the union of his two natures could he offer the obedience that God requires and offer himself to atone for the sins of humanity. However, this assertion had never been denied from Augustine to Stancaro. The traditional argument began with the hypostatic union and claimed that, while the divine nature enabled Christ's mediation through his obedience and expiatory death, it was the human nature which was obedient and died, and which thus mediated. Therefore, for Calvin to successfully refute Stancaro, he would need to offer a logic affirming not merely that Christ's divinity enabled his mediation, but that it was directly involved with it. To do this, he would need to make a dramatic break with the tradition.

The Word as Mediator

In a bold gambit that opens both treatises against Stancaro, Calvin argues that to properly understand how Christ is Mediator, we must first understand that even before the issue of the incarnation as a response to our fall arises, Christ was Mediator in relation to creation as God's eternal Word. "[F]rom the beginning of creation he already truly was Mediator, for he always was Head of the Church, had primacy over the angels, and was the firstborn of every creature."[40] Paul's language in Colossians and Ephesians teaches us that Christ's mediatorship entails a broad set of duties: as the

---

[40] Tylanda, "Christ the Mediator," p. 12 (*CO* 9:338).

first-born of creation, he is the "mode of communication from which otherwise hidden source, the grace of God flowed to men";[41] he is a mid-point (*medium*) between the Father and creation;[42] and, as Head of the angels, he maintains them under his command and unites them to God.[43] Each of these roles precedes Adam's fall, our need for reconciliation that arises from it, and Christ's incarnation as a response to it. They are roles fulfilled by the Word in his divinity alone.

This theme of the Word's mediatorial activity before the incarnation is not new to Calvin's thought but appears several times within the *Institutes*. In his discussion of the deity of the Word, Calvin argues that Moses describes the eternal Word as the "intermediary" in the creation of the universe, and Calvin contends that only such an intermediary does justice to God's glory in the act of creation.[44] Indeed, all of God's speaking – in creation and through the prophets – is grounded in this substantial Word or Wisdom of God. Without such a foundation, the Father's outreach to the world absurdly would seem to be a "merely fleeting and vanishing utterance."[45] Likewise, Calvin appeals to the Ephesians' claim that Christ is Head over the angels as well as the Church when arguing with Servetus about Christ's eternal sonship.[46]

Calvin immediately acknowledges in both letters that Adam's fall and the resultant alienation of humanity from God form the primary context for speaking of Christ as Mediator, so that we develop our notion of his mediation under the rubric of his incarnation, "as he is God manifest in the flesh."[47] Thus, although references to the mediation of the Word do appear prominently in the letters to the Polish Brethren and in the *Institutes*, this theme does not figure centrally in Calvin's Christology. But Calvin, nonetheless, begins his discussion of the Mediator with the role of the Word in mediating creation and as the Head of the angels to quickly reframe the debate in which he is engaged, turning the twelve-century-old debate about Christ as Mediator on its head. Rather than accepting that incarnation was necessary for mediation to take place, and then arguing for one of the two options entailed by this assumption, he begins by implicitly repositioning the Trinitarian grammar behind this assumption in its relation to Christological discussion, arguing that mediation stands at the heart

---

[41] Tylanda, "Calvin's Second Reply," p. 147 (*CO* 9:350).

[42] Tylanda, "Christ the Mediator," p. 13 (*CO* 9:338).

[43] Tylanda, "Christ the Mediator," p. 13; "Calvin's Second Reply," p. 152 (*CO* 9:338, 354). See also Willis, *Catholic Christology*, p. 7.

[44] *Inst.* xiii.7, p. 129 (*Opera Selecta* [hereafter *OS*] 3:117).   [45] Ibid.

[46] *Inst* II.xiv.5, p. 489 (*OS* 3:466).   [47] Tylanda, "Calvin's Second Reply," p. 147 (*CO* 9:350).

of God's activity toward us. Calvin wants to reorient this Trinitarian grammar on the basis of certain methodological commitments and the insights they entail, and the remainder of this chapter will seek to illumine this effort as Calvin develops his own understanding of why and how Christ is Mediator.

The outlines of his position are already discernible in what we have seen so far. In the first place, Calvin's talk of Christ as Mediator is shaped by the language he finds in Scripture – in this case the Christological hymns from Ephesians and Colossians. The doctrine of the Trinity may suggest that we should be wary of identifying the Word as Mediator before the Word is incarnate, but that is not the way that Paul speaks of the Word. We must follow Paul and find another way to protect the natural equality of the Word alongside the Father. How Calvin will accomplish this second task we will see in time.

Secondly, the language of Scripture directs us to give the notion of mediation a broader scope than the theological tradition had come to accord it. The tradition in the medieval West conceived of Christ's mediation primarily in relation to his appeasement of the Father on account of Adam's sin, so that Stancaro, in the end, focused only on this aspect of Christ's work; but Christ's role as first-born of creation and Head of the Church and the angels suggests that he is Mediator as Head as much as expiator. A considerable portion of Calvin's argument following the opening sections of the letters will be devoted to the sense in which Christ's mediatorial headship requires not just his human nature, but also his divine nature.

Finally, in the midst of all this talk of natures, the implicit logic in Calvin's discussion is that mediation as an activity is carried out by a person, not by his natures, though this person certainly is only able to carry out this activity on the basis of his natures. If the Word mediates between the Father and creation, it cannot be his nature that mediates, for he shares that nature with the Father. Rather, it is the Word, as a person distinct from the Father, who mediates), though he is only able to perform this mediation on the basis of his divine nature, through which the hidden grace of God can be poured out upon us and by which we can be united to the Father. So, too, it is a person, Christ, who mediates, Calvin argues, but he mediates only on the basis of both of his natures, each of which is essential.

With this pivotal introduction to his Christology in place, Calvin then asserts that we should think about Christ primarily as he has become incarnate in response to Adam's sin. Calvin thus makes the transition from the office of the Word to the office of Christ as Mediator, and from here he will pick up the threads that he has already introduced and expand on them as he examines how the complete person of Christ, in his divine and human natures, is required to fulfil the entire scope of this office.

The complete office of the Mediator

Calvin first wants to establish that Christ's divine nature is required for his activity as the Mediator between God and humanity, filling out in the most obvious way the constricted picture of the Mediator that Stancaro had developed. To make his case, he must argue that the divine nature is needed not merely as a prerequisite for the human nature's fulfillment of Christ's mediatory task, but rather by the task itself – that Christ's divinity, in other words, does not simply enable Christ's humanity, but is itself involved in the very act of mediation.

In order to argue for the necessity of the divine nature in the act of mediation, Calvin must first broaden the scope of what is understood as Christ's mediatorial office, as he had begun to do in his declaration that the Word from the beginning had fulfilled this office of Mediator. Stancaro starts with the assumption that Christ mediates as he is obedient to God's law and suffers an atoning death. If one accepts this premise, then it is difficult to argue against the limitation of his mediation to his human nature, given that, within a sixteenth-century western framework, neither obedience nor suffering could be attributed to the divine. Calvin therefore responds that Christ's atoning sacrifice, though it is a part of his mediatorial activity, does not exhaust it:

Christ did not fulfill all the duties of his office by expiation and sacrifice. What does it mean to overcome death? To rise in the power of the Spirit and receive life from oneself? To unite us to God and to be one with God? Without doubt, these will not be found in Christ's human nature apart from the divinity, yet they do come into consideration when it is a question of the Mediator's office.[48]

In answer to Stancaro, Calvin begins by expanding the contours of Christ's office to include a number of attributes and functions, spoken of in Scripture, that Calvin will relate to Christ's headship over us. Christ overcomes death, gives life, defends and protects us, and guides and unites us to the Father. In all of these ways, Christ mediates between us and the Father, not to the exclusion of his priestly sacrifice but in conjunction with it; and so Calvin includes them under the rubric of Christ's headship

---

[48] Ibid., p. 153 (*CO* 9:355).

with the priestly functions of Christ in his description of the office of the Mediator.[49]

At the end of this discussion, he summarizes that Christ "is made king and appointed priest over the Church." He goes on to add that he also "governed the prophets by his spirit."[50] The full scope of the Mediator's office is grasped not merely as it is seen in its priestly dimensions, but also as it includes Christ's headship or kingship and his inspiration of the prophets. We understand, therefore, all that Christ has done, and so who he is in light of what he has done, only as we accept this threefold character of his office and explain his being and work in relation to it.

Of course, Calvin is not the first to note the full scope of Christ's office, but, by bringing this full scope of Christ's office under the rubric of his mediation (which is a *novum* as far as I can discern), he consolidates Christo-logical talk and thus allows it to achieve a clearer focus and a more complete expression. Christ's royal office is not simply mentioned but is explored in detail as one dimension of Christ's work overall.[51] This will lead to a more potent Christocentrism in Calvin's thought, which is a thesis of this book as a whole.

The mediation of the complete person of Christ

Indeed, as this expansion of Christ's mediation produces a more robust picture of Christ's work, it also allows Calvin to more easily demonstrate why Christ cannot be Mediator in his human nature alone. All of the attributes and functions of headship that Calvin lists require from Calvin's perspective Christ's divine nature. Christ can unite us to God and show us the way to the Father only because he is already one with God. Likewise, Christ overcomes death and gives us life only because he, in his divinity, has life in himself. For Calvin, Christ's headship involves both a preeminence and an ability that cannot be rightfully ascribed to the human; thus, it

---

[49] Tylanda, "Christ the Mediator," pp. 13–14; "Calvin's Second Reply", pp. 147–9 (*CO* 9:338–339, 350–352).

[50] Tylanda, "Christ the Mediator," p. 14 (*CO* 9:340).

[51] I have already noted Thomas' largely undeveloped attribution of the threefold office to Christ (*ST* III.22.1, ad. 3), but a more interesting example of a medieval exploration of this idea is found in John de La Rochelle's "Introduction to the Four Gospels" (*Franciscan Christology*, Damian McElrath, ed. [St. Bonaventure, NY: Franciscan Institute Publications, 1980], pp. 46–58). There we find an exposition of the character of each Gospel under the rubric of the attribution to each Gospel of one of the animals (lion, human, ox, and eagle) from Ezekiel's vision (Ezek. 1:68). De La Rochelle uses the categories of Christ's threefold human prerogatives (kingly, priestly, and doctoral) to characterize the three Synoptic Gospels, drawing on Augustine's earlier discussion of Christ's royal and priestly *personae* (Augustine, *De consensu evangelistarum*, Book I, ch. 6, n. 9). But, again, though we find these categories operative in this work, they are little developed and are not used to structure any broader thinking about Christ in the context of theology.

ideally makes his case for the necessity of Christ's divinity, especially when Calvin can tie to it arguments that Christ's priestly being and activity require his divinity.[52]

In its narrowest sense, Calvin's debate with Stancaro revolves around the place of Christ's divine nature in his mediating task. His discussion, therefore, is formulated to show the necessity of that nature in fulfilling that task, but this does not mean that Calvin ignores Christ's human nature entirely. Calvin is clear that, after Adam's fall, Christ's mediation includes his humanity; but he consistently pairs requirements for humanity with requirements for divinity. Christ is our brother, through his human nature, and is also our guide to the Father, through his divine nature.[53] A sense of the necessity of both natures for mediation emerges from the totality of Calvin's discussion, and that he does not mention the human nature more is presumably attributable to the fact that he assumes its role in the debate.[54]

Overarching this talk of each nature's necessity in Christ's mediatorial activity is the fact that we speak of these natures only in the complete person of Christ.[55] In the Christological hymn in Philippians 2, Paul speaks simply neither of the human nature of Christ nor of the divine, but "[he] places before our eyes a complete person composed of two natures."[56] Christ is able to mediate because in his person divinity and humanity are united; but it is the person of Christ, and not his natures, who mediates.

Calvin draws out this emphasis on Christ's person most clearly when he takes up the question of the proper Christological hermeneutic for interpreting Scripture. Following his argument in the *Institutes*, Calvin tells us that there are some passages in Scripture that apply chiefly to Christ's humanity and others that apply chiefly to his divinity. This is consistent with the so-called Antiochene hermeneutic, mentioned earlier in this chapter, and a possible corollary to this hermeneutic is the application of scriptural passages that speak of Christ's mediatorial activity to Christ in his humanity. Calvin, however, moves in another direction and argues that passages referring to Christ's mediation should be read not in relation to either nature, but with reference to his complete person as the God–human, the Word incarnate – a teaching that resembles more what I have described as the Alexandrian approach to Scripture.

[52] Tylanda, "Christ the Mediator," pp. 13–14; "Calvin's Second Reply," pp. 147–149 (*CO* 9:338–339, 350–352).

[53] Tylanda, "Calvin's Second Reply," p. 148 (*CO* 9:351).

[54] Calvin dwells at more length on the necessity and significance of Christ's humanity in the *Institutes* ii.xiii, as I shall explain in chapter 6 (pp. 208–210).

[55] See, for example, Tylanda, "Calvin's Second Reply," p. 148 (*CO* 9:351).

[56] Ibid.

In John's Gospel, which, for Calvin, is directed to the meaning of Christ's office as Mediator,[57] "[Christ] claims for himself what does not belong to either nature but concerns the complete person."[58] The immediate context of this assertion is Christ's statement in John: "I am in the Father and the Father is in me" (John 14:11). "There to the life," Calvin tells us, "is the picture of a Mediator!"[59] It is a picture in which Christ's humanity allows for the revelation of his divinity; such that the revelation (mediation) takes place not in either nature alone, but only in the unity of Christ's person.[60]

To make his case for the relation between Christ's person and office, Calvin began by breaking down this office to highlight how its different aspects require his divinity and his humanity, each in their own right; but once this is done he continues that "all the actions which Christ performed to reconcile God and man refer to the whole person, and are not to be separately restricted to only one nature." Calvin is wont to describe Christ as "God revealed in the flesh," implying a linking or bonding of the two natures indicated therein by the action of revelation or mediation such that neither is grasped in its significance without the other. It is in a dynamic personal unity that mediation occurs. Indeed, as we shall see in chapter 6, there is for Calvin an organic connection between the concepts of person and activity that intertwines the two in his thinking.

Once Calvin has made his case for this relation of person and office in Christ's mediation, he turns his attention to Stancaro's objections. Calvin, not surprisingly, is largely dismissive of Stancaro and his concerns; he describes them as "foolish" and as "absurdities."[61] Stancaro is a prime example, for Calvin, of one who is guilty of bad logic by allowing his theological preoccupations to cloud the witness of Scripture.

Scripture as witness to God's gracious economy

From Calvin's perspective, Stancaro's primary failing is that he is a poor reader of Scripture, particularly because he does not allow Scripture to provide the framework for articulating doctrine. His neglect of Christ's

---

[57] "The Deity of Jesus Christ," *The Deity of Jesus Christ and Other Sermons*, Leroy Nixon, trans. (Grand Rapids: Eerdmans, 1950), p. 16 (*CO* 47:468).

[58] Tylanda, "Calvin's Second Reply," p. 149 (*CO* 9:352).   [59] Ibid.

[60] *Comm. John* 14:11, II.47. Quotations from Calvin's commentaries will rely on the English translations in the Calvin Translation Society edition of Calvin's commentaries (*Commentaries of John Calvin*, 46 vols. (Edinburgh: Calvin Translation Society, 1843–55; reprint, Grand Rapids: Eerdmans, 1948–50) which are adequate for the purposes of this book. I will cite these commentaries by Scriptural reference, volume, and page number. Parenthetical references to the Latin text of Calvin's commentaries will follow, taken from *Ioannis Calvini Opera quae supersunt Omnia*, ed. Baum, Cunitz, and Reuss (Brunswick, 1863–1900).

[61] Tylanda, "Christ the Mediator," p. 15; "Calvin's Second Reply," p. 150 (*CO* 9:340, 353).

headship exhibits most clearly his inattention to how Scripture speaks of Christ, Calvin argues, but underlying this particular neglect is a general refusal to allow how Scripture speaks of Christ – that is, primarily in God's economy for our salvation – to provide the context for understanding the implications of Trinitarian doctrine. Fundamental to Stancaro's case is the logic traced above: if Christ in his divine nature is one with the Father, then he can be said to mediate between humanity and God in his humanity, but not his divinity. Calvin acknowledges the first step in this argument – that Christ in his divinity is one with the Father – but he refuses to accept that the rest follows necessarily.

We must distinguish, he tells us, between God's essence – who God is in and for Godself – and God's revelation of Godself in God's economy – who God is for us. Calvin agrees that in God's essence, the Son is eternally one with the Father and so is in all respects equal to the Father; but that does not mean that this unity and equality must rule our talk of the relation of the Father and the Son in God's economy for our salvation. It need not mean this, for it is the prerogative of the Father and the Son for the Son to subordinate himself to the Father to mediate between God and humanity. And we should be careful that it does not mean this. God's essence is a profound and unfathomable mystery that we must revere; thus, we should speak of it simply, seldom, and with great care. We understand only vaguely the mystery of the Trinity, for it is beyond our comprehension and God has not chosen to reveal its depths to us. But God in Scripture has spoken copiously of the economy whereby God has related to us through God's Son; and so we must turn to Scripture and to the divine activity toward us of which God speaks therein, to learn what God would teach us of Godself. Calvin writes: "Therefore, there is no safer way than to bid farewell to profane subtleties and speculation, and by means of [God's] words hold our minds fixed on that admirable dispensation in which the Father is said to have sent his only begotten Son."[62] And elsewhere:

If, properly speaking and according to the usual mode of Scripture, Christ is Mediator between God the Father and us, that cunning speculation of his only entangles and obscures what is otherwise clear . . . Leaving aside that profound and incomprehensible mystery [the doctrine of the Trinity], we only count what we have learned from the Scriptures and the sacred lips of Christ.[63]

Calvin makes a set of methodological points here that also run throughout the *Institutes*. Our concern in theology is primarily not with God's essence but with God's activity toward us, especially as God has been active

---

[62] Tylanda, "Calvin's Second Reply," p. 151 (*CO* 9:354).   [63] Ibid., pp. 152–153 (*CO* 9:355).

in Jesus; and our thoughts about that activity should be shaped by the witness of Scripture. Stancaro ignores both of these axioms when he allows his elaboration of the doctrine of the Trinity the primary role in determining his Christology, and the result is invidious in its limitation and impoverishment of Christ's mediation. A primary claim of this book will be that Calvin takes both of these points seriously to the degree that we can understand his Christology only as we grasp it in its relationship to Scripture's witness to God's economy for our salvation – only, that is, as it emerges from the narrative of God's relationship with God's Church as it is contained within both Israel's history and the Gospel history which form the backbone of the Old and New Testaments.[64] I explore this point in more detail in the next chapter.

The condescension of the Son

If we listen to Scripture and its testimony to this economy, Calvin has explained, we find that Christ's mediatory office involves a wide range of activities fulfilled through his two natures in the totality of his person. This implies that in his person as the God–human Christ is subordinate to the Father; and, we should add here, given what Calvin writes of the mediation of the Word in creation and as Head of the angels, the person of the Word, as it is active in God's economy before and apart from the incarnation, is also subordinate to the Father. But, from Calvin's perspective, in neither case is this subordination a threat to the unity and equality of the Son with the Father in eternity, for, again, we must separate God's essence from the economy that God has ordered for our salvation. Calvin writes:

As long as Christ sustains the role of Mediator he does not hesitate to submit himself to the Father. He does this not because his divinity has lost its rank when he was clothed in the flesh, but because he could not in any other way interpose himself as intermediary between us and the Father without the Father's glory, in the present dispensation, becoming clearly visible in the person of the Mediator.[65]

---

[64] Calvin's turn from what he would term speculative questions to an attention to God's economy, especially as it is revealed in biblical history, brings Calvin's theological approach into some congruence with that of Irenaeus, mentioned briefly above. Susan Schreiner notes this relationship and articulates it as concern for Christ's redemption of history: Susan E. Schreiner, *The Theater of His Glory: Nature and Natural Order in the Thought of John Calvin* (Grand Rapids: Baker Academic, 1991), pp. 108–11. This is right, but the focus of this book goes more deeply into the heart of this relationship, I believe, with its emphasis on Christ's redemption through history. This is what validated history in the context of Irenaeus' dispute with Marcion and the Gnostics, and it is the center of Calvin's work, as well.

[65] Tylanda, "Christ the Mediator," p. 15 (*CO* 9:340).

Christ's subordination to the Father in God's economy is a necessity of his office. Only as his divinity is veiled in his humanity can he be present among us in such a way that he can lead us back to the Father. In commenting upon the central text of those who argue that Christ is Mediator only in his humanity, 1 Timothy 2:5 ("There is one God, and there is one Mediator between God and men, the man Jesus Christ"), Calvin contends that Paul calls Christ "man" in this text because he is set out as "our ordinary approach to the Father." Calvin expands on this argument in the *Institutes* and explains that Christ in his divinity would be too glorious for sinful humanity to approach, but in his humanity we can approach him as our brother without fear.

The subordination, then, which Calvin describes, refers not to the ontological relationship between the Father and the Son, but rather to a loving decision shared by the Father and the Son. Calvin here picks up on a theme described earlier in Athanasius, that the Son in his mediation of the relationship between God and the world condescends to be the condition of the possibility of that relationship. He becomes the medium through which that relationship is transacted based on his willingness to stand between the Father and the world, and this willingness speaks to the humility of the Son and manifests the love of the Father. It is a warrant for Christ's exaltation, not a sign of his imperfection.

The Son's subordination through his condescension is not accidental to Calvin's theology, proceeding only out of his commitment to hearing how Scripture speaks of Christ and to the integrity of the complete person of Christ in his office as Mediator. Rather, it is essential to his articulation of the theme of "accommodation" that runs throughout his thinking.[66] Fundamental to Calvin's theology is an intuition of the infinite gap between God and humanity, a gap grounded in our creatureliness and exacerbated by our sin. We have no capacity for God, so God capacitates Godself to us (playing off Willis' helpful formula, *infinitus capax finiti per accommodatio*).[67] God in Christ brings Godself down to our level so that God might communicate God's will and grace to us. God in Christ condescends.

Calvin, in his letters to the Polish Brethren, is deeply committed to a Christology that is doctrinally correct. Trinitarianism is not negotiable on the basis of biblicism, but doctrine is properly sounded and heard only

---

[66] Ford Lewis Battles' article "God Was Accommodating Himself to Human Capacity" is, of course, the classic expression of this insight into Calvin's theology (in *Interpretation* 31 [1977]:19–38; reprinted in R. Benedetto, ed., *Interpreting John Calvin* [Grand Rapids: Baker Books, 1996], pp. 117–138).

[67] David Willis, "Rhetoric and Responsibility in Calvin's Theology," in *The Context of Contemporary Theology: Essays in Honor of Paul Lehmann* (Atlanta: John Knox, 1974), pp. 43–64.

within the greater context of God's witness to Godself in Scripture. In relation to Christology, that witness testifies to Christ's work in his person as the Mediator through his threefold office as priest, king, and prophet – this is the substance of God's economy for our salvation, with which Scripture is concerned. Calvin's point, in the end, is not that Stancaro is too Trinitarian, but that he has not understood that doctrine in all of its richness because he has listened to it in isolation. Within the realm of Scripture, Trinitarian thinking tells us not what God cannot do – mediate through the divine nature of the person of the Word – but what God graciously has done – condescend in love.

This is a theological point worthy in itself, but I introduce this book with it to alert us to the underlying methodological approach which Calvin brings to Christology. Faithfulness to the Church's doctrine is maintained throughout; Calvin not only adheres to dogmatic statements and theological traditions, but explores them at length in both his commentaries and the *Institutes*. However, these doctrines find their final place in his Christological thinking only when they have been placed in the greater context of Scripture's witness to God's economy for our salvation. Hence, we begin our detailed exposition of Calvin's understanding of this economy in its relation to Christology in the next chapter.

CHAPTER 2

Christ and the covenant history

In his letter to the Polish Brethren, Calvin directs his readers to Scripture as the source for shaping Christology, but he does not tell us to look in the first place for Christological definitions there. Rather, he asks us to begin by attending to God's witness in Scripture to God's economy for our salvation. We are first to consider how God, who is the author of history and of the scriptural texts which record it, administers God's relationship with the world and with God's Church in particular. From there we are to draw images, concepts, and the dynamic that give form to how we speak of Christ. We do this because there is an intimate relationship between this economy and who Christ is; we can even say that Christ is the substance of the economy.

Our task in this chapter is to examine how Calvin describes this economy – to find the rubrics under which he construes God's redemptive relationship with the world – so that we might begin to identify the Christological vision that emerges out of such a description. By proceeding in this way, we are taking Calvin at his word that Christology follows and is determined by the understanding of this economy that we have been given in Scripture. We look not for abstract definitions of this economy, taken apart from Scripture, any more than we would begin with abstract Christological definitions; rather, we look to the scriptural testimony to discern the picture of God's economy inherent within it.

When Calvin reads Scripture and its depiction of God's economy, he finds there, first and foremost, the history of the covenant. In Abraham, Calvin would argue, God revived the Church, which was lost in Adam's fall, through an eternal covenant; this covenant was renewed in Moses and the Law and in David and the kingship before it was finally fulfilled in Christ. God thereby gave God's people a land, a Law, and a king, through which God enacted and manifested God's mercy toward them in spite of their disobedience. Moreover, in and through these gifts and promises, God called the Church to look for a yet greater enactment and manifestation of

God's mercy that was to come in Christ. God wills relationship with God's chosen, and the covenant was the means to and the form of this relationship. In the *Institutes*, Calvin identifies what he calls the "very formula of the Covenant": "I will be your God and you shall be my people" (Lev. 26:12).[1] Scripture is dedicated to recounting the formation of the bond this formula entails, and, if we are committed to beginning theology by attending to Scripture's witness to God's economy for our salvation, then for Calvin we must begin here with the covenant history.

In this chapter, we begin our exploration of Calvin's Christology by attending closely to Calvin's understanding of the covenant history as he develops it in his commentaries on the Old Testament and as he finds it fulfilled in Christ's Gospel history. Calvin's Old Testament commentaries unfold the story of God's covenant with God's chosen, and we find in this unfolding constant reference to Christ as the Mediator on whom this covenant depends and to whom it looks. Thus, we begin to get a sense of the shape of Calvin's Christology if we attend first to his relation of Christ to Israel's history. Following this introduction, I outline three principal features of the covenant history for Calvin: its unity, its gracious character, and its relationship to Christ as its Mediator. I then develop a more full-bodied picture of this story as Calvin sees it narrated in Scripture, paying special attention to the initiation of the covenant in the story of Abraham, in which we find the essential characteristics of the history best illustrated, and its development through the giving of the Law and the Davidic kingship, as well as in the work of the prophets. Through this exegetical work, we discover the central pattern of Calvin's Christology – that Christ mediates the covenant in history through his threefold office of priest, king, and prophet. This pattern structures the following three chapters of this book.

This discussion of the Old Testament history also begins to give dimension to the relationship between Christ and the covenant history, dimensions that I further sketch out in the following section of the chapter. There we probe the significance of Calvin's marriage of Christology to history. Insofar as "history" can refer us both to the enacted events of which history consists and to the crafted narratives that record these events, we see that Calvin's historical Christology includes activist and rhetorical dimensions. That is, it is focused on what Christ has done and on the manner in which the narrative of that doing shapes us to respond to Christ in his activity. Moreover, this understanding of the relationship of Christ to history demands a more complete perspective on Calvin's insistence that we read

---

[1] *Inst.* II.x.8, p. 434 (*OS* 3:409).

Scripture in its historical sense. The historical sense of Scripture, for Calvin, refers to the sense intended by Scripture's authors, but only in light of the broad shape and course of the history which Scripture narrates. Since that history is essentially Christological for Calvin, the historical sense is not antithetical to or in tension with the Christological sense; rather, the two are the same.

In the final section of this chapter, I examine in broad strokes how this template of the historical, covenantal character of Calvin's Christology drawn from his Old Testament commentaries fits Calvin's exposition of Christology in his commentaries on Christ's Gospel history. My intention is to demonstrate the aptness of this model for understanding Calvin's Christological focus as it is embodied in the Gospel commentaries, recognizing that Calvin wrote his commentaries on the four Gospels before he turned to the Old Testament. We find, therefore, that Calvin emphasizes the genre of the Gospels as history (both in its dimension as enacted event and as rhetorically crafted presentation of these events) and that he connects this Gospel history to God's covenantal history as its fulfillment, especially as Christ has fulfilled the threefold office of priest, king, and prophet. As we shall see, all of this is indicative of Calvin's so-called soteriological concern – that is, that his Christology turns not on questions of who Jesus was, but rather around the axes of what Christ has done to save. This, he explains, is the soul of the Gospel.

This chapter, then, is quite involved, but it should establish what I argue is the fundamental framework for understanding Calvin's Christology: that it is essentially an historical Christology, with all that this entailed for Calvin, focused on Christ's role as the Mediator of God's covenant history with God's Church through the threefold office of priest, king, and prophet. This framework serves us in the following three chapters of the book, as we analyze the content of this Christology by examining Calvin's explication of each of Christ's three offices, looking at material from both his Gospel commentaries and the *Institutes*, always with an eye to the historical form in which Calvin believed this material to be embodied.

An implicit assumption in my approach is that the theme of the covenant history serves as an authentic organizing principle to these commentaries. Enough has been written on this topic elsewhere that I can make this case simply by means of illustration.[2] But a second assumption entailed by this thesis I want to articulate explicitly here at the outset: that this

---

[2] Hoekema and Bierma explore the importance and meaning of covenant in Calvin's theology, while Parker, Neuser, and Muller locate Calvin's discussion of this topic in the context of his commentaries. Anthony Hoekema, "Calvin's Doctrine of the Covenant of Grace," *Reformed Review* 15 (1962), 1–12;

emphasis on God's covenant history as it is fulfilled in Christ's Gospel history is foundational also to Calvin's *Institutes*, at least in their final form. This simply suggests that Calvin carries out in practice the theological method that he preaches to Stancaro, that the shape of Scripture should determine the shape of one's theology. As a method for understanding Calvin's theology, it suggests that we best invert Calvin's precept in the preface to the *Institutes* – that they were written as a guide for understanding Scripture – and work forward from his broader understanding of Scripture reflected in the commentaries to the *Institutes*. What Calvin finally sets down in the *Institutes* is drawn from Scripture, and so we best understand it if we turn first to its source. My claim here is not that Calvin presents in the *Institutes* an elaborate analysis of the concept of the covenant, but that the form of the covenant history in its intimate relationship to Christ's work as the Mediator of the covenant is inscribed on the very structure of the text.[3]

The attractiveness of this proposal is only augmented if we attend to the fact that the *Institutes* were given their definitive form in the years immediately following Calvin's work on his Old Testament and Gospel commentaries.[4] Thus, when Calvin comments that he is only satisfied with the *Institutes* "arranged in the *ordo* now set forth," we might suspect that this satisfactory *ordo* was shaped by his work on the commentaries.[5] Let me describe briefly what I have argued at more length elsewhere, that one force defining the shape of the 1559 *Institutes* is Calvin's attempt to express in Book II of the *Institutes* the theme of the covenant history that culminates in Christ's Gospel history, a theme that emerges for Calvin in his work on Scripture. Three central developments in the structure of the 1559 *Institutes* suggest that this is the case: (1) Calvin's separation of the material concerning our knowledge of God the Creator in Book I from

Hoekema, "The Covenant of Grace in Calvin's Teaching," *Calvin Theological Journal* 2 (1967), 133–161; Lyle D. Bierma, "Federal Theology in the Sixteenth Century: Two Traditions?" *Westminster Theological Journal* 45 (1983), 304–321. T. H. L. Parker, *Calvin's Old Testament Commentaries* (Edinburgh, 1986), p. 83; Wilhelm Neuser, "Calvins Verständnis der Heiligen Schrift," *Calvinus Sacrae Scripturae Professor: Calvin as Confessor of Holy Scripture*, Wilhelm Neuser, ed. (Grand Rapids: Eerdmans, 1994), pp. 43ff.; Muller, *The Unaccommodated Calvin*, pp. 154–145.

[3] Hence I agree with Muller that Calvin offers no extended discussion of his concept of covenant, but Muller misses the manner in which this concept undergirds the text as a whole: Muller, *Unaccommodated Calvin*, pp. 154–155.

[4] In the decade immediately preceding the publication of the 1559 *Institutes* Calvin published commentaries on Isaiah (1551/1559), the Gospel of John (1553), Genesis (1554), the harmony of the Synoptic Gospels (1555), the Psalms (1557), Hosea (1557), and the minor Prophets (1559); At the time of the publication of the 1559 *Institutes*, Calvin had set about work on a commentary on the last four books of Moses.

[5] *Inst.*, "To the Reader," p. 3 (*OS* 5).

the material concerning our knowledge of God the Redeemer in Book II
and his account of this separation; (2) Calvin's creation of a new chapter
discussing the mediation of Christ, evident in the history of the covenant
in the Old Testament (ii.vi); and (3) Calvin's new placement of the chapters
discussing the relationship of the Old and New Covenants (in ii.ix–xi). A
brief consideration of these three structural *nova* in the *Institutes* not only
outlines the coherence of this work with the general pattern of Calvin's
commentaries, but also begins to make evident that the *Institutes* in their
final form have altered the previous form of the *Institutes*, which centered
on the doctrine of justification by faith, to a new form, oriented to God's
history with God's Church, centered on Christ's Gospel history – what
Christ has done to enact God's relationship with us.

The literary history of the *Institutes* is marked by two fundamental shifts
in the structure of the text. In Calvin's initial expansion (1539) of his original (1536) text, the catechetical form of the text is augmented through
the addition of new material and the expansion of briefer discussions,
while its catechetical function is supplanted by a new concern to serve as
a set of *loci communes* providing instruction on the essential theological
questions that emerge for the student of theology in the interpretation
of Scripture.[6] Richard Muller has argued persuasively that the conjunction of Calvin's own work on Paul's Romans epistle and the influence of
Melancthon's Romans-inspired theological vision has placed a determinedly
Pauline soteriological stamp (as Paul was read by the Reformers) on the new
form of the 1539 *Institutes*, a form Calvin refines in future editions of the
text through to 1557. The skeleton of this new structure is expressed by
Muller in the movement sin–law–grace–the people of God in the Old and
New Testaments–predestination, with justification by faith (as a primary
thesis in the discussion of grace) serving as the heart of the whole alongside
a more expansive rendering of the Gospel in a chapter on faith and the
Creed.

But how do we account for the second structural shift in the *Institutes*,
as Calvin reorders the entire text under the four creedal topics. We should
look first to Calvin's opening discussion in Book II, where he shifts from
the topic of "The Knowledge of God the Creator" to "The Knowledge of
God the Redeemer in Christ, First Disclosed to the Fathers under the Law,
and Then to Us in the Gospel." Commentators on Calvin have struggled to
account for Calvin's decision to position his discussion of sin here at the start

---

[6] From Muller's helpful discussion of the shift in Calvin's thinking behind the 1539 revision of the
Institutes and its later cousins (*Unaccommodated Calvin*, pp. 119–130).

of Book II. It does not fit either the creedal structure or the structure of the twofold knowledge of God, which the titles of the two books portend, and it breaks his consideration of theological anthropology in two – allocating the understanding of humanity as created to Book I and humanity as broken by sin to Book II. But we should notice that Calvin begins Book II not so much with a discussion of sin in general as with a discussion of the Fall.[7] We have moved, Calvin informs us, from a consideration of the "original nobility" that God bestowed on Adam in creation to "Adam's desertion that enkindled God's fearful wrath" (*Inst.* ii.i–iv). We are located in Scripture here by Calvin, in Genesis, at the turn in the narrative between chapters 2 and 3, when the story of Adam, Eve, and the "apple" sets the course of the grand story of God's redemptive history with God's people. Calvin attempts repeatedly to signal this location in Genesis, explaining, for example, in Book I, that there he is only discussing the creation, and that he has not yet advanced "to the fall of the world," or its remedy, "that covenant by which God adopted to himself the sons of Abraham."[8] If we recognize this location, then we understand the division in Calvin's anthropology between Books I and II: it is the division between Genesis 1 and 2, the creation of humanity in the image of God, and Genesis 3, Adam's fall. Through this recognition, we can grasp that the introduction of sin in Book II signals not a doctrinal transition, but a cosmic cataclysm that will open out onto an inestimable blessing. We thereby gain an appreciation of the dynamism inherent in the *Institutes*.[9]

Our perception of the historical bent of Calvin's text is confirmed when we turn to the sixth chapter of Book II, the chapter added to the 1559 *Institutes* to follow immediately upon his initial discussion of sin. Calvin picks up the thread from the previous discussion – "The whole human race perished in the person of Adam" – as an introduction to the topic of redemption. The focus of this discussion is our need of Christ, the Redeemer, who renews in us a knowledge of God as Father, while the

---

[7] There is a discussion of sin here, to be sure, but it is a discussion that begins with original sin – which is to say Adam's sin. This could simply indicate that Calvin is following a typical systematic pattern of describing sin, in general, through attention to its primal, and so definitive instantiation, and this surely is a part of his procedure. The general pattern of the argument in Book II, however, supports my claim that Calvin's move here is not one of mere theological conformity, but is an evocation of the history narrated in Genesis, which places his entire discussion of sin in a broader framework, the history of God's redemption of the Church.

[8] *Inst.* I.vi.1, p. 71 (*OS* 3:61); see also *Inst.* I.x.1, p. 97 (*OS* 3:85). These passages were crafted specifically for the 1559 version of the text, fit to its new form.

[9] We should note that Book I introduces the principal characters to Scripture's narrative and provides the essential backstory from which this narrative makes sense. This is, of course, in addition to its purpose of reflecting Scripture's witness by beginning where Scripture begins – with creation.

context for this discussion is a broad, fast-paced, but inclusive survey of Israel's history with God from Abraham through the Law to David and the prophets, cast as God's saving response to Adam's fall. The point that Calvin drives home is the work of Christ manifested throughout Israel's history – that "apart from the Mediator, God never showed favor toward the ancient people" – and this serves as an occasion to rehearse the high points of that history, each of which is Christological in its own right.

Thus, Calvin broaches the subject of our need for the Mediator not through a full-throated exploration of the Chalcedonian implications of such a need (that waits for chapter xii), nor with an exposition of Christ's Gospel as the fulfillment of this need (chapter xvi), nor with an explanation of how we are justified through faith, which is our recognition of this need (Book III); rather, Calvin, having completed his commentaries on Genesis, the Psalms, and the prophets and just beginning his commentary on the last four books of Moses, crafts a new chapter to his story, making it for the first time the story that Scripture tells from the start. It is the story of humanity lost in a fall from paradise and then restored through God's relationship with a peculiar people, a relationship founded on, pointing to, and culminating in the story of Christ, the Mediator of this relationship.[10] Calvin is clear that Scripture's first story – the story of the Church founded in God's promise to Abraham – is a Christological story. But, more significantly for our purposes, he declares that if we are to understand this latter story, on which our identity as Christians depends, then we must begin here, with the history of Israel; here, with God's original adoption of God's people; here, with Christ's ministrations, dimly but clearly lit, before they burst forth like the noonday sun.

The historical progression of Calvin's narrative in Book II continues unabated in his exposition of the Law, where he deals at length with the center of God's covenant history with Israel; and again, when he introduces this topic, he first locates it within the broader framework of the history. It comes some four hundred years after the promise to Abraham, he tells us, not to wipe out this promise but to renew it. After this exposition of the Law, Calvin is ready to turn to Christ's Gospel, but he orders a smooth transition from Law to Gospel by the interposition of the three chapters on the relationship of the Old and New Covenants. Calvin achieves two goals with this new location of these chapters. First, he strikes another blow in

---

[10] The relationship between this new form of the *Institutes* to Calvin's work on his commentaries is most clearly apparent if we notice the striking resemblance between the form and content of the *Institutes* and summary of Scripture's story that Calvin offers in his *Argumentum* to his Genesis commentary. See *Comm. Gen., Argumentum*, pp. 64–65 (*CO* 23:11–12).

his mission against the too easy interpretation of Paul that sets Law and Gospel against one another, arguing instead for a unitary narrative view of Scripture in which the Gospel fully reveals, completes, and so fulfills what was the substance of the Law and the whole of the Old Covenant from the beginning – the mercy of God realized and manifested in Christ. Second, these chapters serve not only as a theological transition, but also as an historical transition – they are the book of Malachi or John the Baptist, if you will – summarizing the substance of the Old Testament history from which we have tasted Christ, but in such a way that we cannot rest content there, but are driven on in hope and desire to find the full banquet laid before us in the Gospel.

When Calvin argues in these chapters that Christ is the substance of God's economy both as it is expressed in the history of God's covenant with Israel and as it is fulfilled in his Gospel (ii.x.2), we can see that in the 1559 *Institutes* this comment has moved from being an occasional observation to being a summary of the structure of Book II of the *Institutes* in its entirety. The impact of this shift on our understanding of Calvin's Christology is at least twofold. First, it supplies and demands that God's covenant history with Israel be taken as the proper context for doing Christology. If you are going to explore our knowledge of God the Redeemer, Calvin's avowed purpose in Book II, then you must begin your discussion with Adam's fall and God's response through Abraham, Moses, David, and the prophets – each of whom, again, is Christological in their own right.

This reorientation toward the covenant history bears one very specific implication for Calvin's Christology. If we accept that the title of Mediator is central to Calvin's understanding of Christ, then we must heed his order of teaching in which this title is first introduced, not in chapter 12 of the second book with an analytic discussion of what is implied in such a title, but in chapter 6, under the rubric of Christ's work as the Mediator of the covenant to the church of the Old Testament – again, in a chapter written precisely to provide this coloring in the new shape of the 1559 *Institutes*. Calvin, in other words, has replaced a theoretical discussion of this topic, attentive primarily to the theological discussions of the previous five centuries, with a Christological narration of Scripture's history as the normative framework for understanding Christology.[11] Calvin does not disdain the theoretical discussion. He maintains it in ii.xii, but only as it is contextualized by ii.vi. This was our conclusion in the previous chapter.

---

[11] Note Muller's discussion of Calvin's purpose in ii.xii (Muller, *Christ and the Decree*, p. 28).

This norming effect of Scripture's history is most evident in the *Institutes* in Calvin's discussion of Christ's threefold office (ii.xv) – another discussion broadly reframed for the 1559 *Institutes*. In this new chapter Calvin offers the rubric of Christ's threefold office – each office being introduced through its relation to the instantiation of that office in Israel's history – as the means by which we might most expansively grasp Christ's work for us. This chapter now serves as a gateway into Calvin's broader discussion of Christ's work in his Gospel history (ii.xvi), thereby ordering our understanding of that discussion. Covenant history, read as Christological history, becomes for Calvin in the 1559 *Institutes* the story with which a Christian theologian must begin if they are to rightly convey a Christian knowledge of God the Redeemer.

This leads us to the second impact of the shape of the 1559 *Institutes* on our understanding of Calvin's theology: it rivets our attention on Christ's history, and through that history on Christ himself. The newly minted chapter 6 proclaims first and foremost that redemptive knowledge of God is *sola Christi*; and it offers an exposition of the covenant history in this context not to turn us away from Christ, toward that history, but to focus our attention on finding Christ in God's history, in the place where Christ has enacted and manifested God's fatherly love for God's Church. This focus on finding Christ in the history that Christ enacts is brought to a climax in the final paragraph of ii.xvi (before the appendix of chapter xvii, refuting Socinus), in Calvin's grand but concise proclamation of the Gospel history which is "a rich store of every kind of good [that] abounds in [Christ]" (*Inst.* ii.xvi.19). Look here, Calvin implores, for the foundation and fulfillment of your faith.

If we accept Muller's claim that the *Institutes* in their previous instantiations are shaped fundamentally by Paul's logic in Romans (and his analysis on that account makes a great deal of sense), then we must surely argue that this logic has been displaced (not replaced, but moved aside and reoriented) by this second logic of Christ's Gospel history as the fulfillment of God's covenant with God's people. This is to take seriously Calvin's comment that Paul's epistles are themselves Gospel only in a corollary fashion, only as their teaching is conformed to the Gospel per se, which is the "continuous history which shows how God sent his Son."[12] Calvin is deeply concerned with the right of order of teaching in his *Institutes*, and in the definitive version of the text he has turned from Paul's order to the order he found inscribed by God on Scripture as a whole.

---

[12] "Deity of Christ," p. 15 (*CO* 47:467).

THE COVENANT HISTORY

Calvin relates the covenant history in Scripture as the story of God's one covenant with the Church, beginning with Abraham in the twelfth chapter of Genesis, through which God works out the Church's redemption. (He annexes the first eleven chapters of Genesis to this covenant history as a kind of prologue.[13]) However, in his attention to Scripture's witness to this covenant, Calvin is clear that its history is defined by multiple instantiations. As I described it above, what was promised to Abraham was enacted under types through Moses and the Law and David and his kingdom before it was fulfilled in Christ. In Mosaic Law, God gave to the Church the rule of life, whereby the people could live into the holiness that God required, and established the way of salvation in priestly sacrifices, whereby the people were reconciled to God. In the Davidic kingdom, God anointed a king and promised an eternal kingdom through which God would provide for the safety and prosperity of the Church. In Christ, then, the reconciliation typified in the Law and the blessing typified in the kingdom were fulfilled by the one who could accomplish these both fully and finally.

Although we can speak of these separate instantiations of God's covenant with God's Church, Calvin never describes these as new or separate covenants; rather, they are renewals of the one eternal covenant that God made with Abraham when God initially called him to go into the land of Canaan. So the prescription of circumcision to Abraham and the Law given to Moses were bound to God's original covenant and were intended to recall it to the minds of the people that it might be etched there with certainty.[14] Calvin summarizes the progression of renewal through Israel's history in his comments on Isaiah 55:3 ("I will make an everlasting covenant with you, even the sure mercies of David"); there he states: "The Lord had indeed entered into a covenant with Abraham (Gen. 15:5, 17:7), afterwards confirmed it by Moses (Exod. 2:24, 33:1), and finally ratified this very covenant in the hand of David, that it might be eternal."[15] For Calvin, each new covenantal instantiation initiated on God's part is only the confirmation and, in some sense, the elaboration of the covenant that God originally made with Abraham.

---

[13] In this I differ from Parker (*Calvin's Old Testament Commentaries*, p. 83), who argues that the concept "covenant" seems to leave the first eleven chapters of Genesis hanging. My contention is that Calvin, in his discussion of Creation, does not set it apart from the narrative of the covenant, but, rather, in intentional relationship to it. See, for example, his *Argumentum* to his Genesis commentary (1.64 [*CO* 23:11–12]).

[14] See *Comm. Gen.* 17:2, 1.444–5 (*CO* 23.235) and *Comm. Exod.* 19:1, 1.313 (*CO* 24.192).

[15] *Comm. Isaiah* 55:3, IV.161 (*CO* 37.285).

Even the work of Christ is seen by Calvin as the renewal of the covenant with Abraham. Puzzling over why God stated that he should be remembered from eternity as the God of Abraham, Isaac, and Jacob (in Exod. 3) when he is revealed so much more clearly in Christ, Calvin concludes that, "since the coming of Christ the truth of the covenant made with Abraham was shewn forth, and was thus demonstrated to be firm and infallible, its memory was rather renewed than destroyed; and that thus it still survives and flourishes in the Gospel, since Abraham even now ceases not to be the father of the faithful under the one Head."[16] Calvin reads Scripture as the story of God's one covenant, begun with Abraham and completed in Christ, through which God has worked out God's redemptive economy for the world.

Moreover, this single covenant is, for Calvin, always and everywhere a covenant of grace. Indeed, "whenever the word 'covenant' appears in Scripture," he tells us, "we ought at the same time to call to remembrance the word, 'grace.' "[17] He is thus careful to distinguish what he calls the "peculiar" character of the Mosaic Law, that it demands perfect righteousness (it is this peculiar sense that led Paul to oppose it to the covenant made with Abraham) from its more general testimony to God's gratuitous adoption of the people conditioned only on God's mercy.[18] And indeed, even this peculiar character of the Law is subordinated to the gracious aspect of the Mosaic covenant. The demands of the Law were to drive the people, even in Moses' day, to look for their salvation in God's mercy alone. God's covenant with the Church, then, insofar as it is a redemptive covenant, is a covenant of grace, enacting and manifesting God's mercy in all its aspects.[19]

---

[16] *Comm. Exod.* 3:15, 1.75 (CO 24.45).   [17] *Comm. Isaiah* 55:3, IV.161 (CO 37.285).

[18] *Comm. Exod.* 19:1, 1.313 (CO 24:192). I discuss the peculiar nature of the Mosaic Law more fully below.

[19] On these two points, the unity of the covenant and its gracious aspect, Calvin differs from the so-called federal theologians who followed him. James Torrance presents a helpful summary both of the basics of federal theology (drawn largely from David Weir, *The Origins of Federal Theology in Sixteenth Century Reformation Thought* [London: Oxford University Press, 1990]) and of Calvin's understanding of "covenant" as it is distinct from federal theology. See Torrance, "The Concept of Federal Theology," in *Calvinus Sacrae Scripturae Professor*, pp. 15–40. Torrance draws a particularly helpful contrast between the federal theologians and Calvin on this point of the gracious aspect of God's covenant. For the former, the covenant of grace is subordinated to an initial covenant of Law, which was made at the time of Creation and broken in Adam's fall. The covenant of grace is, in fact, worked out only within the context of the Law, such that the Law provides the framework for Christ's gracious activity. For Calvin, God's gracious initiative in Christ, first disclosed in God's covenant with Abraham, forms the broader framework for understanding our redemption, and the Law is only understood within this framework as a gift disclosing the way of life to God's people and as a burden, driving them to Christ, when they cannot fulfill its requirements. See Torrance, *Calvinus Sacrae Scripturae*, pp. 30–32. See also Willem J. Van Asselt, *The Federal Theology of Johannes Cocceius (1603–1669)*, Raymond Blacketer, trans. (Leiden: Brill, 2001), who provides a more nuanced view of one thread of federal theology, while still maintaining Calvin's distinctiveness from this later development.

Of course, essential to the grace enacted and manifest within this covenant is the work of the Mediator.

God's covenant with Abraham is the historical foundation of the covenant, while God's grace and mercy are the theological foundation; but Calvin's attention to the covenant history led him also to the instrument by which it was founded, the end at which it aimed, and the substance of which it consisted, which was the Mediator, or Christ. Fundamental to Calvin's understanding of the covenant is that the initial covenant – that in Abraham all the families of the earth would be blessed – included within it the promise of Christ. That is to say, God's initial promise to Abraham was a promise of a Mediator who would remedy humanity's alienation from God and without whom we would have no access to God.[20] Thus, the faith that God's promises elicited, from the Patriarchs and from all who came after, was always faith in this Mediator. For Calvin it was obvious that the Mosaic Covenant, bound up as it was with the giving of the Law, set forth this Mediator in the ceremonies of reconciliation by which the people were taught to trust themselves to God's mercy. Neither the ceremonies nor the priests who performed them were efficacious in themselves; rather, they directed the people to the Mediator with his true sacrifice who still lay in their future.[21] Likewise, David's kingdom was established "to be a figure or shadow in which God might represent the Mediator to his Church."[22] Just as the Law promised a Mediator who would reconcile Israel to God, so in David God promised a Mediator or Messiah who would protect them from their enemies and secure for them a kingdom as their inheritance. Furthermore, these promises did not simply offer to Israel a future for which they could hope; the Mediator's grace was active and established through them – forgiveness was offered in the sacrifices of the Old Testament and the Church was protected from its enemies through David's reign. God's people, then, could participate in the grace of the Mediator by faith in anticipation of its fulfillment in Christ.

Thus, when Calvin writes in the *Institutes* that "apart from the Mediator, God never showed favor toward the ancient people, nor ever gave hope of grace to them," he is referring to Christ's role not only as the foundation on which God's covenant was promised and the end to which it was directed, but also as the very substance of the covenant in which God's people were engaged, by which God's grace was active in their lives.[23] The story of the

[20] See *Comm. Ps.* 89:30, III.440 (*CO* 31:822).
[21] See Exod. 12:21, I.221 (*CO* 24.136), Num. 3:5, II.221 (*CO* 24.449), Lev. 1.1, II.324–325 (*CO* 24.507), and Exod. 25:8, II.154–5 (*CO* 24.404–5).
[22] *Comm. Ps.* 89:30, III.440 (*CO* 31.822).   [23] *Inst.* II.VI.2, p. 342 (*OS* 3:321).

covenant is in at least one sense the story of God's promise of a Mediator to God's Church and of the manner in which that promise and its various fulfillments served to nurture and preserve the Church with God's grace until the coming of Christ. Thus, we see that the covenant history is the context for Calvin's Christology not only because it is the central focus of Scripture's witness to God's redemptive economy, but also because this history is essentially Christological. It is the history of the Mediator. With that in mind, we can now turn to an extended examination of Calvin's vision of the covenant history and the illumination it brings to this project.

Prologue

Scripture's narration of God's relation to humanity begins with what Calvin calls the history of the creation of the world in Genesis. In creation God proclaimed God's glory and mercy to a newly formed humanity so that humanity might respond with love and obedience. As Calvin puts it: "After the world had been created, man was placed in it as in a theatre, that he, beholding above him and beneath the wonderful works of God, might reverently adore their Author."[24] God established a rightly ordered relationship with humanity; but, as the story goes, humanity soon fell away, and a new, salvific initiative was required on God's part. Calvin insists that Genesis is properly understood only as these things are connected:

[T]hat the world was founded by God, and that man, after he had been endued with the light of intelligence, and adorned with so many privileges, fell by his own fault, and was thus deprived of all the benefits he had obtained; afterwards, by the compassion of God, he was restored to the life he had forfeited, and this through the loving-kindness of Christ; so that there should always be some assembly on earth, which being adopted into the hope of the celestial life, might in this confidence worship God. The end to which the whole scope of the history tends is to this point, that the human race has been preserved by God in such a manner as to manifest his special care for his Church.[25]

Calvin is sensitive to Scripture's exposition of God's relationship with humanity as one that begins with creation. So Calvin not only begins the *Argumentum* to his Genesis commentary with creation but also introduces the *Institutes* with a consideration of this same topic. But the story there begun quickly turns when humanity alienates itself from God; and the rest of Genesis and, indeed, the rest of Scripture occupies itself chiefly with God's proffered salvation in the call of the Church – what Calvin calls

---

[24] *Comm. Gen., Arg.,* 1.64 (*CO* 23:11–12).   [25] Ibid.

"the history of [humanity's] restoration, where Christ shines forth with the benefit of redemption."[26] The initial chapters of Genesis, then, form a kind of prologue to this history of restoration, a prologue set in the theater of creation, in which God in God's glory and kindness is introduced, along with humanity, created by God for proper relationship but fallen through their own willfulness.

For Calvin this prologue bears only indirectly on Christology. It does introduce a third character on the stage, the eternal Word of God, who is the Mediator of creation.[27] But Christology, for Calvin, is chiefly concerned with God's redemptive plan for God's Church – in the *Argumentum* to Genesis, Christ's name only arises with respect to the history of redemption. As Calvin says in the *Institutes*: "We know why Christ was promised from the beginning: to restore the fallen world and to succor lost men."[28] This prologue of the history of creation bears most directly on Christology, then, as it sets the scene for this restoration, which begins with the covenant that God makes with Abraham, founded on the promise of the Mediator. In reading the opening chapters of Genesis, we are especially to observe:

> [T]hat after Adam had by his own desperate fall ruined himself and all his posterity, this is the basis of our salvation, this the origin of the Church, that we, being rescued out of profound darkness, have obtained new life by the mere grace of God; that the Fathers . . . are by faith made partakers of this life; that this word itself was founded upon Christ; and that all the pious who have since lived were sustained by the very same promise of salvation.[29]

Creation, for Calvin, at least within the context of his commentary on Genesis, serves not so much as the basis for the relationship of the pious with God, but rather as the condition from which humanity fell, necessitating its redemption and restoration in Christ. Thus, we now turn to the beginning of the history of restoration in God's promise to Abraham.

The promise to Abraham

The story of God's promise to Abraham in the first half of Genesis is seminal for the covenant history: it initiates the history, and it serves as a model by which the rest of the history can be understood. Indeed, from Calvin's perspective, the story of Abraham contains in summary form every

---

[26] Ibid., 1.65 (*CO* 23.65)
[27] See *Comm. John* 1:1, 1.25 (*CO* 47:1) and *Comm. Gen.* 1:3, 1.74–75 (*CO* 23.16) for the Word's mediation of creation.
[28] *Inst.* II.xii.4, p. 467 (*OS* 3:440).   [29] *Comm. Gen.* 1.65 (*CO* 23:11–12).

ingredient essential to God's covenantal relationship with God's people.[30] It was a relationship in which God constituted a Church as adoptive children through the interweaving of God's grace and Abraham's response. The foundation for this relationship was laid through the promise of a Mediator, by whose expiatory act the relationship might be restored and through whose blessing the faithful were made children of God; and Abraham's participation in this relationship hinged on his grasp of this fundamental promise in all of its dimensions.

God's covenant was established with Abraham in three iterations in Genesis. Initially, God called Abraham out of his country to a new land, promising to make of him a great nation (Gen. 12); God later expanded on this promise and sealed it, once with a ceremony of covenant (Gen. 15) and once with the sacrament of circumcision (Gen. 17).[31] For Calvin, these stories and not the story of Pentecost relate the birth of the Church: "It is wonderful," Calvin writes, "that a man miserable and lost, should have the preference given him, over so many holy worshipers of God; that the covenant of life should be placed in his possession; that the Church should be revived in him, and he himself constituted the father of all the faithful."[32] Calvin consistently refers to Israel as "the Church," insofar as they are Abraham's descendants, and he is clear that the Gentiles were admitted into this Church because they were "united to the one family of Abraham."[33] "[T]o be children of God," he elsewhere writes, "we must be reckoned members of his tribe."[34]

Abraham, as the father of the faithful, serves as a prototype for the Church in his relationship with God.[35] This relationship was marked by grace from the beginning – Abraham was "plunged in idolatry" when God first called him[36] – and this grace took the form of command and promise. Abraham, in turn, responded with obedience and faith. The complexity of God's relationship with Abraham and the Church emerged out of this interaction.

The motive force behind the drama of Genesis derived from God's commands requiring Abraham's obedience – that he leave his country to wander in a strange land, that he sacrifice the son on whom the promise depended. It was a life of almost unmitigated suffering, as Calvin describes it.[37] But Abraham was able to maintain such a life through his faith in God's promise

[30] See *Comm. Gen.*, Dedication, p. 1, v. 1.
[31] Note Calvin's understanding of Genesis 12 as a covenant story (*Comm. Gen.* 12:3, 1.347 [*CO* 23.177]).
[32] Ibid., 12:1, 1.343 (*CO* 23:177).   [33] Ibid., 17:7, 1.447–450 (*CO* 23:237–238).
[34] *Inst.* II.x.II, p. 437 (*OS* 3:411).   [35] See *Comm. Gen.* 12:1, 1.343 (*CO* 23:174) and *Inst.* II.x.II, p. 437.
[36] See *Comm. Josh.* 24:2, pp. 272–273 (*CO* 25:563–564).   [37] *Inst.* II.x.II, pp. 437–438 (*OS* 3:411–412).

that God would sustain him, bless him, and provide him with a great family. If God's commands, then, were the motive force behind the drama, the promises were the foundation on which the drama was staged.[38]

In Calvin's development of this understanding of the covenant as the intertwining of grace and response, the personal character of the relationship emerges as the focus of Calvin's thought.[39] So, he explains that Abraham's belief was, in the end, not simply a belief in the promises, but extended to a belief in the God who promises. Calvin writes:

> It is, indeed, to be maintained as an axiom that all the promises of God, made to the faithful, flow from the free mercy of God, and are evidences of that paternal love, and of that gratuitous adoption, on which their salvation is founded. Therefore, we do not say that Abram was justified because he laid hold on a single word . . . but because he embraced God as his Father.[40]

Abraham's faith was constituted by his embrace of God, and his obedience was derivative from this embrace. Indeed, it was only proper obedience if it sprang from this embrace and the reverence for God that it entailed:

> The foundation, indeed, of the divine calling, is a gratuitous promise; but it follows immediately after, that they whom he has chosen as a peculiar people to himself, should devote themselves to the righteousness of God. For on this condition, he adopts children as his own, that he may, in return, obtain the place and the honour of a Father.[41]

This is the reality to which the whole of the covenant history drives: that we might know and honor God as Father.[42] For this God created the world, but through Adam's fall, our trust in and honor of God were effaced. The covenant, then, is God's initiative toward the reconstitution of God's family, the Church.

Indeed, God's promise to Abraham was, in the first place, the promise of a Church. When God says in Gen. 12, "I will make of thee a great nation," Calvin understand this to entail God's separation for himself of a "peculiar

---

[38] *Comm. Gen.* 12:2, 1.346 (*CO* 23:176).
[39] The narrative of the covenant history in Genesis, with this emphasis on grace and response, forms, I believe, the most helpful framework for a discussion of the bilateral covenant in Calvin. It picks up clearly the themes that Hoekema develops around mutuality in Calvin's understanding of the covenant. See Hoekema, "Calvin's Doctrine of the Covenant of Grace," and "The Covenant of Grace in Calvin's Teaching"; Bierma, "Federal Theology in the Sixteenth Century: Two Traditions?" and Peter A. Lillback, *The Binding of God: Calvin's Role in the Development of Covenant Theology* (Grand Rapids: Baker Academic, 2001).
[40] *Comm. Gen.* 15:6, 1.407 (*CO* 23:212).   [41] Ibid.
[42] Calvin's commitment to the Fatherhood of God is drawn out ably in Brian Gerrish, *Grace and Gratitude: The Eucharistic Theology of John Calvin* (Minneapolis: Fortress Press, 1993). See esp. pp. 22–31.

people," distinguished by God's special love.[43] This promise is essential for Calvin because it reversed the situation of a fallen humanity, alienated from and abhorrent to God in their sinfulness. But God's pledge of a special love to Abraham's race had no foundation unless the curse of the Fall was first addressed. In the light of the biblical history, only a Mediator could alter the situation, appeasing God and conveying God's fatherly love to humanity, and so God's promise of the Church to Abraham must have included a promise of this Mediator; in fact, it entailed it.

Calvin argues at length that at the time of God's original covenant with Abraham, God not only promised Abraham a family and a land, but also the Mediator on whom the salvation of the world would depend. When God promised "in thee shall all families of the earth be blessed" (Gen. 12:2–3), Calvin understands this to include the promise of the Mediator – a reading grounded in Paul, both as historian and theologian. Calvin takes Paul's assertion that God promises Christ 430 years before the gift of the Law (Gal. 3:8–17) as an accurate rendition of history. He thus concludes that although this promise of the Mediator might be seen most clearly later in Genesis, when God proclaims that the nations will be blessed in Abraham's seed (the verse to which Paul refers), a precise accounting of Paul's chronology would place the promise at the time of God's initial call to Abraham.[44]

History, then, suggests that this promise lay at the foundation of God's covenant, while theology demands it. Calvin, describing the remedy that the Mediator offers to our alienation from God, writes:

Now Paul assumes it as an axiom which is received among all the pious, and which ought to be taken for granted, that the whole human race is obnoxious to a curse, and therefore that the holy people are blessed only through the grace of the Mediator. Whence he concludes that the covenant of salvation which God made with Abram is neither stable nor firm except in Christ.[45]

Calvin does not immediately specify the content of the Mediator's grace, but he is clear that there was no possibility of a relationship between God and the Church even at the level of call and promise unless the Mediator was integral to them both.

Indeed, Calvin's claim is not merely that God promised a Mediator, but that Abraham understood, at some level, the thrust of this promise. Abraham's earliest sacrifice to God (Gen. 12:7) derived from an

---

[43] *Comm. Gen.* 12:2, 3, 1.347–8 (*CO* 23:176–177). See also *Comm. Gen.* 17:7, p. 448 (*CO* 23.237).
[44] *Comm. Gen.* 12:3, 1.348–9 (*CO* 23.177).
[45] Ibid. 12:3, 1.349 (*CO* 23.178). See also *Comm. John* 8:33, 1.343 (*CO* 47:203).

understanding of the need for a sacrifice to gain access to God, and, perhaps more significantly, that such a sacrifice was effective only as his faith was "directed to the blood of Christ."[46] No sooner had Abraham been promised the Mediator than he turned his faith toward him and even had some recognition that the Mediator's grace was connected to his expiatory act. For Calvin, God's promise functioned from Abraham's side of the relationship as well as from God's.

Much of the plot of Abraham's story turns for Calvin on Abraham's awareness that this Mediator would come from his loins. When, for example, in Egypt Abraham acted to preserve his own life at the expense of Sarah's virtue, Calvin concludes that he did this not out of disregard for Sarah, but rather out of his knowledge that the hope of salvation was centered in himself and in his seed.[47] Indeed, if we pay attention to Calvin's explanation of the narrative related in Genesis, we see that this specific promise of the Mediator who would spring from Abraham's line and not the more generic promise that he would have descendants is the driving force behind the story. As he explains in the *Institutes*, many of Abraham's descendants fall out of the story (Ishmael, Esau, the unfaithful in Israel), but the story itself pushes on toward the advent of the Mediator.[48] He is the foundation of all of God's promises.

The Church that God would build on this foundation has also been directed toward a specific end. Within the Abraham story, God's promise of the land leaps out as "the leading article of the covenant,"[49] but on Calvin's reading this promise stood primarily as a token or symbol of God's "paternal favor," a concrete sign that pointed beyond itself to God's greater blessing, the gift of eternal life.[50] Calvin emphasizes in his Genesis commentary the same theme that is evident in the *Institutes*, that God's covenant with Abraham was, from the first, a spiritual covenant through which Abraham was directed to spiritual blessings.[51] The land, then, served as "a mirror and a pledge" of the celestial inheritance that God could not yet set "plainly before the eyes of the fathers," for Christ, the Mediator, in whom this promise would be realized, had not yet been manifested.[52]

This final promise of eternal life bends back around to the first – the promise of the Church. God's promise to be the God of Abraham and

---

[46] *Comm. Gen.* 12:7, 1.355 (*CO* 23.181).
[47] *Comm. Gen.* 12:11, 1.359 (*CO* 23.184). Calvin is sure that it grieved Abraham's heart to risk the ruin of his wife's character, but he never connects the promise of the Mediator in Abraham's seed to Sarah.
[48] See *Inst.* II.vi.2, pp. 342–345 (*OS* 3:321–323).   [49] *Comm. Josh.*, *Arg.*, xviii (*CO* 25:422).
[50] See *Comm. Gen.* 27:27, II.91–92 (*CO* 23.378); *Inst.* II.xi.2, p. 451 (*OS* 3:424–425).
[51] *Comm. Gen.* 17:8, 1.450 (*CO* 23.239); *Inst.* II.x.11–13, pp. 437–441 (*OS* 3:411–414).
[52] *Comm. Gen.* 27:27, 1.91–92 (*CO* 23.378).

his descendants was the promise that separated the Church out from the nations as it vouchsafed to them God's gracious love. But if God is God of the living and of the dead, then this promise to be their God does not cease at death but stretches into eternity. In other words, what finally was promised in both God's calling the Church and God's granting eternal life was a relationship with God, adoption as children out of God's fatherly love; and this relationship is eternal, binding God's chosen to God in this life and the next.

This promise of eternal life, like the call of the Church, was also founded on the promise of the Mediator. Each was a consequence of our adoption by God, and this adoption is a fruit of the Mediator's grace.[53] But the promise of the land and life provides a variant shading to Calvin's picture of the Mediator. Abraham's faith in the Mediator when he made sacrifice begins to sketch out the priestly character of the still inchoate image of the Mediator and his grace. Correlatively, in Calvin's commentary on Isaac's blessing of Jacob, we are told that the eternal life in which Abraham, Isaac, and Jacob had put their hope is the spiritual kingdom of Christ, the Mediator.[54] This suggests a second, royal aspect to the Mediator's office – that the realm into which the Church is brought by its adoption is the realm over which the Mediator has asserted his dominion.

The sacerdotal and monarchial dimensions of the office of the Mediator and Abraham's awareness of them are most evident in the story of Abraham's dealings with Melchizedek, King of Salem (Gen. 14:18–20). Melchizedek was an obscure character in a minor story in the midst of the Abraham saga, but his significance within the broader biblical tradition was heightened first by a reference to him in Psalm 110, "The Lord has sworn and he will not recant: 'You are a priest for ever after the order of Melchizedek' " (Ps. 110:4). The letter to the Hebrews then picked up this theme and argued for the preeminence of Christ's Messianic priesthood given this claim of its origin in Melchizedek (Heb. 5:10, 6:20, 7:1–11).

Calvin reads the story in Genesis in light of the later two passages; but in his Genesis commentary, he is most interested in what the encounter with Melchizedek meant to Abraham and not the more extended typology of Hebrews.[55] This more narrow focus, however, does not in any way obscure Melchizedek as a type of Christ, for Calvin claims that Abraham was aware of the image of the Mediator in this king and priest before any of the later

---

[53] See *Comm. Gen.* 22:2, 1.563, 565 (*CO* 23.313, 314).   [54] *Comm. Gen.* 27:27, 11.91 (*CO* 23.378).

[55] See his comments on Melchizedek's lineage in *Comm. Heb.* 7:3, pp. 157–158 (*CO* 55: 83–84) and *Comm. Gen.* 14:18, 1.387–388 (*CO* 23.200–201).

writers.[56] Indeed, Calvin argues, David was able to write of Melchizedek and the Messiah as he did in the Psalms only because this awareness of Abraham's had been passed down through the generations.

Melchizedek is identified as a priest and king, and Calvin finds it extraordinary that this one man possessed both offices – not only is it exceptional in the context of the story,[57] but it also sets Melchizedek and the Messiah of whom he is a type apart from the priests and kings under the Mosaic Law, by which no person could ever hold both offices. This was the central point manifested to Abraham by Melchizedek as a type of the Mediator – that he (the Mediator) would fulfill both offices. Calvin claims that these two offices stand at the heart of Christ's mediatorship, for through them he secures our relationship with God and our standing in a fallen world:

> The sum of the whole is that Christ would thus be the king next to God, and also that he should be anointed priest, and that for ever; which it is very useful for us to know, in order that we may learn that the royal power of Christ is combined with the office of priest. The same Person, therefore, who was constituted the only and eternal Priest, in order that he might reconcile us to God, and who having made expiation might intercede for us, is also a King of infinite Power to secure our salvation, and to protect us by his guardian care.[58]

The Mediator as priest reconciles us to God and intercedes for us before God. The Mediator as king secures our salvation and defends us from our enemies. Through these two roles, God's covenant with Abraham and the Church was enacted.

Moses and the Law

When we turn to Calvin's discussion of the Mosaic Law, we find many of the same patterns as we found in his presentation of the story of God's promise to Abraham. Calvin discusses the Law primarily in its connection to the covenant history. The Law and its prelude in the deliverance of the people from captivity concretized the relationship that God initiated with Abraham, not only through its clarification of God's commands and promises in its promulgation of "the rule of life" and "the way of salvation," but also in its enactment of this covenantal way through the ceremonial Laws. In the ministry of the priests, the performance of the sacrifices, and the presence of the tabernacle, God typologically presented to God's chosen the Mediator, and through this representation of the Mediator's grace enacted the covenant, reconciling the people to God as it drew them

---

[56] Ibid.   [57] Ibid.   [58] *Comm. Gen.* 14:18, 1.389 (*CO* 23.202).

to God in faith. Thus, we shall see that in the Law, as in the promises to Abraham, the Mediator shaped the life of the Church in its relationship with God.

The connection Calvin sees between the Law and the covenant history is evident in his very shaping of the biblical texts in which it is recorded. In his commentaries on the last four books of Moses, Calvin rearranges the material of the books into two continuous, chronological narrative sequences with the whole of the Law, organized under the rubric of the Ten Commandments, sandwiched in between. In this way, the narrative forms a framework for understanding the Law. He then characterizes the narrative as relating the history of God's deliverance and sustenance of God's Church out of God's gracious, fatherly love;[59] it is, again, the history of the covenant. Through Israel's deliverance from Egypt and the gift of the Law, God renewed God's covenant with Israel, and this renewal for Calvin carries with it overtures of rebirth.[60] This renewal was tied especially to the gift of the Law, in which the covenant was "engraved upon the tables of stone and written in a book, [so] that the marvelous grace which God had conferred on the race of Abraham should never sink into oblivion."[61] Calvin's context, then, for reading the Law is God's gracious relationship with God's Church enacted through the covenant.

Obviously, though, the Law did more than reaffirm and solidify the covenant made with Abraham. It also began to expound and clarify that covenant as it revealed to Israel "the perfect rule of life" and "the way of salvation."[62] On the one hand, by giving the Law, God held up, as in a mirror, "the image of the renewed Church," by which the Church might order its life.[63] On the other hand, the Law also offered the way of salvation. "[T]he Law is a testimony of God's gratuitous adoption and teaches that salvation is based on His mercy,"[64] and it did so by leading the people through types and figures to Christ, making the remission of sin offered in him clearly manifest.[65] In the proffered rule of life and way of salvation we find again God's gracious commands and promises, eliciting from the people obedience and faith.

Calvin argues, in fact, that the commands, as well as the promises, led Israel to place their faith in Christ. The Law, in its "peculiar office" showed Israel their unrighteousness through its perfect rule of life. By their mortification Israel was taught to implore God's mercy and seek salvation only in Christ (as he was typologically presented in the sacrifices of the Law).[66] In

---

[59] *Comm. Moses*, Introduction, I.xv–xvi (*CO* 24:5–6). [60] *Comm. Exod.* 12:1, 1.458 (*CO* 24:268).
[61] Ibid. 19:1, 1.313 (*CO* 24.192). [62] *Comm. Jer.* 31:31, IV.127 (*CO* 38:688).
[63] *Comm Exod.* 19:1, 1.313 (*CO* 24.192). [64] Ibid. [65] *Comm. Jer.* 31:31, IV.127 (*CO* 38:688).
[66] *Comm. Exod.* 19:1, 1.313–315 (*CO* 24.194). See also *Inst.* II.viii.1, p. 367 (*OS* 3:344–345).

God's renewal of the covenant with Moses, just as God's promise of mercy catalyzed the Church to obedience of the Law, so the Law in turn drove the people to look for God's mercy.

Calvin gives the function of the Law to condemn us and drive us to Christ its due in his discussion, but his emphasis, in line with his overall conception of the covenant history, is on the gracious aspect of Law as both rule of life and way of salvation. Within this broader discussion, it is Calvin's exposition of the ceremonial Laws, in which the Mediator was set before Israel under types, that is our concern for now, for there we see how Christ, the Mediator, was made present to and functioned for the people of Israel under the structures of the Law.

Calvin clusters the ceremonial Laws almost entirely under the second commandment and its proscription of graven images. Here Calvin discusses the sacrifices, priests, and tabernacle, defining the spiritual nature of each in accordance with the principle of the commandment.[67] Neither the blood of beasts (the sacrifices) nor the work of ordinary sinful men (the priests) could reconcile Israel to God.[68] Rather, they pointed to a higher truth, as signs or figures directing Israel to God's grace and to eternal life. This meant, for Calvin, that "Christ was represented in them, since all the promises are in Him, yea and amen (2 Cor. 1:20)."[69] Israel, in their worship of God through the tabernacle, the priesthood, and the sacrifices, entrusted themselves to God's gracious presence because these ceremonies turned them to Christ, the Mediator.

The ways in which Christ was prefigured in Israel's worship are so commonplace for Calvin that he does not bother to enumerate them in the *Institutes*;[70] but in his commentaries, he develops the typology in a number of directions. He discusses the purity of the priests, the singularity of the High Priest, the meaning of both the goat who was sacrificed and the scapegoat on the day of Atonement, and the spiritual pattern of the tabernacle, which was found in Christ.[71] The one theme that runs through this discussion most clearly is the need for a pure offering to atone for the sins of the people – a need to which the ceremonies of the Law pointed, but which in Christ was fulfilled.

[67] *Comm. Exod.* 20:4, II.106–107 (*CO* 24.376–377); *Comm. Deut.* 12:4, II.129 (*CO* 24:390–391). See also *Comm. Exod.* 28:1, II.191 (*CO* 24:426), and *Comm. Lev.* 24:5, II.291 (*CO* 24:488).

[68] *Comm. Exod.* 25:8, II.154–155 (*CO* 154–5); *Inst.* II.vii.1, p. 349; *Comm. Exod.* 27:1, II.191ff (*CO* 24:418).

[69] *Comm. Exod.* 25:8, II.155 (*CO* 155).   [70] *Inst.* II.vi.2, pp. 342–3 (*OS* 3:321).

[71] *Comm. Exod.* 29:1, II.210 (*CO* 24:437–438); *Comm. Num.* 3:5, II.221 (*CO* 24:444); *Comm. Num.* 19:3, II.39 (*CO* 24:334); *Comm. Exod.* 12:21, I.221 (*CO* 24:136); and *Comm. Exod.* 29:28, II.295 (*CO* 24:439); *Comm. Lev.* 16:7. II.316 (*CO* 24:502); *Comm. Deut.* 12:7, II.132 (*CO* 24:392); *Comm. Exod.* 25:2, II.145–147 (*CO* 24:399–402); *Comm. Exod.* 25:8, II.150 (*CO* 24:446–447); *Comm. Exod.* 30:25, II.224 (*CO* 24:446–447); *Comm. Exod.* 26:31, II.176 (*CO* 24:417).

Christ, then, was typologically present to Israel under the tabernacle, the priesthood, and the sacrifices. But to what end? Calvin argues that just as we, the Church today, can trust that our sins are forgiven in Christ, so, too, did Israel find expiation for their sins through these sacrifices, for "God is placable toward all, who trust that their sin is forgiven them by the sacrifice of Christ."[72] The ceremonial Laws, as "external representations of grace" mirror the "spiritual effect" of Christ, and so realize this effect in the historical reality of Israel. The sacrifices therefore expiated the people's sin as they were bound to Christ's sacrifice, and through this expiation, they instilled faith. Their repetition not only turned them to the Mediator, but in this turning, reminded them of their constant need of God.[73] This was the difference between the sacrifices offered by the Jews and those offered by the pagan religionists around them. They were "exercises of faith and repentance" because they were commanded by God and directed to the Mediator.[74]

It is this coupling of effect – the presentation of Christ's redeeming death and the elicitation of faith from the Church – that leads Calvin to describe the sacrifices as being sacramental in nature. Calvin writes:

> Now, since this promise could not have been at all delusive, it must be concluded that in the ancient sacrifices there was a price of satisfaction which should release them from guilt and blame in the judgment of God; yet still not as though these brute animals availed in themselves unto expiation, except insofar as they were testimonies of the grace to be manifested by Christ. Thus, the ancients were reconciled to God in a sacramental manner by the victims just as we are now cleansed through baptism. Hence it follows that these symbols were useful only as they were exercises unto faith and repentance, so that the sinner might learn to fear God's wrath and to seek pardon in Christ.[75]

The sacrifices cleansed the people of their sins through Christ's atoning death, but only as this was joined to their testimony and its evocation of faith and repentance. These two dimensions of the sacrifices express the reality of Christ that they mediated in Israel's midst. This is the culmination of the testimony that Calvin finds to the Mediator's office of reconciliation (which we explore in more detail in the next chapter.) Now we turn to the testimony Calvin finds concerning the Mediator's royal office, especially as that office was reflected in God's call of David to be king over Israel.

---

[72] *Comm. Lev.* 6:1, II.357–358 (*CO* 24:526).
[73] See *Comm. Exod.* 29:38, II.295–296 (*CO* 24:490).   [74] *Comm. Exod.* 25:8, II.154 (*CO* 24:404).
[75] *Comm. Lev.* 1:1, II.324–325 (*CO* 24:507). See also *Inst.* IV.xiv.17, p. 1292 (*OS* 5:274) and *Inst.* IV.xiv.23, p. 1299–1300 (*OS* 5:280–281).

The Davidic kingship

In the *Argumentum* to his Joshua commentary, Calvin muses over Israel's need for a leader, a head who could give the body of the Church godly direction. Joshua had been established as such a leader after the death of Moses, lest Israel remain "as a body with its head chopped off,"[76] but in the course of the story, the people at times appear rudderless. This deficiency, however, was a part of God's larger purpose: "The apparent failure reminded the children of God that they were to look forward to a more excellent state, where the divine favour would . . . shine forth in full splendor. Hence their thoughts were raised to Christ, and it was made known to them that the complete felicity of the Church depended on its Head."[77] This passage takes up the theme of Christ's kingship or headship, which was a second role of the Mediator in the covenant history. God's covenant entailed not only that the Church would be reconciled to God, but also that they would be blessed by God; and the mediation of this blessing was enabled by the king or head of the Church. Ultimately and eternally, this king would be Christ, but within Israel's history, the paradigm of this headship was David. So Calvin continues in the passage from the Joshua commentary: "The same thing was exemplified in David, who bore a typical resemblance to Christ, and in whom it was shown that the divine promises were only established and confirmed in the hand of a Mediator . . . [I]n the person of David the image of the Mediator on whom the perfect felicity of the Church depended was visibly held forth to view."[78] David, as king, was a type of Christ; indeed, he (and his posterity) was made king, Calvin explains, "not so much for his own sake, as to be a type of the Redeemer."[79] David's role was both to guide the Church in its hope, directing them to their true head, and to serve as an earnest for that hope, functioning as head of the Church in Christ's stead, enacting in a limited but concrete manner God's promised covenantal blessings upon the Church.

The office of the king was to rule, protect, and provide for the welfare of God's people, and David fulfilled this office with aplomb during his reign.[80] By doing so, David took God's part in God's relationship with the people. God, Calvin reminds, is the "King and Protector" of Israel, not merely because God is sovereign, but because "he had taken upon him the

---

[76] *Comm. Josh., Arg.*, xix (*CO* 25:422).　　[77] Ibid., *Arg.*, xxii (*CO* 25:423).　　[78] Ibid.

[79] *Comm. Ps.* 2:1, 1.1 (*CO* 31:43). Calvin is clear that, in fact, God's promise of the throne to David and his seed from eternity was a promise of Christ. See *Comm. Isaiah* 9:7, 1.315 (*CO* 36:199); *Comm. Ps.* 18:50, 1.307 (*CO* 31:193–194); and *Comm. Matt.* 1:1ff., 1.83 (*CO* 45:58).

[80] *Comm. Luke* 1:69, 1.69 (*CO* 45:46–47); *Comm. Ps.* 63:11, 11.443 (*CO* 31:598); *Comm. Ps.* 18:43, 1.298–300 (*CO* 31:189–190).

government of the Jewish people, in order to preserve and maintain them in safety."[81] David functioned in the role of king, then, only because God appointed him to it, and David fulfilled this role only because God worked through him in it. Calvin comments, "God illustrated his power in David, by exalting him with the view of delivering his people."[82] David thus took on the office of the Mediator.

Calvin writes in his Isaiah commentary: "The Prophet does not speak of David as a private individual but as a holy king whose throne was established by the hand of God under whose guidance the Church would continue to be safe, and in short who would be the Mediator between God and the Church."[83] David mediated between God and the Church by securing for the Church those blessings that God had promised – a land, prosperity, and safety. This office was, therefore, a second means by which God enacted God's covenant with the Church, and we should note that this second office bore a different function in the relationship between God and God's people than did the priestly office. The latter office enabled that relationship, reconciling the Church to God. Through the kingly office, that relationship became a source of divine blessing. This distinction recalls Calvin's discussion of Melchizedek – that through the office of priest we are reconciled to God and through the office of king our salvation is secured. In these two offices, the central activities of the Mediator of God's covenant are established.

Within Israel's history, the office of the king included a second dimension, however, for in the temporal blessings that the kings bestowed, they were also to point beyond themselves to Christ and his eternal kingdom. This is why Calvin is sure to distinguish David from the office that he holds; he serves as king only as a type of Christ. Calvin writes:

Now to move to the substance of the type. That David prophesied concerning Christ is clearly manifest from this, that he knew his own kingdom to be merely a shadow. And in order to learn to apply to Christ whatever David in times past sang concerning himself we must hold this principle, which we meet with everywhere in all the prophets, that he with his posterity was made king not so much for his own sake as to be a type of the Redeemer. As David's temporal Kingdom was a kind of earnest to God's ancient people of the eternal kingdom, which at length was truly established in the person of Christ.[84]

That David directed Israel to Christ is evident for Calvin in the fact that David could never fulfill many of the attributes prophesied of David and his kingdom – eternity, victory over death, and the like. David and

[81] *Comm. Ps.* 74:12, III.173 (*CO* 31:697). [82] *Comm. Ps.* 68:18, III.26 (*CO* 31:628).
[83] *Comm. Isaiah* 37:35, III.143 (*CO* 36:640). [84] *Comm. Ps.* 2:1ff., I.11 (*CO* 31:42–43).

his descendents, rather, were to point the people to Christ by providing a down-payment on these blessings. Throughout the Psalms commentaries, there are allusions to David's function as a type of Christ, as the pattern of David's life or David's distress led beyond him to Christ; and similar things could be said of Solomon or David's other descendents.[85] Through these types, God taught Israel about Christ and, more importantly, through this teaching beckoned them forward in their history, with all of its tumult and suffering, in faith and hope in Christ.

David's kingdom equally served this typological function. The temporal kingdom presented an image of the eternal kingdom that Christ would bring: "It is the design of the Spirit, under the figure of the temporal kingdom to describe the eternal and spiritual kingdom of God."[86] Because it did so, the people were expected to look past the temporal to the eternal.[87] (This is the burden of the discussion of the similarities between the Old and New Testaments in *Inst.* II.x.) In this way, David's kingdom was "a mirror" into which the people looked to see this future inheritance "prepared for them in heaven."[88]

David and his kingdom, then, served as a type of Christ, but not merely on account of the similarities between the two; rather, in the promise that God attached to David's kingship, this kingship became the foundation for Christ's royal work.[89] There was, in fact, a certain continuity between David's temporal kingdom and Christ's eternal kingdom in this relation of foundation to fulfillment. The second arose out of the first, so that Israel upon the downfall of David's kingdom was to seek its renewal in Christ.[90] David and his kingdom were a realization of the covenant, but a realization adapted to the childhood of the Church, presenting in a material, temporal fashion Christ's spiritual blessing.

We find this same pattern in Calvin's interpretation of the later prophecies concerning the Messianic king. Such prophecies pointed both to a present or near-future blessing that Israel would receive from God and the eschatological blessing to be brought by the coming Messiah.[91] There exists a duplex relationship between the two dimensions of such a promise. Pedagogically, the contemporary blessing – for example, the return from exile – led the people to look for the Messianic kingdom.[92] But the contemporary blessing of the return not only pointed to Christ's kingdom, it

---

[85] *Comm. Ps.* 118:25, IV.391–392 (*CO* 32:210); *Comm. Ps.* 22:15, 1.372 (*CO* 31:228); *Comm. Ps.* 45:6, II.180–181 (*CO* 31:453–454).

[86] *Comm. Ps.* 118, *Arg.*, IV.375 (*CO* 32:202).   [87] *Inst.* II.xi.1, p. 450 (*OS* 3:423).

[88] *Inst.* II.xi.1, p. 450–451 (*OS* 3:424).   [89] See, for example, *Comm. Matt.* 1:1, 1.83–84 (*CO* 45:58).

[90] *Comm. Ps.* 118:25, IV.391 (*CO* 32:210).   [91] *Comm. Isaiah* 9:2, 1.299 (*CO* 36:189–190).

[92] *Comm. Joel* 3:1–3, *Minor Prophets* II.112–114 (*CO* 42.581).

also initiated it: "The return from the captivity in Babylon was the commencement of the renovation of the Church which was completed when Christ appeared; thus there is no absurdity in an uninterrupted succession [between the two]."[93] The return and renovation of God's people was a part of the continuous work of God that concluded with the salvation that Christ effected.[94]

The prophets

In his commentary on Psalm 78, Calvin argues that Christ's royal and sacerdotal offices stand at the center of God's covenantal relationship with God's Church. He writes: "After having made mention of the temple the prophet now proceeds to speak of the kingdom; for these two things were the chief signs of God's choice of his ancient people, and of his favour toward them; and Christ also hath appeared as our king and priest, to bring a full and perfect salvation to us."[95] In this section I take up the prophetic office and its relation to the history of the covenant within the Old Testament, both locating the function of this office and then exploring its relationship to Calvin's Christology. We discover that the prophets were interpreters of the Law who explained God's promises and clarified God's commands. The prophets thereby called the Church into a deeper relationship with God, especially as they led God's chosen to place their faith in the salvation enacted through the royal and sacerdotal offices. This prophetic office, Calvin maintains, was fulfilled by Christ and continues in the ministry of the Church's pastors and teachers to this day.

At the beginning of the preface to his Isaiah commentary, Calvin binds the prophetic office to the Law, "from which they derived their doctrine, like streams from a fountain." This Law, he continues, consists of "the doctrine of life," "threatenings and promises," and "the covenant of grace, being founded on Christ." The role of the prophets, then, was to illustrate the doctrine and to "express more clearly what Moses says more obscurely about Christ and his grace, and bring forward more copious and more abundant proofs of the free covenant."[96] They needed to recall and clarify for the Church God's will expressed in the Law because of the Law's brevity and the people's capriciousness.[97] They needed to make more plain God's promise of the Mediator in order to encourage the Church in difficult times.[98]

---

[93] *Comm. Isaiah* 9:6, I.306 (*CO* 36:194).   [94] *Comm. Isaiah* 43:19, III.343 (*CO* 37:95–6).
[95] *Comm. Ps.* 78:70. III.280 (*CO* 31:745).   [96] *Comm. Isaiah*, Preface, I.xxvi (*CO* 36:19).
[97] See *Comm. Isaiah*, Preface, I.xxvii–xxviii (*CO* 36:20–21).   [98] *Comm. Isaiah*, I.xxix (*CO* 36:22).

The prophets proclaimed and described the reign of the coming Messiah, but always with an eye to the reassurance of God's people in their present struggles, binding the people in faith and hope more tightly to God's covenant, to which the promise of the Messiah was attached.[99] Indeed, inherent in the future promise was always a present promise – release from captivity in Babylon, for example – and the present reality of the Church's adoption by God. The prophet, then, sought to bind the Church to God not only by speaking of what Christ would do, but also of what he had done and was doing in the Church's midst. Again, Calvin writes:

> After having treated of the future deliverance of the people [Isaiah] comes down to Christ under whose guidance the people were brought out of Babylon . . . The former prophecy must have been confirmed by this doctrine; because they would scarcely have hoped that the Lord would deliver them if they had not placed Christ before their eyes, by whom alone desponding souls can be comforted. For from him they ought not only to expect eternal salvation, but ought equally to expect temporal deliverance.[100]

The prophets were thus to guide the people in and hold them to their participation in the covenant, rallying Israel in their faith in God through the promise of the Mediator while demanding of them obedience to God's commands. Now, faith in God's promises and obedience to God's commands were the two dimensions to God's covenant with Israel, and so the prophets were given very broad responsibility for the mediation of Israel's relationship with God. In fact, Calvin notes that God had appointed the prophets to be "substitutes" for God in teaching the people,[101] and this responsibility was so significant that Calvin maintains repeatedly that God would never leave God's Church bereft of such teachers, left to drift aimlessly amidst the hopeless superstitions of the pagan nations surrounding them.[102] Indeed, Calvin argues that this teaching office continues in the Church to the present day in the offices of pastor and doctor.[103]

Such a mediatorial office is implicitly Christological for Calvin in all of its aspects; not only is Christ, ultimately, the source of the Law,[104] he is also the head of all of the Law's teachers,[105] and he rules the Church by their

[99] Ibid. [100] *Comm. Isaiah*, 49:1, IV.8 (*CO* 37:190).

[101] *Comm. Deut.* 18:21, 1.448 (*CO* 24:280).

[102] See *Comm. Deut.* 18:15 I.434 (*CO* 24:272–273), *Comm. Isaiah* Pref., I.xxviii (*CO* 36:20–21), and *Inst.* II.xv.1, pp. 494–495 (*OS* 3:472).

[103] This is seen clearly in Calvin's discussion of the ministers of the Church in *Inst.* IV.iii. We will return to this and consider it in some detail in chapter 5, 167f.

[104] See *Comm. Heb.* 2:1, p. 52 (*CO* 55:21), *Comm. Gal.* 3:19, p. 102 (*CO* 50:216), and *Comm. John* 14:24, II.99 (*CO* 47:334).

[105] *Comm. Heb.* 3:3, p. 80 (*CO* 55:37).

ministry.[106] But to say that Christ is their head and they his instruments is to set them in a particular relationship to Christ and his mediatorial work – a relationship in which they work with Christ rather than in place of him.[107] This means, on the one hand, that the prophets had authority only in their relationship to Christ, their head, and that they were chiefly employed in directing the people to Christ. On the other hand, the prophets had a place alongside Christ – and not just the prophets, but also the apostles and, presumably, other teachers of the Church – as they have contributed to making known Christ's benefits. Each has had their own part in the educative task.

We thus begin to see a distinction between the Christological role of the prophets and that of the priests and kings. The latter fulfilled their office in Christ's place – they took his part as types and no longer had a role in God's Church once Christ had come, but the prophetic office, carried out alongside Christ, did not cease once Christ had come. The prophets before Christ and the apostles and other teachers in the Church after Christ, share with Christ the ministry of leading of the Church into faithful participation in the covenant.

Calvin makes a second distinction between the prophetic and the sacerdotal and royal offices, vital for understanding his Christology. In a passage from his Isaiah commentary, Calvin discriminates between the publication by the prophets of God's promised blessings and the accomplishment of those blessings in Christ. Christ accomplished blessing as Christ reconciled the people to God and established God's kingdom in their midst – that is, through the Mosaic priesthood and the Davidic kings. This priesthood and kingship, then, can be said not only to turn the people to Christ, but also to actualize in a sacramental sense God's covenant. In contrast, the prophet's task is less the enactment of the covenant and more the proclamation of it, that through their proclamation the people might enter more fully into the covenant enacted by the priests and kings.

In this distinction between the prophetic office and that of the priests and kings, we see a fundamental dynamic running throughout the story of the covenant as Calvin has understood it. On the one hand, the covenant relationship between God and God's Church relies wholly on what God has done. God reconciles the people to Godself through the ministry of the priests and God blesses the people through the ministry of the kings. Covenant in this sense is simply and fully the grace of God that God

---

[106] *Comm. Heb.* 2:13, p. 69 (*CO* 55:31).   [107] See, for example, *Comm. Isaiah* 61:1, IV.303 (*CO* 37:371).

establishes in the midst of the chosen. God promises without our merit and God fulfills despite our unworthiness.

On the other hand, the covenant relationship between God and God's Church requires the Church to live into that relationship, to respond to God with faith and obedience.[108] The office of the prophet is to lead the chosen into this life, to make plain and rhetorically powerful what God has done (that they may believe) and what God requires (that they might follow). As much as the covenant stands upon God's graceful enactment of blessing, it is complete only when God's people respond to that grace; and for Calvin, the opportunity to respond to grace is itself an aspect of grace. The goal of the covenant was that the Church might know God as Father (a parent), and such knowledge implies response.

These distinctions, however, need a little blurring in relationship to this threefold office of mediation. Prophets can be said to enact the covenant, insofar as they, through their teaching, lead people to complete the relationship. Conversely, Calvin repeatedly emphasizes that in the history of the royal and sacerdotal enactment of the covenant, the grace of God was displayed in a manner that itself was rhetorically powerful. The prophetic explanation of this display is therefore meant to heighten this impact, not supply its want.

In these last points, we begin to see the formal implications of the connection of Christology to the covenant history. This connection means not only that we understand Christ's work under the rubric of the threefold office through which the covenant was mediated to Israel, but also that Calvin's Christology is fundamentally historical. It has to do with God's enactment of covenant in history, with the people's response to that enactment, and with the manner in which the enactment of the covenant leads to the faithful response. It is to this broader connection of Christology to history that we now turn.

CHRIST IN HISTORY

Given Calvin's view of the covenant history that I have outlined above, we must now consider more completely what is entailed theologically for Calvin in this relationship of Christology and history. Through this relationship Calvin has interpreted Israel's history Christologically and he has defined his Christology historically. What are the implications of this?

---

[108] Here we find another set of texts that might contribute to the discussion of the bilateral covenant in Calvin. See Muller, *The Unaccommodated Calvin*, p. 155.

An activist Christology

To answer this question, we first need to be clear on two different senses of "history" that are operative in this relationship with Christ. As noted previously, "history" can refer to both the events of history and the narratives that record and explain those events. Thus for Calvin, our understanding of Christ is wrapped up, first, in our understanding of Christ's involvement in history as event. It focuses our attention on Christ's activity, what he does as a part of this history to shape it and move it along. This is why Calvin directs us to seek the historical sense of the biblical text (as I explain below) – because the significantly Christological material in Scripture concerns the manner in which Christ, as the Mediator, has enacted God's covenant in history. Christ reconciles humanity to God through his sacrifice, he bestows God's blessings upon God's Church through the establishment of his kingdom, and he teaches the Church to understand this reconciliation and blessing aright. In this description, the significance of Calvin's development of his Christology in its relationship to the covenant history emerges, for we see that the question of what Christ does in this history predominates over the question of who he is as the God–man.

This focus on Christ's enactment of our salvation in the covenant history also ties our understanding of and relationship with God to this enactment and this history. We should not, therefore, look to some previous activity of God, such as creation, for access to God, nor should we seek to understand God and our standing with God through our grasp of God's decision for us in eternity apart from this history. This history, and Christ's activity within it as its constituting force, is the venue in which our salvation is accomplished. It demands our attention. Calvin's Christology in this sense instills a dynamic quality into his theology as a whole. It tells us that although the covenant between God and Israel is an eternal covenant, it is not worked out in eternity, but in the dynamic history of God's economy of salvation. Likewise, Christ and Christology have significance for God's people precisely because Christ makes history – because he enacts God's grace in and through the events and activities of which the covenant history consists. It is on the basis of this enactment that God's people are able to come to a recognition of God's grace as it touches their lives.

Christological history and authorial intent

To say that Calvin's Christology is historical also means that Christ and his work for us are *presented* to us in history or as a history. It brings to our awareness not only what Christ has done, apart from us, to enact God's grace and effect our salvation, but also the manner in which, from Calvin's perspective, God has drawn us into the covenant through the exhibition of this grace. Again, history refers both to the events enacted and to the presentation of those events in a history – in this case the biblical history – authored in such a way as to shape its readers through the vision of the world imparted within this history. If we accept the fact that Calvin in his schooling and his scholarship was fundamentally a humanist – that he, at the least, was trained in the humanist arts of rhetoric, linguistics, and historiography – then we can see that Calvin viewed history, insofar as it is a literary product, not merely as the record of the events it reports, but as a narrative of these events intentionally and rhetorically ordered to shape its readers for the better.[109] For the humanists, history was a form of rhetoric, and, for Calvin, this rhetorical intentionality underlay both Scripture's presentation of the covenant history and God's original authoring of that history. Calvin's Christology is historical, then, not only in the content it recounts, but in the form of this recounting.

Commentators on Calvin's exegetical method have noted the analytical methods he employs and recommends to others for understanding particular texts. The exegete should attend to the author's intention behind the text as determined by philological understanding, the historical and geographical context of the author, and the literary context of the text. Calvin most likely came upon these principles in his legal studies under Bude and Alciati, but they are more generally a part of the heritage of humanist historiography.[110] Alongside these analytical principles, however, humanism also placed a certain synthetic imperative on the historian. Humanist history sought not merely to convey to its readers information about the past, but by this conveyance also to offer them some useful service in the present.[111] Bruni wrote: "The careful study of the past enlarges our foresight

---

[109] Battles offers an excellent discussion of Calvin's background as a humanist in his article, "Calvin's Humanist Education," in *Interpreting John Calvin* (Grand Rapids: Baker Books, 1996), pp. 47–62. See also Olivier Millet, *Calvin et la dynamique de la parole: Etude de rhétorique réformée* (Paris: Librairie Honoré Champion, Editeur, 1992), pp. 39–48.

[110] Alciati and Bude are noted as leaders of the *mos gallicus*, the new historical school of law, that emphasized the importance of understanding Roman legal texts within their original historical context. See Battles, "Calvin's Humanist Education"; Lauro Martines, *Power and Imagination: City-States in Renaissance Italy* (New York: Vintage Books, 1979), p. 209; Millet, *Calvin et la dynamique*, pp. 40–42.

[111] Indeed, the conveyance of information and useful service stood at some tension with each other in fifteenth- and sixteenth- century historiography. In the fifteenth century a debate arose among humanist historians over the relative importance of truth-telling vs. ethical relevance in historical accounts. Some early humanists, out of their desire to write edifying, rhetorically well-crafted

in contemporary affairs and affords to citizens and to monarchs lessons of incitement or warning in the ordering of public policy. From history also we draw our store of examples of moral precepts."[112]

To serve these ends, a history needed to be rhetorically well crafted and ordered to make its point clearly and concisely: "Only through the genius of eloquence exercised in the arrangement and disposition of the material could historians save events and individuals from the ravages of time and make fully effective the lessons to be learned."[113] Thus, in contrast to medieval annals, in which the reader would find a compendium of numerous events (some more relevant than others for any particular purpose) ordered only by their chronology, humanists would pick and choose among the events they related and would order them (generally, but not always, with chronological accuracy) in a manner that would draw out their argument clearly.[114] The historian was telling a story, a story with a purpose, and that purpose gave the story its shape.[115]

Calvin's concern for these historiographical canons is evinced in his treatment of the biblical writers, for he attributes to them the production of just such intentionally structured, purposeful narratives. When Calvin speaks of authorial intentionality, for example, he is referring not merely to the intended meaning behind any one piece of text, but also to the intention and meaning of the text as a whole, evident in its narrative structure. Thus, he distinguishes the purpose behind the three Synoptic Gospels, which were written to show that Christ was the Mediator, and John's Gospel, which taught us what it meant for Christ to be the Mediator,[116] and he

pieces, soon divorced their "histories" from any meaningful connection to what actually happened, devoting themselves more to the composition of moving speeches and to the structuring of their narratives around symbolically pregnant, if fictive, events. Others like Valla, however, maintained the importance of adhering to the truth in writing history through attention to factual detail. This latter school eventually won the day. Calvin's commitment to the actuality of history and the truth of the biblical accounts is notable in light of this earlier dispute. See Peter Burke, *The Renaissance Sense of the Past* (London: Edward Arnold, 1969), pp. 105–124; Myron Gilmore, "The Renaissance Conception of the Lessons of History," in *Facets of the Renaissance*, Wallace Ferguson, ed. (New York: Harper Torchbooks, 1963), pp. 92–98.

[112] Lionardo Bruni, *De studiis et literis,* from Martines, *Power and Imagination,* p. 195.

[113] Gilmore, *Facets,* p. 86.

[114] Note Hans Baron's discussion of the purposefully structured narratives of the fifteenth century over against the chronicles that preceded them. Hans Baron, *The Crisis of the Early Italian Renaissance: Civic Humanism and Republican Liberty in an Age of Classicism and Tyranny* (Princeton: Princeton University Press, 1966), pp, 169, 170.

[115] This is not to argue that there was no shaping purpose behind medieval histories – from chronicles to the lives of the saints – but historians of historiography argue that this is a distinctive emphasis of fifteenth- and sixteenth-century humanism (see Ernst Breisach, *Historiography: Ancient, Medieval, and Modern* [University of Chicago Press, 1983], pp. 127–128, 153–170).

[116] See *Comm. Harm.,* 1.xxxvii (*CO* 45:2–3); *Comm. John, Arg.,* 1.21–22 (*CO* 47.VII). See also his sermon on the deity of Christ (p. 16 [*CO* 47:468]).

explains the narrative structure and content of each Gospel in terms of these differing purposes.[117] Similarly, Calvin notes that, in the final four books of Moses, there are places where the narrative seems misordered, and that on the whole it is confusingly ordered, especially in the admixture of Law with narrative and the giving of the Law over the course of several books with no organizing principle. But he asserts that the Spirit led Moses to order the narrative as he did, for in this way it was "perfectly adapted for the instruction of the people."[118] The biblical writers, when writing history, ordered their narratives in a manner that suited their rhetorical or theological purposes, and Calvin did not chastise them for this.[119]

Rather, Calvin held up these purposes as vital to the understanding of the history which expressed them. Thus, at the beginning of his commentaries on both the book of Genesis and the last four books of Moses, Calvin introduces his readers to these texts with an explanation of the purpose manifest in them – that through their relation of their respective histories they might orient their readers more piously toward God. Moses' account of the history of creation is not simply a chronicling of the order of events through which the world was brought into being, but the exhibition of God's grace through the narrative so that we might recognize and be moved by this grace.[120] Likewise, the narrative of Israel's deliverance from Egypt and forty-year journey to the promised land functions as a mirror, reflecting "the incomparable power, as well as the boundless mercy of God in raising up and, as it were, engendering his Church."[121] On the one hand, the loving-kindness of God evident in the text should serve as a "source of confidence" and teach us "to be bold in prayer"; on the other hand, "the terrible punishments which are everywhere recounted, instruct us in reverence toward God, and inspire our hearts with awe."[122]

For Calvin, the biblical histories, especially as they are occupied with the narration of the covenant history, serve not merely to report the events that they recount, but also, through this recounting, to draw their readers more deeply into relationship with God; and, insofar as the covenant history is Christological, these biblical histories draw the faithful to God through

[117] See, for example, *Comm. John*, 6:1, 1.226 (*CO* 47:130); "Deity of Christ," p. 15 (*CO* 47:467). Millet discusses Calvin's attention to narrative intent in the construction of the biblical histories (*Calvin et la dynamique*, p. 267).

[118] *Comm. Moses*, Preface, 1.xiv (*CO* 24:5–6).

[119] Although Calvin can admit that at times the biblical writers have misordered sequences of events, this option is precluded when characters within the narrative speak to the given order. See, for example, his discussion of the timing of the Last Supper in his commentary on the Gospel harmonies (III.194–195 [*CO* 46:698–699]).

[120] *Comm. Gen., Arg.*, 1.58–60 (*CO* 23:5–6).   [121] *Comm. Moses, Arg.*, 1.xv (*CO* 24:5–6).

[122] Ibid., 1.xvi (*CO* 24:5–8).

their presentation of Christ in his activity as the Mediator of the covenant, thereby focusing the Church on Christ as its object of faith. This is a second consequence, then, of Calvin's relation of Christology to history: that we attend to the biblical history for the manner in which its authors have intentionally presented Christ to their readers through their narrative. Where it becomes most interesting with Calvin, however, is that when he speaks of Christ's intentional presentation in history, he refers to history as texts and events. For Calvin, the events of history are just as much authored and intentionally structured by God's providence as are the texts that report these events. Thus, he wants to understand history as rhetorically purposeful on this more fundamental level as well.

The divine historian

For Calvin, the divine hand is evident throughout the individual stories of Scripture – God tempts Abraham; God shuts the door on Noah's ark; God insures that the children of Israel maintain a separate identity during their sojourn in Egypt.[123] But Calvin is more interested in the broader sense in which history is the field on which the divine plan, and not just the plans of humans, is worked out. Just as individual events or small clusters of events are understood on the basis of the activity and intentionality of the human actors who participate in them, so, too, history, as a whole, must be understood in relation to the intentionality of the one whose activity pervades it, whose motivations and causal reach extend far beyond the limited effect of human causality and motive. History must be related in a way that makes sense of this overarching level of motivation and intentionality, and so Calvin describes God as the author of history. History is written by human historians who recount the passing events in subservience to their various purposes; but it is also written by the divine historian who has determined its course in accordance with his merciful purpose.

This means that to ask about authorial intent concerns not only the intent behind various historical texts, but also the intent behind historical events, authored as they have been authored. History as event has been scripted to shape our lives. One implication of this belief is that the broad sweep of divinely authored history forms the context in which biblical events and characters as well as biblical texts must be understood. Thus, Calvin argues that to understand what David writes in the Psalms in their historical sense, we must see David and the Psalms not merely in the narrower context of David's immediate history, but also in the broader context of the history

[123] See Parker, *Old Testament*, p. 96.

of the covenant – a history into which David has been written as a type of the Messiah to come. And thus, to ask how Christ functions within the biblical history – the question from which we begin to understand Calvin's Christology – we should not, from Calvin's view, initially be asking how Calvin read Christ into this history, nor how the biblical authors saw Christ in relation to this history. Rather, we should first be interested in how God wrote Christ into the history through promises, prophecies, and types, and, finally, in the incarnation. The question is: how did God use Christ to work out God's merciful purpose within the context of God's covenant relationship with the Church?[124]

Christology and the historical sense

The relationship of Christology to biblical history is manifest most clearly in the coherence Calvin sees between the Christological and historical senses of Scripture. Calvin is known to have emphasized the need to interpret Scripture for both its historical sense – which he defines as the sense that its human authors intended and that its original readers were meant to hear – and its Christological sense – that we must read the Scriptures "with the express design of finding Christ in them."[125] Calvin's critics, and some of his friends, have perceived a tension between these two readings of Scripture, at least as applied to the Old Testament, and the assumption behind this perception is that the Jewish authors of the Old Testament, writing to Israel, offered to God's chosen people little or no Christian vision of Christ, so that a Christological sense of the text must be read into it.[126] Given my argument thus far, it is clear that Calvin would reject this assumption. For Calvin, Christology is not simply native to Israel's history, it is its very substance, so that we understand what moves characters within the history as well as God's purposes behind the history only when we grasp this relationship.

Calvin accepts the Jewish challenge as it was issued in his day that the prophets must be understood in their historical context. Indeed, he rejects many traditional Christological readings of both the Old and New Testaments because they are "allegorizing" and make no sense within the text's

---

[124] Calvin, of course, recognized God's providential guidance behind all of history; God's authorship is bound to no particular volume in the temporal library. But he was not optimistic about the possibility of reading authorial intent from the wider history of the world (see Schreiner, *Theater of his Glory*, pp. 113–114). Sacred history is fit for such interpretive contemplation, but not secular history, arguably because it alone has been provided with its proper interpretation in the textual histories that record it.

[125] *Comm. John* 5:39, 1.218 (*CO* 47.125).

[126] See Puckett's description of this reality (David Puckett, *John Calvin's Exegesis of the Old Testament* [Louisville: Westminster/John Knox, 1995], pp. 4–12).

history.[127] Such readings not only jeopardize Christian apologetic concerns, making what Calvin regards as nonsensical arguments, but they also misdirect Christian theology from its focus on what God was doing in history. However, Calvin also rejects Jewish arguments that there is no Christological sense of the text as false to Scripture's history. For Calvin, Scripture only makes sense in its relationship to the Mediator. If you read the Mediator out of the history, then you are left with a narrative that has no grounding and no goal.[128]

The intimate relationship between the Christological and historical senses of the Old Testament can be best understood if we briefly consider Calvin's reading of two passages. When Calvin discusses the sacrifice of Isaac in his Genesis commentary, he omits any Christological interpretation of the text on the basis of figuration – the ram as a type of Christ because he was sacrificed in Isaac's place, for example.[129] Such interpretations have no grounding because they are not required to make sense of the story, nor is there any indication, from Calvin's perspective, that Abraham had any sense of such meanings implicit in the event.

That is not to say that the story has no Christological dimension for Calvin. Rather, this dimension is what drives the story in its depth and poignancy. What is at stake for Abraham in God's command for him to sacrifice Isaac is not merely his son, Calvin explains, nor even the promise that he will have a great family. No, what is at stake is his salvation and the salvation of the world, for God's own command has threatened God's promise of a Mediator. Calvin writes:

If God had said nothing more than that his son should die, even this message would have most grievously wounded his mind; because whatever favour he could hope for from God was included in this single promise, "In Isaac shall thy seed be called." Whence he necessarily inferred that his own salvation and that of the whole human race would perish unless Isaac remained in safety. For he was taught by that word that God would not be propitious to man without a Mediator . . . Whence however could he have had this hope but from Isaac? . . . Yet not only is the death of his son announced to him, but he is commanded with his own hand to slay him; as if he were required, not only to throw aside, but to cut in pieces, or cast into the fire, the charter of his salvation, and to have nothing left for himself, but death and hell.[130]

---

[127] Puckett explores in some detail Calvin's rules for texts that may be properly allegorized (*John Calvin's Exegesis*, pp. 106–113).

[128] See, for example, his discussion of the Christological sense in Daniel (*Comm. Dan.* 7:27, II.74–78 [*CO* 41.85]).

[129] See *Comm. Gen.* 22:13, I.571 (*CO* 23:318).   [130] *Comm. Gen* 22:2, I.563 (*CO* 23:313).

This interpretation may not pass for the historical sense of the text for many modern exegetes, but it nonetheless illustrates clearly the tie between Calvin's Christological understanding of a text and his concern for the history with which the text deals. History, as seen from the perspective of the actors within it, becomes the primary frame of reference for reading the text. This text has a Christological dimension for Calvin not because it prefigures in any way Christ's passion, but because of its place within the history of God's covenant with Abraham and the promise of the Mediator upon which that covenant was founded. Moreover, the Christology to which the text speaks is also apparently historical; it is bound to the covenant history not only as its foundation and end, but also as its motive force. Abraham's activities are determined by his concern for and relation to the Mediator promised by God. Calvin's Christological/historical reading of this passage thus exemplifies the relationship between his Christology and history as event that I spoke of above.

Calvin's reading of a second text, Psalm 45, picks up on the second aspect of the relationship between Christology and history mentioned above, the manner in which history is scripted and reported to shape its observers/hearers. Calvin states that this psalm was composed for the occasion of Solomon's wedding to an Egyptian wife, and his exegesis occupies itself first with the explication of the text in its connection to this historical setting, but he then turns to a Christological reading of the text, arguing that the history to which the text refers requires such a reading. The psalm attributes to the king qualities that neither Solomon nor any of Israel's kings possessed; thus, if the text speaks truly, and Calvin takes for granted that it does, these most superlative of attributes must refer to the Mediator or Messiah who is to come.

This discussion is most pointed when Calvin turns to the sixth and seventh verses of the psalm ("Thy throne, O God, is forever and ever . . . because God, thy God, hath anointed thee with the oil of gladness above thy fellows"). These verses had figured prominently in the Arian crisis of the fourth century. Both sides in the dispute had argued for a Christological interpretation of the text and claimed that it supported their understanding of the eternal relation of the Father to the Son. The Arians stated that the last clause ("because God, thy God, has anointed thee with the oil of gladness above thy fellows") identifies God's Son or Word as a creature set apart by God to serve as an intermediary between God and humanity. Athanasius responded that the first clause ("Thy throne, O God") clearly shows the eternal divinity of the Word, in unity with the Father. Calvin in his reading of this text agrees with the Trinitarian underpinnings of Athanasius' interpretation, but he argues that both parties mistake the text when they apply it primarily to the relation of the Son to the Father in eternity. Calvin writes:

It is important to notice that Christ is here spoken of as he is "God manifested in the flesh." He is also called God as he is the Word begotten of the Father before all worlds; but he is here set forth in the character of Mediator, and on this account also mention is made of him a little after as being subject to God. And indeed, if you limit to his divine nature what is here said of the everlasting duration of his kingdom, we shall be deprived of the inestimable benefit which redounds to us from this doctrine, when we learn that, as he is the head of the Church, the author and protector of our welfare, he reigns not merely for a time, but possesses and endless sovereignty; from this we derive our greatest confidence, both in life and death. From the following verse also it clearly appears that Christ is here exhibited to us in the character of Mediator; for he is said "to have been anointed of God," yea, even "above his fellows." This however cannot apply to the eternal Word of God, but to Christ in the flesh, and in this character he is both the servant of God and our brother.[131]

Calvin is concerned that this text be interpreted in relation to Christ's activity as king or head of the Church within history and not limited to Christ's eternal relation to the Father because it is in and through his activity in history that he brings the Church confidence and comfort. This was the intent of the psalmist, "to confirm the hearts of the faithful, and to guard them against the terror and alarm with which the melancholy change that happened soon after [the division of Solomon's kingdom soon upon his death] might fill their minds."[132] This same intention is apt for the Church in Calvin's day which is beset, he argues, by Papists who reject Christ and by Turks and Jews who reproach him. The psalm reminds these contemporary readers, "that Christ has no want of sword and arrows to overthrow and destroy his enemies."[133] This intention is fulfilled only when the text is interpreted Christologically, for only the promised Mediator could bring comfort to the Church both in Solomon's day and in Calvin's. It is also fulfilled only when the Christology of the text is understood historically. What brings comfort is the promise of Christ's real activity in history, in that place where we live our lives. The text and the history of which it speaks are rhetorically effective only through this conjunction of Christ and history.

---

[131] *Comm. Ps.* 45:6–7, II.183 (*CO* 31:454).   [132] *Comm. Ps.* 45:6–7, II.179–80 (*CO* 31:452).
[133] *Comm. Ps.* 45:6–7, II.183 (*CO* 31:454).

THE GOSPEL HISTORY

The intimate connection of Christ to the covenant history and the broader relationship of Christology to history that this connection entails are equally evident in Calvin's discussion of Christ as he is revealed in the Gospel. Indeed, my discussion thus far is pertinent primarily for the illumination that it brings to Calvin's discussion of the Gospel, in his Gospel commentaries, insofar as it helps us to structure and highlight key elements of this discussion. We find in Calvin's exposition of the four Gospels first an emphasis on the Gospel as history, again taking history to mean both event or activity and its presentation. The Christology Calvin finds in the Gospel is an historical Christology as much as the Christology found in God's covenant history with Israel. Moreover, Calvin's Gospel Christology is tied not simply to history in general, but specifically to Israel's covenant history, so that we can understand this Gospel only as the fulfillment of the covenant history, most especially as that history is organized under the threefold mediatorial office of priest, king, and prophet. All of this points us to Calvin's central focus on what Jesus has done to save – a focus that permeates his Christological discussion in his Gospel commentaries, as well as in the *Institutes*.

The Gospel as Christ's history

Calvin introduces his commentary on a harmony of the Synoptic Gospels with a definition of *Gospel* taken from Paul, one that illumines the "Evangelical history" he is about to explore. The Gospel is that which "was promised by God in the Scriptures, through the prophets, concerning his Son Jesus Christ our Lord, who was made of the seed of David according to the flesh, and declared to be the Son of God with power, according to the Spirit of sanctification, by the resurrection from the dead."[134] Elsewhere, he defines the term more generally as the word that "declares how God loved us when He sent our Lord Jesus Christ into the world,"[135] or as "the message of the grace exhibited to us in Christ" and "the embassy, by which God reconciles men to himself (2 Cor. 5:20)."[136]

Central to all of these definitions and to every discussion of the term in Calvin is that the Gospel is principally concerned with the history of Jesus Christ; it is the story "of how our Lord Jesus Christ came into the

---

[134] See *Comm. Harm.*, *Arg.*, I.xxxvff. (*CO* 45:1), from Rom. 1:2–4.
[135] "Deity of Christ," p. 13 (*CO* 47:466).   [136] *Comm. John, Arg.*, 1.21 (*CO* 47:VII).

world, he went about, he died, he rose again, he ascended into heaven."[137] The Gospel is Christ's history, both as the events and the narrative of his life, and it is in this history that Christ's person and office are made real for the world. The Gospel "clothes" Christ;[138] its proclamation is his "manifestation."[139] Calvin's emphasis on Christ's history constituting the essence of the Gospel is underlined when he explains the difference between the Gospel, per se, and Paul's epistles, which are not named "Gospel." They are not so named because "there we have not a continuous history which shows us how God sent his Son, how He willed that assuming our nature, He might have true brotherhood with us, how He died, was raised, and ascended into heaven."[140] The Gospel history is fundamental, and Paul's epistles are Gospel, more generally, only as their teaching is conformed to what and who are presented in the history.

Why this emphasis on history, though? Because in this history, God has accomplished and exhibited our salvation in Christ. Calvin calls Christ the "Guarantee" of God's love and of the Church's adoption; in Christ's life, death, and resurrection, "God signed and sealed his fatherly love."[141] Paul's letters are in some sense a commentary on our salvation, procured by Christ, but in the Gospel history we have to do with that procurement in and of itself. It is in that history that sins are forgiven, death is defeated, and humanity is united with God. "All that," Calvin writes, "is comprehended under the name of 'Gospel' because it declares to us how God perfected and accomplished everything which was required for the salvation of men, and it was all done in the Person of His Son."[142] Indeed, this emphasis on what Christ accomplishes in his history also leads Calvin to contrast the Gospel with the promises made in Israel's covenant history with God. Surely the saints of the Old Testament could put their trust in God's promises and surely they knew Christ in and through these promises, but the promises themselves were effective unto life only because they were realized in Christ's Gospel history. "Forgiveness of sins is promised in the covenant, but it is in the blood of Christ. Righteousness is promised, but it is offered through the atonement of Christ. Life is promised, but it must be sought only in the death and resurrection of Christ."[143] Calvin continually returns to Paul's statement that "all of the promises are in Christ, Yea and Amen" (2 Cor. 1:20). In Christ "God, then, ratified all that He had previously said and had promised to men."[144] In Christ, God has

---

[137] "Deity of Christ," p. 14 (*CO* 47:466).   [138] *Inst.* iii.ii.6, p. 548 (*OS* 4:60).
[139] "Deity of Christ," p. 14 (*CO* 47:467).   [140] Ibid., p. 15 (*CO* 47:467).
[141] Ibid., p. 14 (*CO* 47:466).   [142] Ibid.   [143] *Comm. Luke* 1:72, 1.72 (*CO* 45:48).
[144] "Deity of Christ," p. 14 (*CO* 47:466).

accomplished the salvation to which the covenant with Abraham and all of Israel pointed.[145]

A corollary for Calvin to this establishment of our redemption in Christ and his history is that the grace of God thereby accomplished is also presented to the Church therein. In his exposition of Paul's definition of the Gospel, Calvin writes: "Paul means not only that Christ is the pledge of all the blessings that God has ever promised, but that we have in him a full and complete exhibition of them."[146] The Gospel is the fact of Christ's redemptive history, and, in the four Gospels and the preaching of the Church, it is "the good and joyful message" of the same. Through its proclamation the Gospel leads God's elect into the grace which Christ has accomplished. Christ's Gospel history, therefore, is significant for its subjective or rhetorical impact on God's people, as well as for the objective state of affairs that it instantiates; and to continue the train of thought begun in the previous section, the rhetorical intent of the Gospel history was scripted not only into the narratives that record and proclaim that history, but also into the events of the history itself.

Christ's history as the fulfillment of the covenant

Calvin rivets our attention on Christ's history as the very center and substance of the Gospel of God's grace, then, because in that history our salvation has been uniquely and completely established and so through it our salvation is most brilliantly revealed. Thus, Christ's history stands in some contrast to Israel's covenant history as the reality to which the promises point and the blazing sunlight before which the shadows recede. At the same time, Calvin is clear that Christ's Gospel history must be understood in absolute continuity with Israel's history, not only because the covenant depends upon the reality of its Mediator, but also because the history of the Mediator has its sense and impact only in relation to this broader history from which it proceeds.

When John concludes that his Gospel was written that its readers might believe "that Jesus is the Christ" (John 20:31), Calvin explains that John meant thereby that Jesus was the one who "had been promised in the Law and the Prophets, as the Mediator between God and men," and that

---

[145] Indeed, Calvin objects to those who would attach the name "Gospel" to the promises found in the Old Testament. Though Calvin would agree that those promises were equally a part of God's covenant of grace and were, thus, good news, he wants to reserve the term "Gospel" for Christ's history. *Comm. Harm., Arg.,* i.xxxvii (*CO* 45:2).

[146] *Comm. Harm., Arg.,* i.xxxvi (*CO* 45:1).

"[John] included under the name of Christ all the offices which the Prophets ascribed to him."[147] The covenant history, though distinct from the Gospel, provided for both the Gospel writers and readers the categories through which the Gospel should be heard. Calvin elsewhere explains:

[The Gospel writers] had no intention or design to abolish by their writings *the Law and the prophets* . . . On the contrary, they point with the finger to Christ, and admonish us to seek from him whatever is ascribed to him by *the Law and the prophets*. The full profit and advantage, therefore, to be derived from the reading of the Gospel will only be obtained when we learn to connect it with the ancient promises.[148]

Indeed, Christ himself, Calvin tells us, relies on the covenant history to finally explain his person and office to the disciples on the road to Emmaus: "This passage shows us in what manner Christ is made known to us through the Gospel. It is when light is thrown on the knowledge of him by the Law and the Prophets."[149]

For Calvin, the Gospel is distinct from the covenant history of God's promises to God's Church as the fulfillment of those promises, but it is the Gospel of Christ, the one promised in Israel's history, only as it is the fulfillment of precisely those promises. Thus, the understanding of Christ that emerges from Calvin's reading of this Gospel balances the emphasis on the unique accomplishment of God's gracious will for the Church within Christ's history with the need to organize any explanation of that history by the categories provided in the covenant history, which is the prelude to Christ's person and work. Central among these categories for Calvin is the threefold office of priest, king, and prophet, under which the Mediator's work was structured throughout God's history with Israel. Indeed, when Calvin reads the Gospels, he consistently finds evidence that both the Gospel writers and participants within the Gospel histories understood Christ through his threefold office.

Calvin finds that the Gospels testify most abundantly to Christ's status as the Messianic king both promised to and typified by David. In his commentary on the Matthean genealogy, Calvin notes that Matthew specified David to have been "the king" ("and Jesse begat David the king and David the king begat Solomon," Matt. 1:6), "because in his person God exhibited a type of the future leader of his people, the Messiah."[150] The point of the genealogy, for Calvin, is to show that Jesus is descended from David's line and so can be the Messianic king whom God has promised. Moreover,

---

[147] *Comm. John* 20:31, II.281 (*CO* 47:447).   [148] *Comm Harm.*, *Arg.*, I.xxxviii (*CO* 45:3).
[149] *Comm. Luke* 24:27, III.359 (*CO* 45:806).   [150] *Comm. Matt.* 1:6, I.90 (*CO* 45:60).

Calvin argues that within the Gospel narrative itself, those who surround Jesus understand him to be the promised Davidic king, and they saw him as such, in part, because the details of his history gave him over to this interpretation. When Christ is prepared to enter Jerusalem, he sends his disciples to fetch him an ass that he might ride in upon it. This was done, as Matthew notes, to fulfill Zechariah's prophecy: "Lo, thy King cometh to thee, meek, and sitting on an ass" (Zech. 9:9). For Calvin, then, Christ's intention in making such an entrance is precisely to reveal himself as the king, promised of old, who would restore the salvation of his people.[151] And the crowd who received him understood him exactly in this sense. They cry out, "Hosanna to the Son of David," a prayer taken from Psalm 118, Calvin tells us. In the psalm, Calvin continues, David directed his readers to the eternal succession that God had promised to him, and therefore the crowd, by taking these words upon their lips, recognize Christ to be, in fact, the redeemer in whom David's kingdom would be eternally restored. In Mark's Gospel, the crowd continues: "Blessed be the kingdom of our father David, which cometh in the name of the Lord" (Mark 11:10). Calvin writes: "[T]hey speak thus in reference to the promises; because the Lord had testified that he would at length be a deliverer of that nation, and had appointed as the means the restoration of the kingdom of David. We see then that the honor of Mediator, from whom the restoration of all things and of salvation was to be expected, is ascribed to Christ."[152]

Scriptural citations and allusions tying Christ to David and the kingship are most numerous in the Gospels and Calvin's commentary upon them, but we also find references to the ceremonial laws by which Israel's reconciliation to God was established, laws that Calvin organizes under the priestly office of the Mediator in his Old Testaments commentaries. John reports that when the soldiers came to break the legs of the three crucified, they passed Christ by since he had already died. This was to fulfill Moses' command related to the paschal lamb, that "a bone of him shall not be broken" (John 21:36, Exod. 12:46), the lamb being understood as a type of Christ. The basic thrust of Calvin's discussion of this verse is to play upon the distinction between what was prefigured in the sacrifices of the Law and what was accomplished in Christ. On the one hand, we are reminded that the former sacrifices were only figures, devoid of power to save, except as they are bound to their true substance, which is Christ in his death on the cross. But, on the other hand, we behold Christ, in his connection to the paschal sacrifice, to be, "not only the pledge of our redemption, but

---

[151] See *Comm. Matt.* 21:1, II.446–447 (*CO* 45:571–572).   [152] *Comm. Matt.* 21:9, II.452 (*CO* 45:575).

also the price of it, because in him we see accomplished what was formerly exhibited to the ancient people under the figure of the passover."[153] Christ is here revealed as the perfection of the sacrifices of the Law, while these sacrifices, in turn, provide the framework for our perception of who he is.

Finally, we also find Calvin linking Christ's teaching ministry to the category of the prophetic office. We see this most clearly in his discussion of Luke 4:18 ("The Spirit of the Lord is upon me . . . he hath sent me to preach the Gospel to the poor"), a passage that Calvin argues refers to a coming Messianic prophet, which is fulfilled most properly in Christ alone.[154] But, Calvin's understanding of Christ's mediatorship focuses on his activity as priest and king, whereby God's salvation was established, in contrast to Christ's prophetic office, through which this established salvation was made plain.[155] Thus, when Calvin argues most clearly that Christ's mediatorial activity took place and must be understood in continuity with the covenant history, it is the sacerdotal and royal offices that he emphasizes.

At the heart of the Gospel narratives, Jesus asks his disciples: "Who do you say that I am?" And Peter responds: "Thou art the Christ" (Matt. 16:15–16, and parallels). Here Calvin finds an opportunity to discuss the content of this title that defines Jesus' identity:

> The confession is short, but it embraces all that is contained in our salvation; for the designation *Christ*, or *Anointed*, includes both an everlasting Kingdom and an everlasting Priesthood, to reconcile us to God, and, by expiating our sins through his sacrifice, to obtain for us perfect righteousness, and, having received us under his protection, to uphold and supply and enrich us with every description of blessings.[156]

For Peter to have grasped that Jesus was the Christ, that he was the Mediator, implies for Calvin that he understood him, at least tacitly, to be the priest who reconciles us to God and the king who enriches us with God's blessings, the two offices and activities on which the covenant depended.

Calvin's soteriological concern

For Calvin, then, we understand Christ properly only when we understand him as the one in whom God's covenant history with Israel is fulfilled, only when we recognize that he is the Mediator – priest, king, and prophet – promised in that history. This is the burden of the Synoptic Gospels, Calvin explains. They "are more copious [than John's Gospel] in their narrative of

---

[153] *Comm. John* 21:36, II.241 (*CO* 47:422). [154] *Comm. Luke* 4:17, I.228 (*CO* 45:141).
[155] See ch. 5, pp. 156–158, 163–164 below. [156] *Comm. Matt.* 16:16, II.289 (*CO* 472–473).

the life and death of Christ," and in relating this narrative, they are focused on one point, "that our Christ is that Son of God who had been promised to be the Redeemer of the world."[157] But such understanding is incomplete if we only grasp that Christ has fulfilled this role through the threefold office and do not also understand the unique content with which he fills the covenantal form. This unique content Calvin describes as Christ's purpose, and it is found most abundantly in John's Gospel. John's Gospel, Calvin claims, gives more of the teaching of Jesus,[158] and from that teaching we learn: "the charge committed to him by God, his Father, briefly, his virtue, his power, and his goodness toward us." It is on the basis of these that his history is Gospel, that it is good news.[159] The Synoptic Gospels also relate the purpose for which Christ came, but not in the detail that John gives; they include a great deal of Jesus' teaching, but this teaching is less related to an explication of Jesus' office. John, Calvin writes, "is almost wholly occupied in explaining the power of Christ, and the advantages which we derive from him."[160] To sum it up, Calvin tells us, "the [Synoptics] exhibit Christ's body . . . but John exhibits his soul."[161]

For this reason, Calvin makes John's Gospel theologically primary in the construction of his Christology: "The Gospel of John is to us, as it were, a key by which we enter into an understanding of the others. For if we read St. Matthew, St. Mark and St. Luke we shall not know so well why Jesus Christ was sent into the world as when we shall have read St. John."[162] What John tells us of Jesus' office as Mediator is the key for understanding the synoptics and their message that Jesus is the one who fulfills this office.[163] Of course, what we learn from John of Jesus' office, for Calvin, does not stand outside of the Old Testament history and what it has told us of the Christ. Rather, it works within the categories provided by this history, in Christ's threefold office as priest, king, and prophet. Within that history in the Old Testament, however, Christ's priestly, kingly, and prophetic offices are only presented in shadows, while in Christ they have come into the full light of day. Therefore, we come to understand these offices in far richer and more vibrant detail as we pursue their exposition given in the Gospels.

---

[157] *Comm. John, Arg.*, 1.21 (*CO* 47:vii); Comm. *Harm., Arg.*, 1.xxxvii, (*CO* 45:3).
[158] "Deity of Christ," p. 15 (*CO* 47:467).   [159] Ibid., p. 17 (*CO* 47:468).
[160] *Comm. Harm., Arg.*, 1.xxxvii (*CO* 45:2–3).   [161] *Comm. John, Arg.*, 1.22 (*CO* 47:vii).
[162] "Deity of Christ," p. 16 (*CO* 47:468).
[163] Too many commentators have missed this point in their reading of Calvin, and his Christology is popularly associated more with the perspective of the Synoptics than with John. Barth, for instance, repeats and supports a tradition aligning Calvin's Christology with that of the Synoptic Gospels (and the Christology of Antioch) and Luther's with John (and Alexandria) (Karl Barth, *Church Dogmatics*, G. T. Thompson and Harold Knight, trans. [Edinburgh: T. & T. Clark, 1956], 1.2, pp. 15–25).

This is the task of the next three chapters, to explore Calvin's detailing of Christ's work or activity within his Gospel history under the rubric of his threefold office of priest, king, and prophet both in his biblical commentaries (especially the Gospel of John) and in the *Institutes*.[164] This work assumes that the pattern of Calvin's Christology that emerges out of its *locus* within the covenant history holds good for the *Institutes* as well as the commentaries. I have already explained at the beginning of this chapter the manner in which the *Institutes* can be seen to be shaped by the framework of the covenant history; and, in the chapters which follow, the manner in which Christ's threefold office (ii.xv) serves as a faithful pattern for the Christology which culminates in his discussion of Christ's Gospel history (ii.xvi) will become clear. But, before we move on, I want to take a different angle on a central point of this chapter, that Calvin's Christology emphasizes Christ's work to a degree that it makes sense to pursue its exposition before we turn to what Calvin says about Christ's person. Thus far I have made this point through my development of the covenant history as Calvin's chief Christological framework, the point being that the covenant history not only provides the threefold office as the categories under which Christ's work can be organized, but also places unique emphasis on what Christ does within history. History as a Christological framework privileges doing over the metaphysics of being.

But Calvin argues for an emphasis on what Christ has done within history from a second perspective, that of piety, or the theological goal of forming deep and proper Christian faith. Calvin begins the *Institutes* by instructing his readers that it is less significant to know that God is, or what God is, than to know how God is for us, so that we might look to God for all good and revere God for God's glory.[165] He likewise maintains that in knowing Christ – and, thus, in constructing a Christology – it is a barren knowledge that only grasps who or what Christ is without an understanding of why he was sent to us. On the one hand, this is because Christ's divinity is as inscrutable in its hypostatic union with his humanity as it is in the Father in heaven.[166] Thus, although it is Christ's office to make God known – so that, in fact, we can know God truly only in Christ[167] – nonetheless even here he is clear that we know God in Christ only in God's power, only in

---

[164] My intent is not to collapse the categories of Christ's work and office in Calvin, but to argue that, for Calvin, Christ's threefold office exhaustively organizes all that Calvin will say about Christ's work.

[165] See *Inst.* i.ii, pp. 39–43 (*OS* 3:34–37).   [166] See *Comm. John* 14:10, ii.87 (*CO* 47:326).

[167] *Comm. John* 8:19, i.329–330 (*CO* 47:194–195).

the loving works of God toward us. Human persons simply do not have the capacity to know God in God's essence.[168]

But within Calvin's commentary on Christological passages in the Gospels, he is less concerned with the inscrutability of God's essence, and more concerned that the faithful devote themselves to knowing how and why Christ is set in relationship to God's Church, so that they may learn to place their faith in Christ. Calvin fears that, if Christians rest content with the bare knowledge of who Christ is, this knowledge will not elicit a fruitful faith. When Nathaniel confesses Christ to be both the Son of God and the King of Israel at the beginning of John's Gospel (John 1:49), Calvin comments that our faith ought not to be fixed on Christ's essence, alone, simply recognizing him as God's Son, but that we also must attend to his power and office and know that he has been given to us as king: "[F]or it would be of little advantage to know who Christ is, if this second point were not added, what he wishes to be toward us, and for what purpose the Father sent him."[169] We must know not only Christ's essence, but also his kingdom, for the latter is his power and his will to save, and it is this power and will that upholds our faith.

We can label this point of Calvin's Christological focus on Christ's purpose over Christ's metaphysical status as his soteriological concern. This concern is reflected in the dual aspect of Christ's mediatorial office – that Christ enacts the Church's salvation, that he might thereby draw the Church to faith.[170] Just as Christ intends to draw the Church to faith through his activity among us, so, too, does Calvin intend to draw his readers to faith through his presentation of Christ and his history. From Calvin's perspective, to simply know of the presence of the divine essence in Christ, or to know something of the nature of this essence in the eternal relationship of the Father and the Son, could remain a piece of disinterested knowledge, "a very small and cold portion of faith."[171] It is only as we know that God is for us in Christ, insofar as he has enacted our salvation, that we are led to place in him a faith that nourishes our obedience to him and allows

---

[168] See *Inst.* I.v.9, p. 62 (*OS* 3:53).   [169] *Comm. John* 1:49, 1.79 (*CO* 47:36).

[170] Indeed, we will find over the course of this book that Christology and soteriology are bound together, for Calvin, in his understanding of Christ's work, such that his Christology is soteriologically defined, and his soteriology is Christologically defined. Hence, it is difficult to make sense of claims for an incoherence between Calvin's Christology and soteriology (see Van Buren, *Christ in Our Place*, p. 32; Gerrish, "Atonement and Saving Faith," *Theology Today* 17 [July 1960], 184; and Dawn DeVries, *Jesus Christ in the Preaching of Calvin* [Louisville: Westminster/John Knox Press, 1996], p. 96).

[171] *Comm. John* 9:37, 1.389 (*CO* 47:232).

our relationship with God.[172] We need knowledge – knowledge of Christ's saving activity – that is effective in our lives.

We must immediately add, however, that this so-called soteriologial concern does not displace or efface questions of Christ's person for Calvin. There is the obvious point that Christian soteriology, at least as Calvin understands it, necessitates Christological definition. Though our primary interest may be in what Christ has done for us, we cannot properly conceive of this activity if we do not also understand who Christ is. Only as he is the God–human can he enact our salvation in each of its many dimensions. Thus, I argue, Calvin begins his discussion of Christology proper in the *Institutes* (ii.xii–xiv) with a discussion of Christ's identity as the God–human as a way of introducing onto the stage the one who, in his Gospel history, acts to save – this latter discussion concluding the consideration in the *Institutes* of Christology proper and bringing Book II of the work to its culmination.

However, this soteriological concern stands in a more significant relationship to Calvin's talk of Christ's person insofar as its central purpose is to rivet our attention on Christ's person, given that he is the one in whom God is revealed as Father and through whom we come into communion with God. Calvin's soteriological concern, in other words, shapes our attention to Christ's person such that the noetic dimension of this attention guides the affective dimension, that we through faith and love might bind ourselves to Christ and be engrafted into his body. So the next three chapters on Calvin's understanding of Christ's office are not meant to neglect attention to Christ's person, but rather to give substance to what Calvin says about Christ's person – that he is the one who makes God manifest in the flesh.

[172] Ibid.

CHAPTER 3

Christ as priest

Calvin has a great deal to say about Christ's office as king and prophet, but he is nevertheless clear that Christ's work as priest is the foundation to a proper understanding of his role as Mediator. In the *Institutes*, he argues that Christ became incarnate, according to the Scriptures, "to restore the fallen world"; and in this context, Calvin means by restoration that "[Christ] was appointed by God's eternal plan to purge the uncleanness of men; for shedding of blood is a sign of expiation."[1] If we are to understand Christ's purpose, we must begin with his offer of himself through his death to reconcile the Church to God; that is, we must begin with his work as priest. It is only by means of this reconciliation that a way is open for the broader covenant relation between God and the Church. Through his priestly work, Christ opens the way for his work as prophet and king.

This centrality of the sacrificial work of Christ was evident in the Old Testament history, examined in the preceding chapter. We saw at the very beginning of the story that there was, in fact, a history of the Church in its covenant relationship with God only because of God's effective intention to reconcile Godself with God's Church, a reconciliation tied to an expiatory sacrifice. Abraham knew, Calvin concludes at one point, that he would have no access to God apart from such a sacrifice. In the ceremonial Law, handed down by Moses, this need for a sacrifice was codified into Israel's history as the foundation of their relationship with God, through which they could entrust themselves to God's grace in spite of their sin; but, as Calvin repeatedly states, these sacrifices were effective in the life of the Church of the Old Testament only in their connection to Christ's true sacrifice, through which they were fulfilled.

Moreover, we must remember that the reconciliation accomplished by Christ through the ceremonial laws was effective in two dimensions. On the one hand, the sacrifices, through their presentation of Christ's death,

---

[1] *Inst.* II.xii.4, p. 467 (*OS* 3:441).

restored the covenant relationship; God's wrath was appeased and God was present to the people. Reconciliation was objectively established. On the other hand, the Church was led to faith and repentance by the sacrifices; they were moved by the evidence of their need both for God and for God's grace toward them manifest in the Law. Reconciliation, in this sense, was subjectively appropriating. Indeed, we can say that it was appropriated only as it was first appropriating. The Church responded with faith and repentance only because these were elicited through the typological representations of Christ's sacrifice given in the Law. Christ's mediation through these sacrifices was the principal active agent in Israel's faith; Israel was only the respondent.

Christ, then, mediated God's covenant with the Church through the sacrifices in both the objective and subjective dimensions, and we will understand this work fully only as we see that these two dimensions within his work are intertwined. The sacrifices were able to elicit faith from Israel – they impelled the people to seek pardon from Christ within them – only because they offered atonement. The Church can trust in God's promise, as Calvin says, because that promise is not delusive; it is, in fact, active within the life and history of the Church that God has called, reconciling the Church to God so that God can be present among God's people. Likewise, the sacrifices reconcile the people to God only as they become exercises of faith and repentance. Reconciliation, in this sense, is more than God's setting aside God's wrath. It is God's renewal of relationship with God's people. In both of these cases, it is clear that the redemption of the people involves more than a mere healing of the soul or of a metaphysical rift between God and humanity introduced by sin. The redemption wrought by Christ in these sacrifices focuses on the renewal of God's relationship with God's Church in and through their history. This is the effectual activity of Christ that is manifest in the Law.

In this chapter, as we take up Calvin's exposition of Christ's priestly office both within his Gospel commentaries and in the *Institutes*, we find these same themes. We find, first, an explanation of Christ's sacrificial death, in terms of both its place as the foundation of the covenant and its concrete effectiveness in the lives of God's people. We also find the same dynamic of reconciliation in Christ's fulfillment of his priestly role as what I have just described. Given that God in God's righteousness could not recognize creatures stained by sin, Calvin argues, and that, in fact, God's wrath burned against sin, God out of gracious love for God's chosen sent Christ to propitiate God's anger and open the way for reunion. Christ, therefore, suffered in our place, taking the punishment and wrath that we deserved upon himself, objectively expiating our sin; but he also addressed the fear of God that barred our access to this renewed relationship, drawing near to us when we would not draw near to God and taking away God's wrath, the very cause of our fear. Christ thereby removed the barriers to our relationship with God so that this relationship, born out of Christ's priestly work, might come to full fruition through his work as king and prophet. I lay out these themes concerning Christ's priestly office generally through an initial exploration of Calvin's Gospel commentaries and then pursue them more closely through a detailed examination of Calvin's doctrine of Christ's sacrificial Atonement as it is presented in the *Institutes*.

THE SACERDOTAL OFFICE IN THE GOSPEL COMMENTARIES

When John the Baptist calls Christ the Lamb of God, Calvin tells us,

The principal office of Christ is briefly but clearly stated; that he takes away the sins of the world by the sacrifice of his death, and reconciles men to God. There are other favours, indeed, which Christ bestows upon us, but this is the chief favour, and the rest depend on it; that, by appeasing the wrath of God, he makes us to be reckoned holy and righteous. For from this source flows all the streams of blessings, that, by not imputing our sins, God receives us into favour.[2]

Christ's office as king is to bestow upon the Church the blessings of the covenant, most principally the blessing of fellowship with God; but this beatific relationship is only possible as Christ first removes the barriers of sin and unrighteousness that prevent the Church's relationship with God. This he does through his work as priest.

For Calvin, as for most Christian theologians, there exists a fundamental gap between God and humanity. This gap is in some degree derivative from our creatureliness. Calvin is clear, for example, that a Mediator would have been necessary if Adam had never sinned. He notes Paul's comment in his letter to Timothy, that "God dwells in inaccessible light" (I Tim. 6:16), and concludes from this that we can see and know God in any event only as God accommodates Godself to our smallness and makes Godself known through a Mediator.[3] But, within the context of the covenant history, it is humanity's fall into unrighteousness that has wholly cut us off from God, and God was responding to humanity's fall when God promised to bless the Church through Abraham's seed, through the Mediator. Sin is the principal

---

[2] *Comm. John* 1:29, I.63 (*CO* 47.25).   [3] *Inst.* II.xii.1, p. 465 (*OS* 3:438).

barrier standing between God and God's Church, and Christ, through his atonement, must first expiate our sin and restore us to the original holiness for which God created us before the "natural" ontological gap between God and humanity can be addressed.

This expiation and restoration is no mean task. As is obvious on any reading of Calvin, he takes very seriously the degradation of humanity that is a product of sin. We understand the shape of Christ's life, in fact, only in its relation to this degradation. He writes:

> [Christ] came to quicken the dead, to justify the guilty and condemned, to wash those who were polluted and full of uncleanness, to rescue the lost from hell, to clothe with his glory those who were covered with shame, to renew to a blessed immortality those who were debased by disgusting vices. If we consider that this was his office and the end of his coming – if we remember that this was the reason why he took upon him our flesh, why he shed his blood, when he offered the sacrifice of his death, why he descended even to hell – we will never think it strange that he should gather to salvation those who have been the worst of men, and who have been covered with a mass of crimes.[4]

Calvin mentions at the end of this paragraph "the worst of men," but when he earlier speaks of those who are guilty and condemned, polluted, and debased by disgusting vices, he is not singling out a few; he is describing the condition of all humanity, not by nature, but because of sin.[5] And because of sin, we are cut off from God, "who does not recognize as his handiwork men defiled and corrupted by sin."[6] Therefore, we are in need of Christ's priestly mediation, to make satisfaction, so that God might again recognize us.

God is wrathful against humanity's sin; God's vengeance burns against us. Calvin, reflecting the biblical text, uses strong language to describe humanity's estrangement from God because of sin – estrangement rooted in God's active rejection of our sin – consistently resorting to the language of anger. Christ, then, in his priestly work, propitiates that anger by taking upon himself and suffering our punishment in our place. Christ endures God's anger on humanity's behalf, and this is reflected not simply in his death, but in his concomitant estrangement from God on the cross, estrangement through which he is placed, as Calvin writes, "as a guilty person at the judgment seat of God."[7] So, when Christ says that his soul is troubled, in anticipation of his death (John 12:27), Calvin writes:

---

[4] *Comm. Matt.* 9:12, 1.402 (*CO* 45.250).   [5] See *Inst.* ii.i.8,9, pp. 250–253 (*OS* 3:249–252).
[6] *Inst.* ii.vi.i, p. 341 (*OS* 3:320).
[7] Note Calvin's comments on Jesus' experience of God's wrath in his cry of dereliction (*Comm. Matt.* 27:46, iii.318 [*CO* 45.779]).

It was highly useful, and even necessary for our salvation that the Son of God should have experience of such feelings. In his death we ought chiefly to consider his atonement, by which he appeased the wrath and curse of God, which he could not have done without taking upon himself our guilt. The death which he underwent must therefore have been full of horror, because he could not render satisfaction for us, without feeling in his own experience the dreadful judgment of God.[8]

God rejects human sin and demands its punishment. Christ atones for human sin and stands as the true sacrifice, to which all the sacrifices of the Old Testament pointed, as he becomes this sin and is judged before and punished by God in our place, even to the point of experiencing the horror of rejection by God. In this manner, Christ restores the relationship between God and humanity; by satisfying God's righteousness, by "appeasing God's wrath" against our sin, he allows God to again recognize us and to come into covenant relationship with us. This is typically called an "objective" understanding of Christ's Atonement, and it is prevalent throughout Calvin's work, but Calvin consistently balances this with a more "subjective" approach, recognizing that, through sin, we as much cut ourselves off from God, because of fear as God has cut Godself off from us because of wrath. We are alienated and afraid and dare not approach God, for fear of judgment, because we recognize our own degradation and are conscious of God's hatred of the same. Therefore, Calvin emphasizes that Christ, as priest, also reconciles humanity to God through his Atonement by drawing humanity back to God, reawakening us to God's fatherly love.[9]

In his commentary on Matt. 9:6 ("But that you may know that the Son of man hath authority on earth to forgive sins"), Calvin writes:

By these words Christ declares that he is not only the minister and witness, but likewise the author of this grace. But what means this restriction, *on earth?* . . . Christ's meaning was that forgiveness of sins ought not to be sought from a distance: for he exhibits it to men in his own person, and as it were in his hands. So strong is our inclination to distrust, that we never venture to believe that God is merciful to us, till he draws near, and speaks familiarly to us. Now as Christ descended to earth for this purpose of exhibiting to men the grace of God as present, he is said to forgive sins visibly, because in him and by him the will of God was revealed, which according to the perception of the flesh had been formerly hidden above the clouds.[10]

---

[8] *Comm. John* 12:27, II.32 (*CO* 47.290–291).
[9] More on "objective" and "subjective" theories of the Atonement below.
[10] *Comm. Matt.* 9:6, I.396–397 (*CO* 45.246–247).

Christ is the author of our forgiveness through his obedience and death. He thereby accomplishes our reconciliation and also exhibits the grace of this reconciliation, so that we may know that we have been drawn into relationship with God, that we are embraced by God's fatherly love. Thus, through his work as priest, Christ has made God manifest by drawing near in forgiveness so that humanity, in turn, will draw near to God.

I spoke above of God's alienation from humanity – indeed, of God's wrath toward humanity – as well as humanity's alienation from God because of sin, but this is not entirely accurate to Calvin's depiction of humanity's estrangement from God. It seems to indicate an antipathy on God's part toward humanity, until Christ atones for us, while Calvin is clear that God, even in the midst of God's rejection of human sinfulness, still reaches out to those whom God has created in love. That is the whole point of the covenant history – that God is restoring to relationship with Godself those whom God has chosen to love even though they have made themselves, through sin, noxious to God. Calvin writes in the *Institutes*,

God, who is the highest righteousness, cannot love the unrighteousness that he sees in us all . . . But because the Lord wills not to lose what is his in us, out of his own kindness he still finds something to love. However much we may be sinners by our own fault, we nevertheless remain his creatures . . . Thus he is moved by pure and freely given love of us to receive us into grace.[11]

God cannot come into covenant relationship with humanity in its fallen state – God's hatred of sin is real and must be addressed – but God's love and mercy are, nonetheless, the primary causes of Christ's atoning work, which restores that relationship. God's love initializes and does not follow Christ's sacrifice on the cross, for God still wills fellowship with God's chosen creatures. Therefore, God, out of that love, sent Christ to redeem God's chosen. Christ's priestly work is done on behalf of God so that God's merciful plan might be realized within the covenant history.

Calvin, discussing John 3:16 ("For God so loved the world . . ."), reminds the reader at great length that God's love for God's Church from eternity is the ultimate cause for our redemption, and it is the unmerited quality of this love that allows our minds a "calm repose."[12] Our salvation depends on nothing of what we do, but rests in the firmness of God's gracious and unchanging will; but what, then, he asks, of scriptural passages that seem to indicate that God's love for us begins only with the work of Christ, outside of which God hates us? Still upholding the primacy of God's eternal love, Calvin adds to this that:

[11] *Inst.* II.xvi.3, pp. 505–506 (*OS* 3:484).   [12] *Comm. John* 3:16, 1.122–124 (*CO* 47.63–65).

the grace which [God] wishes to be made known to us, and by which we are encouraged to a confidence in salvation, commences with the reconciliation which was procured through Christ. For since he necessarily hates sin, how shall we believe that we are loved by him until atonement has been made for those sins on account of which he is justly offended at us? Thus, the blood of Christ must intervene for the purpose of reconciling God to us, before we have any experience of his fatherly kindness.[13]

Christ's priestly work does not initiate God's love for God's Church; rather, it commences the realization of that love, "the grace which God wishes to be made known to us," within the covenant history. On the one hand, it enables God to work out God's "fatherly love" for the Church, appeasing God's wrath – again, the problem is not only that we are alienated from God, but also that, although God loves us as God's creatures, God cannot recognize us because God must reject our sin. On the other hand, it reveals that love to us so that we might experience it. Christ's priestly work, then, is a playing out of God's eternal love in the covenant history, through which that love is both accomplished and exhibited so that God's covenant with God's Church might be renewed.

There are, obviously, a great many questions that arise over Calvin's understanding of Christ's Atonement implicit within this discussion of Christ's priestly office, among them: whether Calvin offers an objective or subjective theory; how Calvin finally resolves the relationship between God's eternal election of the chosen and Christ's redemption of the same; and how Calvin resolves the relationship between God's love for the chosen and Christ's meriting of that love. We begin to find answers to these questions by pursuing an analysis of Calvin's presentation of Christ's priestly office further, focusing on his development of this doctrine in the *Institutes*.

CHRIST'S SACERDOTAL OFFICE IN THE *INSTITUTES*

Calvin introduces Christ's priestly office in the *Institutes* in one short paragraph, which begins as follows:

Now we must speak briefly concerning the purpose and use of Christ's priestly office: as a pure and stainless Mediator he is by his holiness to reconcile us to God. But God's righteous curse bars our access to him, and God in his capacity as judge is angry toward us. Hence, an expiation must intervene in order that Christ as priest may obtain God's favour for us and appease his wrath. Thus Christ to perform this office has to come forward with a sacrifice.[14]

---

[13] Ibid., 1.124 (*CO* 47.64), translation emended. [14] *Inst.* II.xv.6, p. 501 (*OS* 3:480).

With this statement, Calvin informs his readers that the primary context in which they must understand Christ's work of reconciliation is that given in the Law – that Christ reconciles humanity to God when he, as priest, offers himself to God as a sacrifice. Calvin will eventually discuss Christ's reconciling work under a variety of rubrics – not only is he an expiatory sacrifice, but he also makes satisfaction and bears our punishment. However, all of these approaches are enclosed within the broader framework of the covenant history that Christ, as the Mediator, fulfills; and within this framework Calvin is insisting that we understand Christ in the first place as priest, that is, as the active agent who reconciles humanity to God, and only then as the sacrifice, satisfaction, or substitute that he offers to make expiation. Christ is not merely the instrument of God's reconciliation with the Church; he is its author, so that the covenant between God and the Church finds its fulfillment in the renewed relationship that he effects.[15] Moreover, Christ's priestly agency must be understood in relation to both the subjective and objective dimensions of its effects, as they have just been described. Christ opens the way for covenant between God and God's Church both by covering our sin and making us righteous in God's eyes and by turning us from fear to the recognition of God's love manifest in Christ's sacrifice. In the *Institutes*, Calvin introduces Christ's priestly role at the end of his chapter on Christ's office so that it might serve as a primary rubric (along with Christ's role as king and prophet) under which he develops the content of Christ's work in his exposition of the Creed – how Christ acquired our salvation – and in his discussion of Christ's merit in the following two chapters.

Calvin's theories of the Atonement

The foundation of Christ's sacerdotal work, both as priest and as sacrifice, is his obedience. Only in the righteousness thereby established does he possess the holiness required to serve as priest and the purity to serve as an expiatory sacrifice. Calvin writes: "How has Christ abolished sin, banished the separation between us and God, and acquired righteousness to render God favourable and kindly toward us? To this we can in general reply that he has achieved this for us by the whole course of his obedience."[16] Scripture generally focuses on the atoning power of Christ's death and resurrection, so that the Creed passes from his birth directly to his passion, Calvin notes

---

[15] So, *pace* Van Buren, Christ's substitutionary sacrifice must be understood within the broader priestly framework of his mediation (see Van Buren, *Christ in our Place*, pp. 65, 89).

[16] *Inst.* II.xvi.5, p. 507 (*OS* 3:485–486).

with accord. But we must also understand that the obedience that Christ manifested through the history of his life was vital to our salvation. Paul writes: "As by one man's disobedience many were made sinners, so by one man's obedience we are made righteous" (Rom. 5:19). Calvin continues, therefore: "from the time when he took on the form of a servant, he began to pay the price of liberation in order to redeem us."[17] Christ is a fit covenant partner with God and so can restore us to the covenant relationship because he fulfills God's commands as we could not. Additionally, even his sacrificial death relies on his obedience, for it is only as he lays down his life willingly in deference to the Father that he both demonstrates his love for the Church and manifests his devotion to the Father.

If Christ's obedience is the foundation of his reconciliation of humanity with God, then his passion is the bulk of the structure. In his judgment before Pilate, his suffering, and his death, he covered our sins and made us righteous before God. Calvin's discussion of Christ's propitiation of the Father, however, is complicated by the multiple metaphors that he deploys to explicate this work. He will speak of Christ's death as an expiatory sacrifice offered in fulfillment of the sacrifices of the Old Testament, and I have argued here that this is the formal framework in which Calvin's doctrine should be understood. Yet he also frequently refers to Christ's making "satisfaction" for the debt that was incurred through sin, so that many commentators frequently understand Calvin's doctrine of Atonement as remaining largely in line with Anselm's development of this theory. However, Van Buren is certainly correct in seeing that a fundamental theme that runs through Calvin's discussion is the forensic notion of penal substitution – Christ is the one who was judged and punished in our place – a notion that Anselm specifically rejected. Our task in the next few pages is to follow each of these streams in Calvin's argument to find the common currents that run through each of them.

At the center of Christ's passion stands the cross; and in his commentary on the Creed (II.xvi), Calvin talks about the cross chiefly as Christ's expiatory sacrifice whereby he removes and destroys the sin that stains humanity. Calvin very consciously reads Christ's death on the cross as a curse, for so it is defined in the Law – "Cursed be everyone who hangs on a tree" (Deut. 21:23). Through this death Christ very literally becomes sin, bearing the curse that sin brings upon us, and this is in accord with the Old Testament sacrifices of which his death is the fulfillment. Those sacrifices offered for sins were called "Ashmoth," Calvin explains, which is the word

[17] Ibid.

for sins. So Christ in his sacrifice gives his life as an "Asham," an expiatory offering whereby we are made clean because he takes our sin upon him – our sin is transferred from us to Christ. But Christ does not merely take away our sin, Calvin emphasizes; he also destroys it: "Yet we must not understand that he fell under the curse that overwhelmed him; rather – in taking the curse upon himself – he crushed, broke, and scattered its whole force."[18] Thus, again, even in his passion, Christ is for Calvin, finally, the agent of redemption, not only through his acceptance of his suffering, but also in his activity in the midst of that suffering to destroy sin. If, therefore, the cross is the center of Christ's passion, the turning point in a fallen humanity's relationship with God, then Calvin will describe this revolution chiefly under the rubric of Christ's sacrifice through which the sin that separates humanity from God is removed and obliterated. Thus, we no longer need to fear God's wrath. The sin that God hates has been destroyed and we are clean, washed in Christ's blood.

Having said this, we also must recognize that Calvin's discussion of Christ's sacrificial death is peppered with the language of satisfaction as well. For example, he writes: "Christ was offered to the Father in death as an expiatory sacrifice that when he discharged all satisfaction through his sacrifice, we might cease to be afraid of God's wrath."[19] The satisfaction theory of Christ's Atonement was first articulated by Anselm five centuries before Calvin and has been considered the dominant notion of the Atonement in the West through to the Reformation and beyond. Indeed, most Calvin commentators will remark quite simply that Calvin follows Anselm in his understanding of this doctrine.[20] At the center of Anselm's explanation is the notion that humanity was created owing God perfect obedience, so that, with Adam's sin, an infinite debt was contracted which we were unable to pay and for which we were condemned to death. However, Christ, with his life of perfect obedience, fulfilled God's demands, so that he did not owe God his death, since death is only the wage of sin. He nonetheless offered to God his life through his death on the cross, a life that is of infinite worth because of his obedience, thereby accruing the capital to pay the debt under which we were bound and freeing us from God's judgment. By Anselm's theory, our atonement takes on the air of a transaction between God and Christ, but Anselm is equally clear that Christ's work was undertaken only in and through the merciful initiative of God. There is, in fact,

---

[18] *Inst.* II.xvi.6, p. 511 (*OS* 3:490).   [19] *Inst.* II.xvi.6, p. 510 (*OS* 3:490).
[20] See Wendel, *Calvin*, p. 219, and Battles' footnote: *Inst.* II.xvi.2, fn. 5, p. 505.

for Anselm no division between God and Christ in this work, as has often been popularly assumed.

Again, general references in Calvin to the "satisfaction" that Christ must make pop up throughout his discussion of Christ's passion, but it is only in his discussion of Christ's merit (II.xvii) that the full vocabulary of satisfaction emerges. There Calvin speaks repeatedly of Christ paying for us what we could not. "What was the purpose of this subjugation of Christ to the law," he writes, "but to acquire righteousness for us, undertaking to pay what we could not pay?"[21] And, elsewhere: "The apostles clearly state that he paid the price to redeem us from the penalty of death."[22] And, again: "[F]or God has given the price of redemption in the death of Christ."[23] Through his sacrifice, Christ has blotted out sin, but the image that emerges in this discussion pertains more to the debt we owe to God because of sin – both the debt of righteousness, which we cannot pay, and the debt of death, which we must pay in its place. Christ, through his obedience and death, redeems us from our indebtedness and sets our account straight with God. By making satisfaction, he has restored our relationship to God.

There is, then, some accuracy to those who would compare Calvin's notion of the Atonement to Anselm's – the language of satisfaction does register in his theology, but also we must note that Calvin often ties this language to a second approach to the doctrine toward which Anselm was quite adverse. For Calvin will frequently argue that Christ paid the price we owed to God by suffering our punishment in our place. He writes: "For unless Christ had made satisfaction for our sins, it would not have been said that he appeased God by taking upon himself the penalty to which we were subject."[24] Indeed, following Van Buren's thesis (see note 15 above), we can say that Calvin in his discussion of Christ's Atonement most consistently articulates this theme of penal substitution – that Christ bears the Father's wrath, the punishment that we deserve, thereby freeing us from its burden.

Calvin pushes this notion most forcefully first in his discussion of Christ's judgment before Pilate. This judgment becomes, in some sense, a staged drama orchestrated by Scripture and history's Author, that through it we might see that the punishment that should have fallen on us was allotted to Christ: "The curse caused by our guilt was awaiting us at God's heavenly judgment seat. Accordingly, Scripture first relates Christ's condemnation before Pontius Pilate of Judea, *to teach us* that the penalty to which we were

---

[21] *Inst.* II.xvii.5, p. 533 (*OS* 3:513).   [22] Ibid., p. 532 (*OS* 3:512).   [23] Ibid.
[24] *Inst.* II.xvii.4, p. 532 (*OS* 3:512).

subject had been imposed upon this righteous man."[25] It is important for Calvin that Christ did not merely die, but that he died having been judged and condemned, though righteous, so that it was clear that he had taken on our guilt:

If he had been murdered by thieves or slain in an insurrection by a raging mob, in such a death there would have been no evidence of satisfaction. But when he was arraigned before the judgment seat as a criminal, accused and pressed by testimony, and condemned by the mouth of the judge to die – we know by these proofs that he took the role of a guilty man and evildoer.[26]

He takes the "role" of a guilty man, he plays out our part – for we are the ones who, in fact, are guilty before God – even though he himself, as Pilate on several occasions publicly proclaims, is innocent: "Thus we shall behold the person of a sinner and evildoer represented in Christ, yet from his shining innocence it will at the same time be obvious that he was burdened with another's sin rather than his own."[27]

Two themes emerge from these passages: that Christ is judged in the place of the guilty, and that the scene enacted before Pilate is deliberately structured to evince this judgment to its observers. The former of these conclusions is obvious and has been drawn by most Calvin commentators, but the quotations given above provide grounds for the latter conclusion as well. Calvin tells us that Scripture narrates this incident "to teach us," that Christ "takes the role" of the evildoer in this scene, that Christ "represents" the sinner, though he has been publicly declared innocent. There are subjective and theatrical overtones to Calvin's discussion of Christ's forensic substitution. The public exhibition of Christ's judgment is vital to Calvin's understanding of Christ's Atonement. It is not enough that Christ takes our place; we must also see and grasp the gracious action on his part.

This is not to say that Christ's Atonement is more show than substance for Calvin, for, in his discussion of Christ's "descent into Hell," he articulates the reality to which Christ's condemnation before Pilate points, that Christ "[underwent] the severity of God's vengeance, to appease his wrath and satisfy his just judgment."[28] It is not adequate that Christ merely die in our place; he must be judged and punished for us, and it is not human judgment before which we stand condemned but God's. In the following chapter on Christ's kingship we see Calvin's exposition of Christ's battle with death; but first we must grasp the context for that battle, that Christ is subjected to death and hell by the Father's judgment, fulfilling the terms

[25] *Inst.* II.xvi.5, pp. 508–509 (*OS* 3:487–488), italics are mine.   [26] Ibid., p. 509 (*OS* 3:488).
[27] Ibid.   [28] *Inst.* II.xvi.10, p. 515 (*OS* 3:495).

of our sentence. In this way he is the Suffering Servant to which Isaiah testified (Isa. 53:5):

A little while ago we referred to the prophet's statement that "the chastisement of our peace was laid upon him," "he was wounded for our transgressions" by the Father, "he was bruised for our infirmities." By these words he means that Christ was put in the place of evildoers as surety and pledge – submitting himself even as the accused – to bear and suffer all the punishments that they ought to have sustained.[29]

Christ's judgment before Pilate directs the believer, then, not to an empty substitution, but to Christ's submission to the wrath and vengeance of God, the full terror of which was the due of sinners but which was borne by Christ.

Therefore, though Calvin speaks of Christ "paying the price" for our redemption, thus taking up the language of satisfaction, we must be clear that he develops this notion in terms of Christ's penal substitution – "that he paid a greater and far more excellent price in suffering in his soul the terrible torments of a condemned and forsaken man."[30] Insofar as this is the case, we should not say with Wendel that Calvin's doctrine is a "classic expression of the doctrine of satisfaction as it had been current ever since St. Anselm."[31] Integral to Anselm's understanding of Christ's work is a rejection of Christ's punishment in our place. What sense is there to God's punishing the innocent, he will ask, to atone for the guilty? Such an act on God's part would not only be ineffective – it would not repay the debt owed by the guilty – it would also be unjust. If Christ is truly innocent, then God's wrath cannot and will not burn against him. For Anselm, then, God is in no way involved in Christ's suffering or death, except to approve of this activity of the Son and to direct him toward it as a means to work out the salvation of humanity. God only receives Christ's death as a gracious gift and rewards him with an infinite merit with which he can cover our debt, precisely so that God's punishment might be avoided. Only Christ's persecutors are responsible for his suffering and death; and because of his suffering and death, no one is made to face God's wrath, except, perhaps, those who choose not to find cover in Christ's grace. Calvin, in contradistinction, argues precisely that Christ was "wounded for our transgressions by the Father," that Christ was punished by God in our place, thereby satisfying the demands not simply of humanity's debt, but of God's wrath.

---

[29] Ibid., pp. 515–576 (*OS* 3:495).   [30] Ibid., p. 516 (*OS* 3:495).   [31] Wendel, *Calvin*, p. 219.

Calvin's distinctive logic

It is worth noting this distinction between Calvin and Anselm not only to set the record straight about the relationship between the two and to clarify the options available to the theologian addressing the doctrine of the Atonement, but also to lead us more deeply into Calvin's thinking as it pushes the question of why Calvin diverged from Anselm so forcefully in just this way. It is not likely that Calvin was simply lazy and did not grapple with the danger that Anselm articulated about his formulation. (I am assuming here that Anselm's concern over the justice and efficacy of God's punishing the innocent to free the guilty carries a great deal of weight.) Nor would I emphasize too strongly the degree to which Calvin was pushed to this doctrine by scriptural considerations – although he does cite the Isaiah text in support of his explanation, the text does not appear to take on a determinative role in his thinking. He never contends that we must come to these conclusions on the basis of Isaiah, but, instead, undergirds an argument that he believes helpful in itself with reference to the Isaiah passage.

Rather, I believe that we can best account for Calvin's divergence from Anselm if we set it in the context of one assumption and two intentions that guide Calvin's handling of this topic. First, Calvin wrote in a different historical milieu from Anselm, and so he brought a different framework to his understanding of the demands made by divine justice because of human sin, a framework defined more by the rule of law than by the rule of honor that governed feudal society. But he also set for himself a broader task in his formulation of his thinking on Atonement: he wished to show not only that Christ had met the demands of justice, but also that he had defeated the enemies that oppressed humanity; and Calvin wished to do both of these things in a manner that would move the human heart to faith through the vivid imagery that God had deployed in the history of Christ and the record of that history in Scripture. These latter two points are more interesting in terms of our discussion of Calvin's Christology, for they speak more to the concerns and methods that determined his thinking; but the former point, concerning the distinctive context in which Calvin conceived his doctrine, is also worthy of note.

The context for Anselm's satisfaction theory was medieval feudal society, a hierarchical society governed by a complex set of relationships between lords and vassals. Simply put, the obligations of and the rights and benefits due to every member of society were defined by their relationship of patronage toward those below them in the hierarchy and their relationship of vassalage to those above. Vassals owed their lords obedience, honor, and service, while lords owed their vassals protection and provision for the necessities of their lives. Anselm read the relationship between God and humanity in this context, so that, while God was responsible to bless and protect humanity, humanity was to give God obedience and service. But, with Adam's sin, this relationship was broken and God was dishonored – this is the debt of honor that humanity owed to God. If humanity could not repay the debt, then God would be forced to reclaim God's honor Godself through just punishment. The demands of justice were determined by this relationship of honor, so that Christ was held accountable to justice in this context. On the one hand, this meant that Christ could atone for humanity through his obedience and his free gift to God of his death, thereby compensating God for the honor lost through Adam's sin; on the other hand, it meant that atonement could not be made through God's punishing Christ in the place of a sinful humanity. What honor is there in punishing the innocent to pay for the guilty? It was this calculus of honor that determined Anselm's championing of the satisfaction theory over penal substitution.

Calvin does not develop his doctrine in the detail that Anselm does (a point to which we later return), he only continually repeats that Christ bears God's punishment in our place; but, at the very outset of his discussion (II.xvi), he suggests the logic that determines the form of his thought. He writes: "Since [God] is a righteous Judge, he does not allow his law to be broken without punishment, but is equipped to avenge it."[32] Here the personal context of feudal relationship appears to have been replaced by the impersonal rule of law. The law, once set down by God, demands that the punishment of the guilty be carried out, and God, the righteous Judge, does not wish to abrogate the law that God has decreed, but acts to fulfill its threat. Within this framework, for Christ to offer his death simply as a payment to relieve us from judgment appears not as the restoration of honor, but as a bribe designed to thwart the intention of the law. Thus, Christ, instead, must take our place as the guilty and suffer the law's demands. Again, Calvin does not develop this line of thinking in any detail, but it does suggest a way to account for his thought.[33]

However, given that Calvin does not pursue the question of why God must demand punishment in response to humanity's crimes, we can presume that although this logic may shape his thinking, it does not drive it. The goal to which he is directing his argument is not the sense in which

---

[32] *Inst.* II.xvi.1, p. 504 (*OS* 3:483).
[33] This is a simple sketch, and further research is needed before this argument could bear much weight.

Christ has reconciled humanity to God in a world governed by divine law. If it were, Calvin would have explored the necessary connection between Christ's death and the law's demand more thoroughly. Instead, his discussion of Christ's substitution consistently veers off in another direction and is governed by separate logic. We understand the weight that Calvin asks his doctrine of Christ's penal substitution to bear only as we grasp this other dynamic.

In his discussion of Christ's descent into hell, through which he suffers God's wrath, Calvin continually turns to the topic of Christ's dread or terror before death. Having explained his interpretation of Christ's descent as his acceptance of God's wrath, Calvin then orients the bulk of his discussion of this topic around two questions: the needfulness or purpose of this suffering by Christ, on the one hand, and the appropriateness of it, on the other. But his answers to these questions converge on the one theme of Christ's fear before this punishment. To say that Christ's descent into hell plays a vital role in our salvation is to say, for Calvin, that it was needful that Christ suffer the dread of death and that it was not inappropriate for the Son of God to suffer such dread. Calvin will describe this fear alternately as the fear of everlasting death and as the fear of abandonment by God – these two, of course, being intimately tied together. So Calvin writes: "[I]t was expedient at the same time for him to undergo the severity of God's vengeance . . . For this reason, he must also grapple hand to hand with the armies of hell and the dread of everlasting death."[34] And again: "Peter does not simply name death [in Acts 2:24] but expressly states that the Son of God had been laid hold of by the pangs of death that arose from God's curse and wrath – the source of death."[35] These are the burden of God's wrath. To say that Christ took our place by bearing God's judgment against us is to say that he faced abandonment by God into everlasting death, and it is because of these that he was overtaken by fear, "the pangs of death." It is in Calvin's explanation of Christ's dealings with this fear that the soteriological implications of his substitution for us become manifest.

In the first place, the claim that Christ bore this fear is the claim that he bore our fear. We were the ones under the threat of wrath; we were the ones who stood to lose our salvation, abandoned by God and consigned to everlasting death. Calvin is addressing a humanity weighed down by fear of these realities, and one of his points in this narration is not only that Christ took on this fear, but that Christ defeated it as well. Calvin consistently refuses to speak of this fear only as Christ's burden, but always

[34] *Inst.* II.xvi.10, p. 515 (*OS* 3:495).   [35] *Inst.* II.xvi.11, p. 516 (*OS* 3:495).

ties together the notion of Christ's bearing this fear with his grappling with it and victory over it. "Therefore, by his wrestling hand to hand with the devil's power, with the dread of death, with the pains of hell, he was victorious and triumphed over them."[36] We pursue this theme, that Christ is the king who defeats our enemies, in the following chapter, but now we discover that he is king in this manner only as he first is priest and sacrifice. Only as he first stands in our place and takes God's wrath upon himself can he face Satan and the armies of hell that threaten us and bind us with fear, for we have these enemies because of God's wrath against our sin. Because Christ is our substitute, he can confront that fear and defeat it. "[Christ] had, therefore, to conquer that fear which by nature continually torments and oppresses all mortals. This he could do only by fighting it."[37] But he could fight it only as he faced it as the outcome of God's wrath turned against him.

Calvin concludes his discussion by maintaining that Christ defeated this fear through faith in God, that even as he cries out in abandonment, he still claims God as his God and entrusts himself to God.

[F]eeling himself, as it were, forsaken by God, he did not waver in the least from trust in his goodness. This is proved by that remarkable prayer to God in which he cried out in acute agony: "My God, my God, why has thou forsaken me?" For even though he suffered beyond measure, he did not cease to call him his God, by whom he cried out that he had been forsaken.[38]

It is Christ, the faithful Son, who defeats the fear that bars us from the Father.

On the one hand, then, we can say that Calvin utilizes this notion of substitution, that Christ bears God's wrath in our place, to emphasize that through his struggle with this terror before God's abandonment he might deliver us from it. His substitution is objectively effective in securing our salvation. On the other hand, Calvin will emphasize equally the subjective effectiveness of this aspect of Christ's priestly work. When Christ is brought low through his experience of God's vengeance and the dread that this experience generates, we are made to see the depth of Christ's love for us in his willingness to join us in our fear, while we at the same time come to recognize the great burden that he has lifted from our shoulders. In other words, when Christ takes our punishment, we are moved both by what he has taken on himself and by what he has taken from us, and thereby we are brought to entrust our lives to him.

---

[36] Ibid., p. 517 (*OS* 3:497).   [37] Ibid.   [38] *Inst.* II.xvi.12, pp. 519–520 (*OS* 3:499).

Throughout his discussion of Christ's descent into hell, Calvin returns to the theme of the depth of Christ's suffering in facing God's wrath. He reminds his readers of the necessity of this suffering – if Christ is to redeem us in both body and soul, then he must face not only physical death, but spiritual death, fearing for his salvation before God's wrath and abandonment. He also calls to our attention the evidence of this suffering – Christ's bloody sweat as he pleads with God to take the cup from him and the need that angels come to minister to him. Calvin describes Christ as "stricken and almost stupefied with the dread of death."[39] Surely we see from all this that "Christ had a harsher and more difficult struggle than with common death"; Christ feared not merely death, but God's curse.[40] In each of these instances, Calvin is defending the reality of Christ's spiritual suffering against those who would deny it; he is maintaining that the creedal assertion of Christ's descent into hell does imply his experience of God's wrath, but he maintains the reality of this experience by emphasizing the necessity and evidence of its depth. If Christ's suffering were not profound, he is arguing, the kind of suffering that arises from the fear of damnation, then we would not be saved and Christ's behavior would be inexplicable. Therefore, Christ did suffer intensely, and Calvin most movingly describes this suffering in words that both he and any of his readers can grasp: "And surely no more terrible abyss can be conceived than to feel yourself forsaken and estranged from God: and when you call upon him, not to be heard. It is as if God himself had plotted your ruin."[41] Calvin is drawing a picture of Christ's devastating alienation from God, our alienation which he has been willing to share and to experience in its fullness that he might redeem us from it. Calvin draws this picture in order to indicate that this redemption proceeds, at least in part, from a mutual sympathy that Christ thereby establishes.

Christ, then, allowed himself to be laid low to raise us who "lay prostrate" in our terror of wrath. Indeed, we can take comfort "for our anguish and sorrow" because "this Mediator has experienced our weaknesses the better to succor us in our miseries."[42] Christ can be sympathetic to us because he has shared devastation, but Calvin also establishes a sympathy on our part with Christ. Insofar as it is our punishment that he has taken and our experience that he has tasted, we, as well, know his suffering and have felt the pain that he was willing to take from us; and to know his suffering is to know his love. It is to know "that he paid a greater and more excellent

[39] *Inst.* II.xvi.12, p. 519 (*OS* 3:498). [40] Ibid.
[41] *Inst.* II.xvi.11, p. 516 (*OS* 3:496). [42] *Inst.* II.xvi.12, p. 518 (*OS* 3:497).

price in suffering in his soul the terrible torments of a condemned and forsaken man."[43] The Scriptures exhibit, the Creed teaches, and Calvin emphasizes Christ's suffering God's wrath so that we might know this price. "[T]his is our wisdom," Calvin writes, "duly to feel how much our salvation cost the Son of God."[44] With this knowledge, we are left to trust ourselves to his love even as he entrusted himself to God in the midst of his suffering. Moreover, as we recognize as our own the suffering that he took upon himself, we should equally awaken to the reality of this burden being lifted from us. Our perception of the depth of Christ's suffering, his abandonment by and alienation from God, is equally the perception that we need no longer face this suffering, abandonment, and alienation in our own lives. We, then, are doubly affected by Christ's substitution for us, relieved of a burden and touched by his love, and this moves us to faith through an awakening to grace.

This, it seems, is finally the most significant reason that Calvin diverges from Anselm and employs the imagery of penal substitution to describe Christ's atoning death. He does wish to open the way for his discussion of Christ's royal defeat of the armies of hell and our fear of death, but more importantly he finds in this language the most powerful metaphor to describe the gracious transaction whereby Christ reconciles humanity to God. However logically consistent Anselm's satisfaction theory may be, it typically strikes most readers as a rather dry, flat rendition of our redemption, as wrath is set aside and suffering not explored. The depth of Christ's passion, the bloody sweat and the cry of dereliction on the cross, are never mentioned. It is the simple fact of Christ's freely offered death that redeems us. Calvin, on the other hand, sees the passion as an action rife with drama, from Christ's judgment as the guilty one by a judge who earlier had proclaimed him innocent to his death as the accursed, hanging on a tree, a drama in which, from beginning to end, he struggles with the overpowering fear of God's wrath and abandonment which in themselves are a consignment to hell. Through this imagery, Calvin presents his readers with a vivid picture of their redemption, a picture in which the horrible fate from which they have been released and the terrible price of their freedom have been made piercingly clear. Indeed, Calvin's approach to Christ's reconciling death is governed thoroughly by his attention to this subjective, rhetorical effectiveness of his language, and he is clear from the very beginning of his exposition that this should be a fundamental principle

---

[43] *Inst.* II.xvi.10, p. 516 (*OS* 3:495).   [44] *Inst.* II.xvi.12, p. 519 (*OS* 3:498).

of his presentation of the Atonement since it had governed God's exposition of these same events in Scripture.

The two dimensions of Calvin's argument

Before Calvin examines the narrative of our redemption as presented in the Creed, he first raises the question: "how fitting [was it] that God, who anticipates us by his mercy, should have been our enemy until he was reconciled to us through Christ?"[45] In other words, how do we resolve the conflict between the foundation of Christ's mission, God's freely given love, and its stated purpose in Scripture, to make us no longer objects of God's hatred? Eventually, Calvin will argue that we must understand that God's love and God's hatred in their relation to us to have different objects. God loves us insofar as we are God's creatures and, on the basis of this love, God undertakes our redemption; but God hates the sin that is within us, and until this sin is accounted for, God cannot receive us completely into God's fellowship. Therefore, God sends Christ to remove sin and reunite us to our Creator.

Before Calvin moves to this second argument, in which the tension of the question is resolved, he first maintains that this tension is integral to our redemption, for through it God has accommodated Godself to our capacity so that "we may better understand how miserable and ruinous our condition is apart from Christ."[46] We only understand the depth of God's mercy if the consequences of that mercy, or lack thereof, are clearly spelled out for us. For example, we might have come to some shallow awareness of God's mercy if we had merely been told that, except for God's grace, God *might* have hated us and cast us off. But how much more moving is the teaching of Scripture:

that [we] are estranged from God through sin, [are] heirs of wrath, subject to the curse of eternal death, excluded from all hope of salvation beyond every blessing of God, the slave of Satan, captive under the yoke of sin, destined finally for a dreadful destruction and already involved in it; and that at this point Christ interceded as [our] advocate, took upon himself and suffered the punishment that, from God's righteous judgment, threatened all sinners; that he purged with his blood those evils which had rendered sinners hateful to God . . . Will [we] not then be even more moved by all these things which so vividly portray the greatness of the calamity from which [we have] been rescued?[47]

---

[45] *Inst.* ii.xvi.2, p. 504 (*OS* 3:483).　　[46] Ibid.　　[47] Ibid., p. 505 (*OS* 3:483–484).

In Christ and in his Gospel story, God did not intend merely to work out our salvation, covering our sins through Christ's death; God also resolved to bring us to so strong an awareness of God's mercy evident in Christ's history, both as we are convicted of the depth of our sin and the peril of our plight and as we are awakened to the intensity of Christ's love for us when he makes our plight his own, that we would effectively be brought to put our faith in God's mercy through the power of the Spirit working within us. Thus, Calvin will utilize the metaphor of penal substitution to present Christ's atoning work to us since through this metaphor we are brought to a profound sense both of the burden that has been lifted from us, especially as we see its terrible effects on Christ in his suffering, and of the love of Christ in his willingness to undertake our redemption. Only in this way will "our hearts seize upon life ardently enough" and "accept it with the gratefulness that we owe."[48]

Therefore, we must now note yet another manner in which Calvin's approach to Christ's Atonement is mistakenly linked too closely to Anselm's by most commentators. Traditionally, theologians have distinguished two types of explanation of Christ's atoning death. There are so-called objective theories of Atonement in which it was necessary for Christ to become incarnate and die on the cross to rectify our relationship with God through a transaction largely between Christ and God, a transaction the fruits of which we enjoy but which takes place apart from us. The emphasis of this theory is both on the necessity of Christ's activity – it was demanded by justice – and its completion apart from our response in faith – it is entirely by Christ's gracious act that our relationship with God is restored. Anselm's satisfaction theory is the typical example of this. There are also so-called subjective theories in which Christ's atoning death is effective insofar as it powerfully manifests God love to the world, turning those who would become believers from the fear of God to place their faith in the love of God that they see in Christ. In this case, while Christ's death is in no sense necessary or demanded by God's justice – God could have simply pronounced us forgiven – it was chosen by God as the best means to communicate God's love and draw the chosen to a faithful response. Thus, by this type of approach, the transaction initiated by Christ not only involves the response of the faithful, it is centered on it. Abelard's "moral influence" theory is usually invoked as a type of this subjective approach. Given this distinction, which is probably more hard and fast than

[48] Ibid.

either Anselm's or Abelard's actual work would justify,[49] most of Calvin's commentators would strongly argue that the Anselmian, objective element predominates and governs his discussion of the Atonement, although they would admit that the subjective dimension is reflected in his work as well.[50]

Nevertheless, from what we have seen of Calvin's discussion of Christ's priestly work, not only in the *Institutes* but especially there, I cannot support this opinion. On the one hand, we can acknowledge the presence and significance of the objective dimension in all of the metaphors through which Calvin views Christ's priestly work. In his expiatory sacrifice, Christ has covered our sin and destroyed it. In his free offer of himself in our place, he has paid the price that we owe and satisfied our debt before God. In his judgment and punishment in our place, he has borne God's wrath for us and defeated the armies of hell and the fear of death that oppress us. Christ in his passion and death has removed the barrier of sin and guilt that separated a fallen humanity from God, without any aid from fallen humanity, and thus opened the way for a renewed relationship with God. In him the covenant has been restored, and this restoration is the foundation for any appropriation of the covenant relationship with which we may be involved.

On the other hand, we must recognize that the subjective dimension plays an equally definitive role in Calvin's writing on Christ's atoning work, that, in fact, this second dimension appears at times to drive his development of this doctrine. So, for example, although he acknowledges the objective purpose of Christ's incarnation and death in chapters twelve and sixteen of the *Institutes*,[51] he begins his explanations of the necessity of the incarnation and of the relation of Christ's death to God's saving love with attention to this subjective concern – it was necessary for the Son to take on a human nature so that we could "hope that God might dwell with us." Scripture speaks of God's wrath toward us apart from Christ so that we might learn "to embrace his benevolence and fatherly love in Christ

---

[49] There are subjective elements in Anselm – for example, the need of the individual believer to apply for Christ's merit through their participation in penitential rites of the Church – while there are also objective elements in Abelard – for example, the grace objectively mediated through the Church's sacraments. The "objective/subjective" distinction makes sense primarily as a schema by which one can highlight predominating elements in various theologies, rather than an exhaustive explanation of Anselm's or Abelard's thought. Hence, the oddity of Gerrish's concern (recently echoed in DeVries) that substitutionary doctrines of Atonement are "objective" to a degree that they are incoherent with any need for human appropriation of what has been objectively won. See Gerrish, "Atonement and Saving Faith," p. 184; DeVries, *Jesus Christ in the Preaching of Calvin*, p. 96.

[50] See van Buren, *Christ in Our Place*, pp. ix–x.

[51] *Inst.* II.xii.3, xvi.3, pp. 466–467, 505–506 (*OS* 3:439–440, 484–485).

alone."[52] This subjective concern is registered throughout Calvin's discussion of Christ's atoning death. We have already noted its presence in his discussion of Christ's substitution in our place, not only in his emphasis on Christ's bearing our punishment, but also in his depiction of Christ's judgment before Pilate. So, elsewhere, Calvin will remind the reader that, "when [Christ] discharged all satisfaction through his sacrifice, we might cease to be afraid of God's wrath."[53] Indeed, Calvin makes the transition from his discussion of Christ's obedience to consideration of his death with just such attention to the effect of that death on us: "But because trembling consciences find repose only in sacrifice and cleansing by which sins are expiated, we are duly directed thither."[54] For Calvin, however much we might say that Christ's passion and death concerned the objective reconciliation of God with humanity, we should equally emphasize that this reconciliation was brought to pass through the effect of his death on the sinful, that through it their fear of God might be removed, their consciences calmed, and their hearts awakened to God's grace.

Of course, there is no evidence that Calvin saw these two dimensions to his thinking in such stark, oppositional terms. Rather, as I have argued all along, the subjective and objective effectiveness of Christ's priestly work are intertwined in Calvin's dealings with this subject. It is from the objective efficacy of Christ's atoning death that its subjective power to move believers arises. Because Christ, and Christ alone, could and did accomplish our reconciliation to God, the chosen are drawn to him in faith; but the power of Christ's death to turn away God's wrath and open the way for relationship with God is empty unless it is coupled with an effect on the chosen, taking away their fear of God's anger and leading them into God's parental embrace. We must remember that the context for Christ's work as Mediator is the covenant relationship that God desires with the elect, and this relationship cannot be enacted simply by Christ's accomplishment of it, for it also must include the participation of God's covenant partners within it. I will return to this again in my conclusion.

The author of salvation

I have spoken loosely of Calvin's "doctrine" of the Atonement, referring thereby to all that Calvin writes of Christ's reconciling of humanity to God through his priestly office, but it is clear from what we have considered

---

[52] *Inst.* II.xii.1, xvi.2, pp. 464–465, 504–505 (*OS* 3:437–438, 483–484).
[53] *Inst.* II.xvi.6, p. 510 (*OS* 3:490).   [54] *Inst.* II.xvi.5, p. 508 (*OS* 3:487).

that Calvin offers no single, unified doctrine or theory of this activity. Instead, he draws from divergent scriptural and traditional theories and images of Christ's atoning work through which he can express the depth and complexity of this work. Calvin's explication of this doctrine is not governed by an adherence to any particular theory of the atonement, but by his desire to communicate effectively the gracious activity of God in and through the work of Christ so that it might have an impact on believers. This is Jones' point when she argues that we will be ultimately frustrated if we approach Calvin hoping to find philosophically rigorous or analytically tight doctrines. Calvin's theological discourse, she writes, "is marked by a double purpose: it seeks to witness to the revelation of God in scripture, and it seeks to do so in a language capable of moving the hearts, minds, and wills of its audience toward an ever-deepening life of faith."[55] So, in Calvin's use and appropriation of these multiple images to describe Christ's atoning work, he is attempting to remain faithful to the diverse images found in Scripture and with these images to lead the chosen to embrace Christ in faith. These are the commitments that drive the formulation of his argument, not his concern to make an airtight case.

However, I must qualify this observation, for there is one logic that does structure Calvin's discussion of the Atonement. As I stated at the outset, Calvin organizes Christ's sacrifice, satisfaction, substitution, and all his work whereby we are reconciled to God under the rubric of his priestly office. This means that they all stand in fulfillment of God's covenant history with the Church, and, more significantly for this discussion, that they also are activities in which Christ is the agent or the author of our salvation. Reconciliation is not something that happens to Christ, but something that he does, that he offers, that he accomplishes. We see this concern in Calvin's penchant for moving from discussion of Christ's suffering, in any context, to the victory that he wins through that suffering. On the cross, when Christ gives himself as a sacrifice for sin, not merely does his blood cover sin, but through his death he destroys it. Likewise, in taking our place before the judgment seat of God, he suffers God's wrath and is overtaken by fear to wrestle with it and defeat it. God does not simply use Christ to work out God's eternally given purposes; God sends Christ, a decision of the Son with the Father and the Spirit, that Christ might enact God's salvific purpose.

This insistence on the importance of Christ's agency in the matter of our salvation undergirds the Christological thrust of Calvin's response to

---

[55] Jones, *Rhetoric of Piety*, p. 187.

Socinius, found in the last chapter of Book Two. Socinius worried over the relation of God's eternal determination of salvation for the Church and the Church's contention that Christ had merited the same. Salvation was either determined in a free and sovereign fashion by God in eternity, Socinius argued, so that no temporal, historical intervention could affect the situation, or else God's decision for salvation was determined by Christ's work so that it was not free and sovereign. Socinius had hit upon a logical conundrum that he resolved to the detriment of the significance of Christ's work. But Calvin responded that Socinius had set up a false contradiction; God's eternal decision and Christ's merit did not function at the same causal level so that only one or the other could be maintained as the true cause of our salvation, but that each in its own way contributed to our renewed relationship with God. "God's love," Calvin writes, "holds first place as the highest cause or origin."[56] There is a history of salvation centered on the work of the Mediator only because God in God's ineffable love was merciful to God's creatures even in their sin and appointed Christ as Mediator to obtain salvation for them. Everything, including Christ's work, is subordinated to God's eternal decree; but Christ's sacerdotal intervention is nonetheless vital as the secondary or proximate cause of our redemption, for through Christ's sacrifice he has removed the stain of our sinfulness so that God can receive us into God's fellowship. Calvin is working with the same distinction with which he began his exegesis of the Creed, that God both loved humanity as God's creatures and was wrathful toward them because of their sin from the time of the Fall. Christ's mission is founded on God's parental love and effectively effaces the barrier of sin so that God might fully embrace God's chosen.

Calvin's discussion is shaped, on the one hand, by his concern for God's sovereignty, that God determines all things by God's eternal decree and, on the other hand, by his emphasis on Christ's agency, through which God's decree takes shape in our midst. Calvin rejects the notion that Christ is only an instrumental or formal cause of salvation;[57] he should be seen, as well, as its material or actual cause. Christ brings God's love to pass when he realizes God's eternal covenant. He not only makes that covenant possible, atoning for our sin; he also makes it actual, for it is through his life, death, and resurrection that God's love is enacted in our history. Calvin writes: "How did God begin to embrace with his favour those whom he had loved before the creation of the world? Only in that he revealed his

---

[56] *Inst.* II.xvii.2, p. 529 (*OS* 3:529).   [57] *Inst.* II.xvii.1,2, pp. 528–530 (*OS* 3:508–510).

love when he was reconciled to us by Christ's blood."[58] This "revelation" of God's love in Christ consists in the first place of the comprehensibility of God's love as it has been expressed in Christ. Christ not only makes it evident – we clearly see God's eternal love because Christ offers himself for us – but he also makes it understandable. God's love for us while we were yet trapped in sin is unfathomable; we can make sense of it only because Christ has covered our filthiness. Christ authors God's love in our history, then, first by making it plain; but, beyond its comprehensibility, Christ also makes God's love tangible for us. Through his obedience, his judgment in our place, his crucifixion, and his battle with the fear of death, Christ has enacted that love and touched us with it. Calvin says that God "begins to embrace" God's chosen through Christ's work because it is there that God not merely wills our salvation, but accomplishes it. Therefore, we are not in faith to look past Christ to God as the eternal Author of life; rather, we find life authored in Christ, insofar as he, in his history, has incarnated God's original mercy for us.

[58] *Inst.* ii.xvii.2, p. 530 (*OS* 3:510).

CHAPTER 4

Christ as king

Writing of Moses' death as Israel approached the banks of the Jordan, Calvin describes the Church as "a body with its head chopped off." Leaderless, the Church could not hope to attain God's blessing – the promised land, prosperity in their lives, and, ultimately, union with God in the promise of eternal life – for it would be directionless, powerless, and more apt to scatter than to undertake unified action. The one who fulfilled the office of the king or head of the Church, then, as typified first by Joshua and, more definitively, by David, was to serve as the Mediator of God's blessings upon the Church – unifying the people under him so that they could enjoy God's blessings of security, abundant life, and unity with God. Through the office of the king, God's covenant promise was enacted. But, as with the priesthood, the truth of the royal office was not contained within the Davidic kingship, for Israel's kings could only bestow blessings that were temporally constricted – Israel eventually lost the promised land – and materially limited – they themselves could not bring the Church eternal life. The true fulfillment of the royal office could only be found in Christ, and David and his descendants only pointed to this truth as they prefigured it in Israel's history.

Calvin's exploration of Christ's royal office in his Gospel commentaries and in the *Institutes* can best be understood with the template of the Davidic kingship before us. Christ, as king, is the one who unites the Church to God, even as he gathers God's chosen to himself, and out of this union he bestows God's blessings on God's Church. To develop his understanding of this office, Calvin employs a number of images to expound the fullness of God's blessing that we receive in Christ. Christ is our Lord, but he is also our brother. He is the fountain through whom God's blessings flow to the Church, and he is the perfect pattern to whom all believers should be conformed. Most importantly, he is the head in whom God loves God's Church. In and through all of these roles, Christ in his office as king is essential to the covenantal relationship that he reestablishes through his work as priest. Indeed, Christ's royal office could be seen as the completion of the sacerdotal, insofar as reconciliation is perfected by the union with God which follows the setting aside of God's wrath and our recognition of God's love. Thus, Calvin writes: "the whole of our salvation consists in this, that Christ should assemble us into one; for in this way he reconciles us to the Father . . . Hence, also, we infer that the human race is scattered and estranged from God, until the children of God are assembled under Christ, their head."[1] Ultimately, Christ's purpose is to draw us into the fellowship of covenantal relationship with God, but this relationship is not individually transacted between God and human persons. Rather, it is effected only as we are united with Christ. Calvin's broad discussion of Christ's headship or kingship revolves around this point.

As I noted in chapter 1, this insistence on the vital role of Christ's royal office in his work as Mediator forms one main thrust of Calvin's attack on Stancaro.[2] Thus, we can understand who Christ is as Mediator only as we fully value both his royal and his sacerdotal offices. Commentators on Calvin's theology have consistently allotted little space to his treatment of Christ's royal office, however, often noting its existence only in passing while devoting the majority of their analysis to Calvin's view of Christ's priestly office.[3] This is not to say that major portions of Calvin's Christology have simply been omitted from these earlier works. Wendel, for example, offers an extended discussion of the necessity of Christians' union with Christ, whereby they receive the grace of the Spirit and are united with God – a topic I file under Christ's royal office – but he does so in his chapter on the work of the Spirit, not in his section on the work of Christ.[4] In doing so, he is simply following Calvin's lead in the *Institutes*, and so my point here is not to fault him. Rather, it is to state up front that in my discussion of Christ's work I reorder Calvin's discussion in the *Institutes* to some degree so that we might gather the whole of his Christological discussion within the Christological framework that he recommends. This move is justified by the differing purpose of this book from the *Institutes*.

In the *Institutes*, Calvin sought to exposit doctrine as a guide to reading Scripture and, through the rhetorical crafting of this exposition, to lead his readers into a deeper piety in their relationship with God. Calvin's text was shaped by these concerns but, for the purpose of this book, as we try to determine the shape of Calvin's Christology and its overall place in

---

[1] *Comm. John* 11:51, 1.454–5 (*CO* 47:274–275).   [2] See pp. 32–33 above.
[3] See, for example, the treatments in Wendel (*Calvin*, pp. 225–226), Willis (*Catholic Christology*, pp. 87–89), and Van Buren (*Christ in our Place*, p. ix).
[4] Wendel, *Calvin*, pp. 234–242.

Calvin's theology, it is important that we gather all that Calvin has to say of Christ's work and person under their proper rubrics. That is why, in this chapter, I offer an extended exposition of Calvin's view of Christ's royal office, examining material not simply from the chapter on Christ's threefold office (II.xv), but from the breadth of the *Institutes*. Only in this way can we grasp Calvin's Christological thinking in all of its heft and focus.

Moreover, it seems obvious, given the content of this book thus far, that this material should be gathered up within the framework of Christ's threefold office. To argue, for example, that we should understand the unity of Christians with Christ apart from this threefold office would either mean that we understand this unity apart from Christ's activity – so that he is in some sense a passive participant in it – or that we understand this activity apart from the covenant history in which the threefold office is situated. Neither of these possibilities would be acceptable to Calvin. Given Calvin's understanding of Christ as the Mediator of the covenant through which God has worked out salvation, we must understand all that we say of Christ in relation to this work of mediation, and we must understand this work to consist in the threefold office of priest, king, and prophet.

The key to this organizational task is the recognition that what Calvin says of about Christ as head of the Church is of a piece with his discussion of Christ's royal office. This recognition has functioned implicitly in what I have said up until now, and it rests on Calvin's interchangeable use of these two terms, "head" and "king," throughout the *Institutes* and the commentaries.[5] The substantive unity of these two terms in Calvin is evident, moreover, from our discussion of the office of king in the Old Testament commentaries. The king not only protects us from enemies, the focus of Calvin's discussion of Christ's royal office in Book II of the *Institutes*, but also unites the Church and pours out God's blessing, the focus of Calvin's Christological references to Christ as head in Book III. This relationship of headship and kingship in Calvin ties together the various Christological discussions covered in this chapter, and our recognition of it is essential for making sense, for example, of my inclusion of Christ's role as the fountain of the Spirit under his royal office.

In this chapter, therefore, I first survey Calvin's discussion of Christ's headship or royal office as it stands in his Gospel commentaries, culling from this material five images of headship. There we find that Christ is brother, beloved of the Father, Lord, fountain of life, and our pattern for

---

[5] See, for example, the introduction to his commentary on Ps. 21 (1.343 [*CO* 31:212]), Ps. 110:1 (IV.298 [*CO* 32:160–161]), and *Inst.* II.vi.2, pp. 343–344 (*OS* 3:322–323).

living. With these images in hand, we look to see how they are woven through Calvin's various Christological musings in the *Institutes*, looking not only at the explicitly Christological sections at the end of Book II, but also at the Christological content of Book III, and its discussion of our reception of Christ's grace. Finally, we examine the implications of Calvin's understanding of Christ's role as head of the Church for his understanding of creation and predestination, teasing out the manner in which Christ's work is integral to Calvin's full conception of both of these theological *loci*.

CHRIST'S ROYAL OFFICE IN THE GOSPEL COMMENTARIES

Christ, our brother

To understand the covenantal reunion that is effected in Christ, we must begin with Christ's relation to humanity as brother, for it is as our brother that Christ will raise us up to God. Calvin's initial premise is that Christ, as the Eternal Son of the Father, is always and already united with the Father. In his comments on John 3:13 ("And no one hath ascended to heaven but he who came down from heaven, the Son of man who is in heaven"), Calvin interprets the phrase "who is in heaven" as referring to the eternal relationship between the Father and the Son, which the incarnate Christ maintains in his divinity and which, therefore, is applied to his whole person. However, Calvin does not focus the intent of this verse on its explanation of the Trinitarian relationship apart from its implications for the Church, but immediately leads his readers to understand that Christ became incarnate to install humanity in this same relationship with the Father: "Christ, therefore, who *is in heaven*, hath clothed himself with our flesh, that, by stretching out his brotherly hand to us, he may raise us to heaven along with him."[6]

Calvin here offers us the patristic notion that Christ took what is ours so that we might enjoy what is his, only Calvin gives it a slightly different sense. For Calvin, Christ took what is ours by becoming our brother, and what we gain of his is a relationship as children to the Father.[7] "This [Christ's incarnation] gives us good reason for growing confidence, that we may venture more freely to call God our Father, because his only Son, in order that we might have a Father in common with him, chose to be our brother."[8] Calvin's logic is that God's chosen are adopted into relationship

---

[6] *Comm. John* 3:13, 1.121 (*CO* 47:62).
[7] See my Conclusion, pp. 230f. below, for a discussion of this.
[8] *Comm. Luke* 1:35, 1.43 (*CO* 45:31).

with the Father through Christ's becoming their sibling – a rather odd approach to adoption.[9]

Calvin clearly thinks of our union with Christ in this case more in social rather than metaphysical terms. Indeed, he seldom explores any sense in which humanity is joined to Christ simply through the act of the hypostatic union, except as a jumping-off point for the discussion of the fellowship that we are able to have with Christ because of his incarnation. It is not human nature or humanity in general that Christ hopes to unite to the divine, but human persons to whom Christ has drawn near by sharing all of which their humanity consists, and who, in turn, can unite themselves to Christ by faith. Christ's charge is to initiate a covenant relationship, not an ontological relationship, between God and the Church.

The first stage in this relationship is Christ's becoming like us, sharing what is ours, except for sin, to the fullest degree by taking on a complete human nature. Calvin emphasizes throughout the Gospel commentaries that Christ took on every aspect of our "frail and perishing natures."[10] He needed to mature physically and intellectually; he suffered from bodily and emotional tribulation; he was ignorant of the future and could be anxious because of this ignorance; he could feel God's wrath, because of human sin, and know the dread terror that this wrath entails.[11] This is the point discussed in the previous chapter, there focusing precisely on Christ's share in our anxiety and terror before God's wrath. Christ, then, shared in every dimension of what we would call the human condition, though Calvin always explains that he did so without sin. He did not indulge in the weaknesses or anxiety that he was experiencing, and he never failed to trust God in his distress.

It has often been observed that Calvin goes to great lengths to preserve the distinction between the two natures in Christ, a comment often buttressed by quotations from the passages I have just mentioned – passages where Calvin argues that in the instances in which Christ was immersed in the human condition, his divinity was "quiescent" in order not to interfere with his humanity taking its natural course. Calvin maintains this distinction, however, not to protect Christ's divinity from the murkiness of humanity. Indeed, he is clear that, in taking on flesh, Christ's divinity has precisely so lowered itself, even degraded itself: "Now, though there be so wide a distance

---

[9] See Brian Gerrrish's discussion on the theme of adoption in Calvin; *Grace and Gratitude*, pp. 87–90.
[10] *Comm. John* 1:14, 1.45 (*CO* 47:14).
[11] Respectively, *Comm. Luke* 2:40, 1.165–7 (*CO* 45:103–105); *Comm. John* 4:6, 1.145 (*CO* 47:78); *Comm. Luke* 19:41, 11.453–454 (*CO* 45:575–576); *Comm. Matt.* 24:36, 111.153–154 (*CO* 45:671–672); *Comm. Matt.* 26:37, 111.226–227 (*CO* 45:719–720).

between the spiritual glory of the Speech of God and the abominable filth of our flesh, yet the Son of God stooped so low as to take upon himself that flesh, subject to so many miseries."[12] The separation of natures is what ensures the lowliness of this flesh – Christ's humanity is fragile, weak, and anxious only as it remains separate from his divinity and can experience reality in a human manner. Christ knows our weaknesses only because his human nature is truly and fully human, not safeguarded from the travail of human experience by his divinity, but immersed in such travail as his divinity refuses to exert any ameliorating influence over him. Calvin emphasizes the separation of the two natures in Christ primarily so that Christ can share our condition.[13]

Calvin is consistently clear that Christ shared in our condition in these ways to reinforce the brotherly bond that he thereby built between himself and us: "There is no doubt whatever, that it was the design of God to express in plain terms, how truly and completely Christ, in taking upon him our flesh, did all that was necessary to effect his brotherly union with men."[14] Again, this brotherly union is not metaphysical; it is a union of love. Christ took on our nature and condition so that he might love us "like a brother," and, more significantly, so that we might see his love for us clearly – especially the mercy and sympathy evident in his suffering with us – and love him in return. It is in this response of love that our union with Christ is achieved as we grasp his proffered brotherly hand in faith.

Calvin writes: "Having been ingrafted into Christ by faith, we obtain the right of adoption, so as to be the sons of God."[15] We place our faith in Christ not simply because he has become our brother and shared our experience, but more specifically because he through his death he has redeemed us from our sin.[16] That was the point in the previous chapter, and it is balanced by the point of this chapter, that Christ's death would be ineffectual unless he also gathered us to himself, so that through him we would be reunited to the Father: "What he possesses as his own by nature, he imparts to us by adoption, when we are ingrafted by faith into his body and become his members."[17] The foundation, then, of Christ's office as head and king is his relationship to humanity as brother, through which he provides for the Church's unity even as under David and his descendants the Israelites were united as God's chosen people.

---

[12] *Comm. John* 1:14, 1.45 (*CO* 47:13).
[13] I return to this point in my discussion of the *extra-calvinisticum* in ch. 6 (pp. 210f. below). This doctrine in Calvin has as much to do with his concern for the integrity of Christ's human nature as with his concern for Christ's divinity.
[14] *Comm. Luke* 2:40, 1.167 (*CO* 45:104).   [15] *Comm. John* 1:12, 1.42 (*CO* 47:11).
[16] see *Comm. John* 6:56, 1.268 (*CO* 47:156).   [17] *Comm. John* 8:36, 1.345 (*CO* 47:204).

The Beloved of the Father

Throughout the Gospels, the reader finds expressions of the Father's love for Christ, his Son. At Christ's baptism ("My beloved, in whom my soul is well pleased"), at the Transfiguration ("This is my beloved Son"), and throughout Christ's many discourses in John ("For the Father loves the Son"), there are references to the special love in which the Father has embraced Christ. Calvin frequently notes in his exposition of these passages that it was the tendency of patristic commentators to interpret these expressions as defining the intra-Trinitarian relationship between the Father and the Son, setting the Son off from all creatures as the one in whom God loved Godself.[18] For Calvin, such interpretations are "harsh and far-fetched." It is abstruse to inquire after the eternal relation of the Father to the Son, and it misses the far more significant point that these passages make – "that in [Christ's] person God the Father embraces in his love the whole Church. As we are all by nature enemies of God, his love will never come to us till it first begin with the head."[19] What is at stake in the Gospel is not the eternal relation between the Father and the Son, but, rather, God's relation to the Church. So expressions of the Father's love for the Son within the Gospels concern Christ not as he is apart from his mission, but insofar as he has been given to the faithful as their head, as the one in whom they are beloved of the Father. When Christ says that the Father loves him, Calvin tells us, "the love which is here mentioned must be understood as referring to us, because Christ testifies that the Father loves him, as he is the head of the Church."[20]

When Calvin says that we are loved by God in Christ, he means two things. In the first place, given all that he has said of Christ's Atonement for us, it is clear that we are loved by God in Christ insofar as he has reconciled us with God and taken away the offense caused by human sinfulness. We are loved by God only in Christ because, apart from Christ, we are God's enemies. That is why Calvin attaches Christ's office as head of the Church to his Atonement: on the one hand, Christ's death is effective only as Christ gathers us to himself so that we might be loved by God as we are ingrafted into him; on the other hand, we are loved by God as we are engrafted into him because he, who is our head, is the one who has atoned for our sins and reconciled us to God. Christ through his sacrifice has appeased God's wrath and opened the way for humanity to participate in covenant

---

[18] See particularly *Comm. John* 5:20, 1.199 (*CO* 47:113); *Comm. John* 15:9, 11.112 (*CO* 47 342); *Comm. John* 17:24, 11.187 (*CO* 47:389–390).
[19] *Comm. Matt.* 12:18, 11.60 (*CO* 45:331).   [20] *Comm. John* 15:9, 11.112 (*CO* 47:342).

fellowship with God, but only for those who, by faith, are united to Christ, so that they, as his body, participate in the love of the Father for their head.

However, Calvin also points out that, in his letter to the Ephesians, Paul describes Christ as the one in whom God's elect were chosen and loved before creation: "With such a love did the Father love [Christ] *before the creation of the world*, that he might be the person in whom the Father would love his elect."[21] The Church is loved in Christ not only as Christ has covered its sinfulness, but also as Christ is the one in whom God chose to redeem the world even when the world was still at enmity with God. Calvin writes:

> And, indeed, Paul informs us that there are two ways in which we are loved in Christ; first, because the Father *chose us in him before the creation of the world* (Eph. 1:4), and, secondly, because in Christ God *hath reconciled us to himself*, and hath showed that he is gracious to us (Rom. 5:10). Thus we are at the same time the enemies and the friends of God, until, atonement having been made for our sins, we are restored to favour with God. But, when we are justified by faith, it is then, properly, that we begin to be loved by God, as children by a father. That love by which Christ was appointed to be the person, in whom we should be freely chosen before we were born, and while we were still ruined in Adam, is hidden in the breast of God, and far exceeds the capacity of the human mind.[22]

We are loved in Christ because Christ, as our brother, has come to us and reached out to us, that we might be ingrafted into his body. But this has two senses: it means that, as we are ingrafted into Christ, our sins are covered and we are reconciled to God; and it also means that Christ came to us as brother in the first place, that he took his office as our head, out of the merciful initiative of God. In other words, God's love for the Church in Christ refers not only to the result of the history that culminates in his death and our redemption, but also to the whole of that history, which was undertaken only on the basis of this love. The covenant history that God inaugurated with Abraham is not merely fulfilled in Christ; it is founded on Christ, the Mediator, in whom, as head of the Church, we were chosen and loved by God before the beginning of the world. This understanding will obviously bear on Calvin's construal of Christ's relation to our election, and I return to it in the discussion of Christology and predestination at the end of this chapter.

For now, it is important to recognize Calvin's emphasis on both of these aspects of God's love for us in Christ, since Calvin will argue that the Church derives confidence which will fund its faith from each. The corollary to

---

[21] *Comm. John* 17:24, II.187 (*CO* 47:390).   [22] *Comm. John* 17:23, II.186 (*CO* 47:389).

God's love for the Church in Christ is the confidence that the Church can take in that love so revealed. On the one hand, this is confidence in the accomplished fact of our redemption. We know that we are no longer enemies of God, and we can rest secure in this knowledge, because we have been joined to Christ, the Father's Beloved.[23] On the other hand, overarching this security, bound as it is to our incorporation into Christ and our accomplished reconciliation to God, is the knowledge that we were loved by God in Christ even when we were still God's enemies. That is, we have a knowledge of God's unfathomable love – a love that is "hidden in the breast of God and far exceeds human capacity" – but only in Christ, for he is the Mediator through whom God pursued God's redemptive agenda with the world. "For he who, without a Mediator, inquires how he is loved by God involves himself in a labyrinth, in which he will neither discover the entrance, nor the means of extricating himself. We ought therefore to cast our eyes on Christ in whom will be found the testimony and pledge of the love of God."[24]

Christ's status as the Beloved of the Father is the corollary to Christ's approach to humanity as our brother. That we are loved by God in Christ, our head, is another way of saying that Christ came to us as a brother so that we would be ingrafted into Christ's body, taking his outstretched hand, and thereby share by adoption the relationship between the Father and the Son. Through both of these images – Christ as our brother and as the Beloved of the Father – Calvin has explored the sense in which the Church is returned to fellowship with God through Christ's royal office; but that does not exhaust Christ's role as head or king over the Church. Through him, the chosen are not only reinstituted into covenant relationship with God, they also receive the benefits or blessings which such relationship bestows. Calvin's exposition of this latter aspect of Christ's kingly office is best grasped through the images of Christ as Lord over the Church and as the fountain of all blessings.

Christ, the Lord

We saw in chapter 2 that Christ's office as king, as typified by Israel's kings, involved primarily his role as the One in whom the Church found protection from their enemies and prosperity in their lives; in this way, he was the One through whom the blessings that flow from God's covenant were bestowed upon the Church. Within the context of the Old Testament

---

[23] Ibid.   [24] *Comm. John* 15:9, II.112 (*CO* 47:342).

history, then, the king's role was primarily martial and governmental. He extended and defended Israel's borders and provided the nation with a steady, firm rule. He oversaw the corporate life of the people on behalf of God in his sovereign capacity.

Within the context of the Gospels Calvin uses these same terms to discuss this one aspect of Christ's royal office. He is fond of describing Christ as God's "vice-regent" or "deputy," and he is clear that it is Christ's office to govern God's Church in the Father's place. Indeed, this is why the title "Lord" belongs to him:

> We know in what sense Scripture gives to Christ the name of *Lord*. It is because the Father hath appointed him to be the highest governor, that he may hold all things under his dominion, *that every knee may bow before him* (Phil. 2:10), and, in short, that he may be the Father's vice-regent in governing the world.[25]

This office of Lordship belongs to Christ, as God manifest in the flesh, until the last day when, having brought all things to submission, "Christ will deliver the Kingdom to God, his Father" (1 Cor. 15:24).[26] Christ in his role as Lord is to reassert God's control over a world that has rebelled from God, drawing those whom God has chosen to return and embrace God's loving rule while crushing those who have rejected and are rejected by God.

Christ, as Lord, exercises God's power and authority over the Church, and his lordship, thereby, entails his roles as both the Church's protector and its master.[27] Calvin saw and experienced a Church beset by enemies. There were rulers of nations and ecclesial leaders who oppressed the faithful in material ways, and, more importantly, there were demonic powers who hoped to seduce or overcome the faithful and draw them from the love of God. But Christ easily defeats humanity's foes and establishes a kingdom in which God's chosen could dwell secure. Therefore, the faithful can have confidence in the face of their enemies, knowing that they have Christ as their Lord.[28] Discussing Zechariah's announcement that, with the advent of God's Messiah, the Church would now know "salvation from our enemies" (Luke 1:71), Calvin writes: "This passage reminds us that, so long as the Church continues her pilgrimage in the world, she lives amongst her foes, and would be exposed to their violence, if Christ were not always at hand to grant assistance. But such is the inestimable grace of Christ, that, though

---

[25] *Comm. John* 20:26, II.277 (*CO* 47:444).   [26] *Inst.* II.xiv.3, p. 485 (*OS* 3:461).
[27] See his *Comm. Matt.* 22:44, III.70 (*CO* 45:618–619).
[28] See *Comm. Luke* 1:71, I.70–1 (*CO* 45:47–48); *Comm. Matt.* 22:44, III.69–70 (*CO* 45:618–619).

we are surrounded on every side by enemies, we enjoy a sure and undoubted salvation."[29] Christ as Lord protects the Church and gives it comfort in a menacing world.

Likewise, he governs the Church with wisdom and mercy, guiding God's chosen into life. Christ claims the title of Master over the Church so that believers are to obey him and subject themselves to his teaching as disciples.[30] Obviously, a good bit of what I might say on this subject is covered in the discussion of Christ's teaching office. What is of note at this point is that Christ, for Calvin, is not merely the Church's teacher, but is its Lord and king, so that he is not only to be heard, but obeyed. His authority extends beyond that of an ordinary teacher, in that he mediates God's rule of the Church. He is the Law's giver before he is its interpreter.

One mode, then, in which Calvin discusses Christ's office as king is in Christ's role as Lord over the Church and the world – a role in which he exercises mastery over the Church while protecting the Church from its enemies. This aspect of Christ's kingship is best represented in Christ's resurrection, through which he has defeated sin, death, and the devil, and in his ascension to the Father's right hand in power. This is Christ as he has been typified by Israel's royal house – Christ in all of his glory. Within the commentaries on the Gospels Calvin balances the glorious image of Christ with the second, more humble image of Christ as our brother, discussed earlier in this chapter. Indeed, Christ is Lord over the Church only as he is our brother, only as he has drawn near to us, shared our lives, and united himself to us. Only as he has gathered the Church to himself, through his participation in the Church's condition, can he then protect the members of the Church as those who have been ingrafted into his body and who have, therefore, set themselves under his care.

But Christ's care for the Church is exhausted neither by his protection of the Church from its enemies, nor by his rulership over the Church through his provision of a righteous law. For, however much Christ may do for the believers entrusted to his care externally, they will only thrive as members of his body as they themselves live into the life that he offers. They must resist sin and the devil through faith; they must embrace Christ's teaching in love. This they do only through the grace and life with which the Spirit fills them. The Church receives the Spirit only through Christ, who has had the fullness of the Spirit poured out upon him, that he might serve as the fountain of all spiritual blessings.

---

[29] *Comm. Luke* 1:71, 1.71 (*CO* 45:48). [30] See *Comm. Matt.* 23:10, III.80–81 (*CO* 45:625–626).

The fountain of life

Christ, as Mediator, spans the expanse of the divine glory between God and creation, both to make God known – he is the lively image of the Father, as I discuss in the next chapter – and to reunite humanity with God. One consequence of his mediatorial activity is the opening of a channel between God and humanity so that the life that dwells with God will be poured out upon those whom God has chosen. Christ in his office as head of the Church is the fountain through which these blessings are poured out.

Calvin describes God (or the Father) as the source of life, righteousness, virtue, and wisdom, but only in such a way that these things are hidden, remote, and inaccessible in God.[31] God's *aseity*, that God exists in and of himself, and God's status as the Creator, the one from whom the existence of all things flows, testify to God's unique possession of life; but we, cut off as we are from God, can in no way know this and, thence, avail ourselves of the blessings that such knowledge would bestow, except as these blessings are manifest in Christ:

> God is said to *have life in himself*, not only because he alone lives by his own inherent power, but because, containing in himself the fullness of life, he communicates life to all things. . . . But, because the majesty of God, being far removed from us, would resemble an unknown and hidden source, for this reason it has been openly manifested in Christ. We have, thus, an open fountain placed before us, from which we may draw.[32]

Christ has been set between the Father and the Church so that the life which dwells with God can flow through Christ to God's chosen.

Calvin tells us that God's Eternal Word, God's Son in his divinity alone, should most strictly be called "life"; he is the fountain from which the life of the world flows.[33] Indeed, we are told in the first chapter of John's Gospel that he is life, and Calvin understands this to mean that he is the source of life and existence for all of creation, not only as he brings the world into being, but also as he sustains it.[34]

Yet, within the context of the Gospel testimony to Christ's redemptive work among humanity, Calvin describes Christ as the fountain of life with regards to his incarnation and not in his divinity alone. Only thus has the life, which in God was remote from us, drawn near, so that we might have

---

[31] See, for example, *Comm. John* 1:16, 1.50 (*CO* 47:16); *Comm. John* 6:57, 1.268–9 (*CO* 47:156). Gerrish discusses both Calvin's description of God as the fountain of life and his attribution of this same title to Christ; Gerrish, *Grace and Gratitude*, see esp. pp. 26–27, 57–59, 132.

[32] *Comm. John* 5:26, 1.207 (*CO* 47:118).   [33] *Comm. John* 6:57, 1.269 (*CO* 47:156).

[34] See *Comm. John* 1:4, 1.31–2 (*CO* 47:5); "Deity of Christ," p. 29 (*CO* 47:478–479).

access to it: "What had been hidden in God is revealed to us in Christ as man, and life, which was formerly inaccessible, is now placed before our eyes."[35] Calvin's thought here is that God, again, has accommodated Godself to humanity and brought life down to our level – God has placed it before us in Christ, our brother, so that we who are unable to mount up to heaven to possess it might have it before us here where we dwell: "And thus, [God] provides for our weakness, when he does not call us above the clouds to enjoy life, but displays it on earth in the same manner as if he were exalting us to the secrets of his kingdom."[36] Christ is both the one through whom life is poured out and the one in whom this life is manifest so that we might draw from it.

When Calvin says that God has revealed and given life to God's Church in Christ "as man," he does not mean that God has offered it in Christ's human nature alone. Rather, by "man," he is referring to Christ as he is God manifest in the flesh. Christ, in fact, can function as the fountain of life only in his two natures, together. Calvin tells us, harking back to John's prologue, that Christ is the fountain of life as he is God's Eternal Word, but that in his flesh he has opened a channel to convey that life to humanity. Or, again: "As the secret power to bestow life, of which [Christ] has spoken, might be referred to his Divine essence, he now comes down to the second step, and shows that this life is placed in his flesh, that it may be drawn out of it."[37] Christ has life to give because of his divinity, but he can give it in a form accommodated to our weakness because of his humanity. [38]

Calvin does, however, emphasize the particular role played by Christ's human nature in his out-pouring of life, or grace, upon the Church. We observed above that Calvin considers Christ's flesh to be the channel through which life flows to us, that "life was placed in his flesh that it may be drawn out of it." For Calvin, Christ's flesh functions as this channel in the first place because, as he says:

[I]n it was accomplished the redemption of man, in it a sacrifice was offered to atone for sins, and an obedience yielded to God to reconcile him to us; it was also filled with the sanctification of the Spirit, and at length, having vanquished death, it was received into the heavenly glory . . . [A]ll parts of life have been placed in it, that no man may have reason to complain that he is deprived of life, as if it were placed in concealment or at a distance.[39]

Life was placed in Christ's flesh, insofar as he, through his humanity, both redeemed us from death into life and exhibited this redeemed life to us.

---

[35] *Comm. John* 5:27, I.208 (*CO* 47:119). [36] *Comm. John* 6:51, I.262 (*CO* 47:162).
[37] Ibid. [38] See *Comm. John* 6:33, I.248 (*CO* 47:143). [39] *Comm. John* 6:51, I.263 (*CO* 47:152–153).

Christ functions as the fountain of life only as he first opens the way for this life to be poured out upon us.

However, Calvin also emphasizes the significance of Christ's humanity in his bestowal of life upon us, more particularly, in that through his humanity, the graces or gifts of the Spirit are given to us. He relies largely on John 1:16 ("Out of his fullness we have all received, grace for grace"), arguing in numerous places that Christ was filled with all the gifts of the Spirit so that he might bestow them upon his chosen as he pleases. So, he will maintain, discussing Luke 2:40 ("And the child grew, and was invigorated by the Spirit . . ."), "Christ received, in his human nature . . . an increase of the free gifts of the Spirit, that 'out of his fullness' he may pour them out upon us; for we draw grace out of his grace."[40] And, elsewhere, "Christ differs from us in this respect, that the Father has poured out upon him an unlimited abundance of his Spirit. And, certainly it is proper that the Spirit should dwell without measure in him, that we may all draw out of his fullness, as we have seen in the first chapter."[41] We possess grace bestowed by the Spirit only as we draw this grace from Christ, who is filled with the Spirit in his humanity. In his divinity he is in eternal fellowship with the Spirit; but in his humanity he was anointed with the Spirit in his birth and at his baptism, so that the fullness of all graces might reside with him.[42]

Finally, we should note that, for Calvin, Christ's work in opening this channel of grace between God and believers does not bear fruit in the lives of the chosen apart from their faith in Christ. Calvin's language consistently emphasizes that Christ has "revealed" or "manifested" this life that God has elected to make available through him, and such manifestation is not, in and of itself, the anointing of believers with God's grace. Rather, it is a display of the riches that are ours in Christ, *if* we will receive them in faith. "[Christ] is ready to flow to us," Calvin writes, "provided that we open up a channel of faith."[43] God's grace is not simply implanted in believers, nor does it flood over them; rather, it is offered to them and accepted by them as they have taken Christ's brotherly hand and been ingrafted into his body. God's chosen receive Christ's blessings as he is their head, in faith. The pouring out of life upon the Church cannot be understood apart from this essential relationship.

Now, to say that we do not receive these blessings apart from faith is not to say that their display in Christ rests passively, awaiting our response. The

[40] *Comm. Luke* 2:40, 1.166 (*CO* 45:104).
[41] *Comm. John* 3:34, 1.140 (*CO* 47:75). See also *Comm. John* 7:38, 1.309 (*CO* 47:182).
[42] *Comm. John* 1:16, 1.51–52 (*CO* 47:18).   [43] *Comm. John* 1:16, 1.50 (*CO* 47:16–17).

whole point of Calvin's depiction of this aspect of Christ's office as a "display of treasures," or as a "fountain," through which the life, hidden with God, has drawn near, is that Christ elicits our faith, enticing or enthralling us with the wealth that God would give. Christ, as the fountain of life, both pours out this life and draws us to it, so that we can enjoy it only in him – only as he has made it available and led us to avail ourselves of it. This aspect of his royal office is not complete if either dimension is excluded from it.

Our pattern and example

Christ comes to the chosen as brother not only that through him they might be united to God and receive God's grace, but also that they might find in him an example by which their lives could be shaped into greater conformity with God's righteousness. He is the external pattern that they should strive to imitate, trusting that the Spirit with which Christ has filled them will effect this godly life within them:

> As we have been elected in Christ, so in him the image of our calling is exhibited to us in a lively manner; and therefore he justly holds himself out to us as a pattern, to the imitation of which all the godly ought to be conformed . . . The conformity between the head and the members ought to be always placed before our eyes, not only that believers may form themselves after the example of Christ, but that they may entertain a confident hope that his Spirit will every day form them anew to be better and better, that they may walk to the end in newness of life.[44]

Calvin most typically speaks of our need to conform our lives to Christ in his patient suffering, or in his moderation of his emotions, by which he avoided any excess that would have been an affront to God. Christ, of course, is able to serve as such an example for us only because he took on a true and complete human nature that was not protected from similar suffering by his divinity. It is only as we are assured that Christ in his humanity suffered as we do that we will find him to be a suitable model for us as we struggle with the obstacles confronting us in our lives. So Christ, for instance, serves as the proper example for the confrontation of death only because death held for him the same dread that it would hold for any human, as Calvin notes, commenting on Christ's statement that his soul was troubled (John 12:27):

[44] *Comm. John* 15:10, II.114 (*CO* 47:343).

If the dread of death had occasioned no uneasiness to the Son of God, which of us would have thought that his example was applicable to our case? For it has not been given to us to die without a feeling of regret; but when we learn that he had not within him a hardness like stone or iron, we summon courage to follow him, and the weakness of the flesh, which makes us tremble at death, does not hinder us from becoming the companions of our General in struggling with it.[45]

Christ, because he is truly our brother, can lead us by his example through the tribulations of this lifetime, and we, seeing that he has trod the same path to which we have been called, will follow him into righteousness. And, indeed, given that Christ leads us into such righteousness, even though it is by the way of suffering, Calvin will say that he sets a pattern of "perfect happiness," for he has exhibited in his humanity that image of God in which we were created but from which we fell away as we were engulfed by sin. Christ, then, by his holy exhibition begins to renew this image within believers as they imitate the form of his life:

Let it be observed here, that, while a pattern of perfect happiness was exhibited in Christ, he had nothing that belonged peculiarly to himself, but rather was rich, in order to enrich those who believed in him. Our happiness lies in having the image of God restored and formed anew in us, which was defaced by sin. Christ is not only the lively image of God, in so far as he is the eternal Word of God, but even in his human nature, which he has in common with us, the likeness of the glory of the Father has been engraved, so as to form his members to the resemblance of it.[46]

Christ fulfills his royal office as he serves as our pattern and our Lord, as he is the fountain from which both life and the blessings of the Spirit are poured out upon us, and as he is our brother and the Beloved of the Father. Obviously, from what we have seen here, Calvin understands Christ's role as head of the Church quite broadly, and in this breadth it is integral to the Christological slant of his theology.

Calvin will say that Christ's work as priest is his "principal office" – that there is a way opened between God and humanity only as he atones for our sin. Indeed, this is the reason that Scripture gives for his incarnation. But, as Calvin works through the panoply of images by which Scripture describes Christ's mediatorial mission, it is clear that his office as king over the Church compasses about his priestly office, both providing its necessary context and serving as its gracious and effective result. The goal of the covenant history is the Church's relationship with God. Through his sacrifice, Christ makes this relationship possible, but the relationship itself is most completely grasped only in its initiation and fulfillment in Christ's

[45] *Comm. John* 12:27, II.32 (*CO* 47:291).   [46] *Comm. John* 17:22, II.184–185 (*CO* 47:388).

work as head of the Church. With the five images of this royal office in hand, we can now turn to Calvin's systematic exposition of this work in the *Institutes* with an eye to the manner in which he pulls them together into the one narrative thread of Christ's realization of God's promised covenant and our integration into the same.

CHRIST'S ROYAL OFFICE IN THE *INSTITUTES*

When Calvin turns in the *Institutes* to the subject of the Mediator (ii.vi), he begins his exposition with a brief rendition of the covenant history, noting that from the time of Abraham God directed the Church to look for their salvation in the one head who would unite the people and deliver them from their enemies into the grace of God's promise. Calvin underlines David, especially, as a type of this head, first in his own history and then in the preaching of the prophets as they proclaimed the coming Messiah who would gather God's scattered children and restore them to David's kingdom. Calvin thereby establishes the covenant history as the context within which his Christology should be understood. Within this context, we see that Christ's ministry to us is not an isolated venture of God toward the Church, since God has always related to the Church through a Mediator. But we also are given an insight into the nature of God's relationship with God's Church; it is a relationship worked out in the covenant history, through the establishment of kingdoms, the defeat of enemies, and the bestowal of blessings, and these are established, defeated, and bestowed by God's Mediator, the king. It is through this enactment of the kingdom by the Mediator that God's covenant is realized as God's promises are fulfilled and God's chosen are led into a faithful relationship with God.

When Calvin turns to address Christ's royal office explicitly (in *Inst.* ii.xv.3–5), he takes up these themes that he found in Israel's history and orients Christ's kingship around the motifs of conquest and beneficence. Christ is, in the first place, "the eternal protector and defender of [God's] Church."[47] Calvin notes God's promise to David, that his throne would stand forever, and argues that, because in Christ this promise has been fulfilled, the faithful can trust his everlasting preservation of the Church, his kingdom. Christ is God's king, "armed with eternal power," so that the Church's enemies can never prevail against him: "Hence, it follows that the devil, with all the resources of the world, can never destroy the church, founded as it is on the eternal throne of Christ."[48] The eternity of Christ's

---

[47] *Inst.* ii.xv.3, p. 497 (*OS* 3:474).   [48] Ibid., p. 498 (*OS* 3:475).

power and of the kingdom that he thereby secures is related to the spiritual nature of his rule. Because his kingdom is spiritual, he is able to fulfill what was prefigured in David and defeat the real enemies of the chosen, that is, death and the devil.

Christ as king, though, not only secures a kingdom for his followers, but he also bestows upon them an abundance of spiritual blessings. Because of the eternity of Christ's kingdom, individual believers can in the midst of struggle look forward to "the full fruit of [Christ's] grace in the age to come."[49] But they can also trust their king to enrich them with "all things necessary for the eternal salvation of souls," and to fortify them "with courage to stand unconquerable against all the assaults of spiritual enemies."[50] Christ is the king who provides for his people; he offers them spiritual gifts because he has been anointed with the Spirit (he is the Messiah, the anointed one) that he might be a fountain from which the Spirit flows abundantly to his members, as from a head to its body.[51]

And along with this protection and provision – indeed, in some sense because of it – Christ is the king who truly rules and governs his people. He is the Father's "deputy," possessing "the whole power of God's dominion," so that we should resolve to obey Christ and obey him with eagerness.[52] With reference to the godly, he is not only king but pastor, gently leading them into the way of righteousness and life. Christ, however, is not a toothless king, as Calvin reminds us, for we also must know that he carries a "rod of Iron to break them [presumably the godless] and dash them all in pieces like a potter's vessel."[53]

Because of these things – Christ's role as protector, provider, and ruler – the Church can find comfort in the king whom God has bestowed upon it:

Thus it is that we may patiently pass through this life with its misery, hunger, cold, contempt, reproaches, and other troubles – content with this one thing: that our King will never leave us destitute, but will provide for our needs until, our warfare ended, we are called to triumph. Such is the nature of his rule, that he shares with us all that he has received from the Father. Now he arms and equips us with his power, adorns us with his beauty and magnificence, enriches us with his wealth. These benefits, then, give us the most fruitful occasion to glory, and also provide us with confidence to struggle fearlessly against the devil, sin, and death. Finally, clothed with his righteousness, we can valiantly rise above all the world's reproaches; and just as he himself freely lavishes his gifts upon us, so may we, in return, bring forth fruit to his glory.[54]

---

[49] Ibid.   [50] *Inst.* II.xv.4, p. 498 (*OS* 3:476).
[51] *Inst.* II.xv.5, pp. 499–500 (*OS* 3:477).   [52] *Inst.* II.xv.5, p. 500 (*OS* 3:478–479).
[53] Ibid., from Ps. 2:9ff.   [54] *Inst.* II.xv.4, p. 499 (*OS* 3:476–477).

Christ, as king, is the true, complete, and spiritual fulfillment of all that had been promised to and prefigured in David. He provides for the safety and welfare of his people and thereby leads them into faithful participation in God's covenant as they entrust themselves to him. Moreover, just as we saw in the previous chapter a concern for both what the Mediator objectively accomplishes and the manner in which he subjectively affects the faithful, so, too, here we find the same thing. On the one hand, Calvin begins quite clearly with Christ's objective accomplishments. He has defeated the Church's enemies, he has provided an eternal kingdom, and he has bestowed upon the faithful bountiful graces. On the other hand, in doing these things, Calvin will equally emphasize, Christ has also shaped the faithful into fit participants in his covenant. He has led the people to place their faith in him, as their "eternal protector and defender," and he has equipped them for their own battles within their own history as God's people by providing them with courage, confidence, and hope. Christ has fulfilled the covenant history and provided for his Church in its own history through the history of his death, resurrection, and ascension.

Death's conqueror

Calvin immediately follows his chapter on the threefold office of Christ with an exposition of Christ's work – how Christ fulfilled the function of Redeemer – through an examination of the narrative of Christ's passion, resurrection, and ascension given in the Apostles' Creed. He notes at the outset that Christ came to save us from our sins and to lead us on to salvation, and in the course of his discussion of the Creed he amplifies these themes both in terms of his atoning sacrifice (discussed in the previous chapter) and in terms of his work as king, whereby he has defeated death and led his Church into righteousness and life. To understand Calvin's exposition of this narrative in relation to Christ's threefold office, we first must grasp that there is no simple correlation between any one office and any of these particular events. Christ's work as priest, for example, includes not only his expiatory death, but also his ascension to the right hand of the Father, from where he intercedes for his Church.[55] So, too, Calvin develops his picture of Christ's royal office in relation to the full narrative of the Creed. Christ's work as king embraces all of his activity through which he wins for us salvation and leads us into it.[56]

---

[55] See *Inst.* II.xvi.16, pp. 524–525 (*OS* 3:504).
[56] In my previous chapter I took a "progressive" approach to the relationship between Christ's offices of priest and king – Christ as priest renews our relationship to God while Christ as king enacts the relationship. This progressive language is helpful at a theoretical level, but not on a historical level. Within his history, Christ acts as both priest and king in all of his work among us.

The most significant theme that emerges from Calvin's exposition of the creed in relation to Christ's kingly office is Christ's defeat of death, and his argument here has several pieces. In the first place, Calvin tells us, we must understand that Christ died and gave himself over to the power of death to deliver us from our bondage to it. But he was not overwhelmed by its power; rather, he laid it low, "when it was threatening us and exulting over our fallen state."[57] As it says in Hebrews (2:14–15), Christ suffered death to destroy the one "who had the power of death, that is, the devil, and deliver all those who through fear of death were subject to lifelong bondage." Through his death, Christ overcomes both death and the devil, and, we should note, he also addresses the human fear of death. For Calvin, the encumbrance from which we must be delivered is not simply our subjugation to death, but also our terror before it and that terror's debilitating effects. His thinking here is obviously quite similar to what we saw in the preceding chapter on God's wrath; and, in fact, we will find that Calvin intertwines these two themes, Christ's bearing God's wrath and defeating the death that is our lot because of this wrath.

Indeed, having discussed the purpose of the Christ's death, Calvin then takes up the second aspect of this discussion, Christ's descent into hell, which, Calvin argues at some length, refers to his suffering the wrath of God and the concomitant terror of death to which humanity is subject because of sin. I have discussed the significance of his struggle with God's wrath, but his interpretation of this struggle as also involving the horrors of death pertains to our present topic. For, to undergo God's wrath includes for Calvin that Christ "also grapple hand to hand with the armies of hell and the dread of everlasting death."[58] Recalling the Hebrew passage, that we are "through fear of death subject to lifelong bondage," Calvin is led to this conclusion:

[Christ], therefore, had to conquer that fear which by nature continually torments and oppresses all mortals. This he could do only by fighting it . . . Therefore, by his wrestling hand to hand with the devil's power, with the dread of death, with the pains of hell, he was victorious and triumphed over them that in death we may not now fear those things which our Prince has swallowed up.[59]

For Calvin, Christ in his death is not only our atoning sacrifice, but also our champion sent out to vanquish the enemies before whom we quake. In doing so, he frees us from death and the devil and from our bondage to ourselves, to our own fears that inhibit us from living into God's proffered life. Again, his death is notable not only for what it accomplishes objectively,

---

[57] *Inst.* ii.xvi.7, p. 512 (*OS* 3:491).   [58] *Inst.* ii.xvi.10, p. 515 (*OS* 3:495).
[59] *Inst.* ii.xvi.11, p. 517 (*OS* 3:496–497).

but also for what it works subjectively in Christ's chosen; he addresses not only external enemies, like the devil, but also the internal enemy of fear. Of course, in making this argument, Calvin must insist on the importance of the involvement of Christ's human nature in this endeavor. Christ is able to defeat our terror before death only because he truly experiences that terror – you cannot defeat an enemy that you have not met in battle; and Christ is able to experience this dread only in his humanity.

The third piece of Christ's defeat of death is given in his resurrection. On the one hand, it is by rising again that Christ has defeated death. There is no victory if death is able to hold him in its ugly maw. On the other hand, through his resurrection, Christ's defeat of death is manifest to believers. Calvin writes: "[A]s he in rising again, came forth victor over death, so the victory of our faith over death lies in his resurrection alone."[60] He continues: "Therefore, we divide the substance of our salvation between Christ's death and resurrection as follows: through his death, sin was wiped out and death extinguished; through his resurrection, righteousness was restored and life raised up, so that – thanks to his resurrection – his death has manifested its power and efficacy in us."[61] If in his death we see his struggle in his humanity with our fear of death, so in his resurrection we see the power of God whereby death is defeated and our faith is secured. Again, for Calvin it is important to emphasize not only what Christ has done, but also how Christ has revealed this to us.

Christ, then, has become our champion through his combat with death. The martial imagery that Calvin has maintained throughout this discussion clearly depicts a king or warrior gone out to battle with his people's foes; and when he turns to Christ's ascension, he continues this theme. For with his ascension into heaven, Christ, the victorious one, "inaugurates" his kingdom.[62] Calvin's immediate point in this context is that, through his ascension, Christ is better able to exercise his beneficent lordship over the Church: "Indeed, we see how much more abundantly he then poured out his Spirit, how much more wonderfully he advanced his Kingdom, how much greater power he displayed both in helping his people and in scattering his enemies."[63] Christ in heaven is no longer limited by his bodily presence as he wields royal power, but is now free through his spiritual presence to rule both heaven and earth more immediately.

Beyond the question of Christ's spiritual presence, Christ's inauguration of his kingdom with his ascension also fits the broader picture we have elicited from Calvin's work. For Calvin here depicts Christ's kingdom

---

[60] *Inst.* II.xvi.13, p. 520 (*OS* 3:500).   [61] Ibid., p. 521 (*OS* 3:500).
[62] *Inst.* II.xvi.14, p. 522 (*OS* 3:501).   [63] Ibid. p. 523 (*OS* 3:502).

not as an eternal entity that exists apart from and above history, a heavenly realm in which we could take refuge from the world's history. Rather, the kingdom that Christ inaugurates with his ascension has a beginning in time, forty days after his death and resurrection; it is the consummation of the kingdom that God initiated with God's promise to David, the coming of which was predicted by the prophets and prefigured in Israel's return from Babylon. That return was the commencement of the renovation of the kingdom, which Calvin now shows was completed with Christ's ascension.[64] It is a kingdom that, though spiritual and everlasting, is the fulfillment of the covenant history; it is a kingdom that was enacted only as Christ first vanquished the Church's enemies and then ascended to take his throne.

Indeed, we again see the historical conditioning of the kingdom, in Calvin's view, in his discussion of Christ's ascension specifically to the Father's right hand. This image, Calvin tells us, is a comparison, "drawn from kings who have assessors at their side to whom they delegate the tasks of ruling and governing."[65] Thus, the Father has delegated to Christ the government of heaven and earth, a position he will maintain until the last day, when he will, as king, also act as judge over all peoples. Christians are to find consolation in this judgment, for the judge is the one who first redeemed them. What head, Calvin asks, would act to scatter his own members? Christ, the God–man, serves as the Church's head when he is appointed vice-regent by the Father over heaven and earth (Calvin quotes Ephesians 1:22, "[God] has made him the head over all things for the church") in fulfillment of the covenant. He rules in the Father's place, even as the Davidic kings had before him.

The steward of the Spirit

Through his death, resurrection, and ascension, Christ inaugurated his kingdom, but that accounts for only a portion of his work. For this kingdom would be of no avail unless there were citizens to populate it. Thus, Christ needed to gather God's chosen into the realm over which he had established himself so that they might enjoy his royal beneficence. As Calvin wrote at the very beginning of his consideration of Christ's role as Mediator, it was not only clear from the start that God's covenant with Abraham would be realized through the one head, but also that "the promised salvation [would not be] realized until Christ appeared, whose task is to gather up what has

---

[64] See *Comm. Isaiah* 9:6, 1.306 (*CO* 36:194).   [65] *Inst.* II.xvi.15, p. 524 (*OS* 3:503).

been scattered."[66] This is the issue to which Calvin turns as he begins the third book of the *Institutes*. Having just concluded his elucidation of the narrative of Christ's passion and resurrection,[67] Calvin writes:

First, we must understand that as long as Christ remains outside of us, and we are separated from him, all that he has suffered and done for the salvation of the human race remains useless and of no value for us. Therefore, to share with us what he has received from the Father, he had to become ours and to dwell within us. For this reason, he is called "our head."[68]

Christ not only needed to establish and inaugurate his kingdom; he also must engage us and make us members within it, and this he does by uniting us with him so that we are engrafted as members into the body of the Church.

We are joined to Christ by faith in and through the work of the Spirit, Calvin tells us. The Spirit is the "inner teacher" by whose efforts we are led to an effective and saving knowledge of Christ.[69] Book III of the *Institutes* could be read primarily for its presentation of Calvin's doctrine of the Spirit, and, indeed, one cannot come to a proper understanding of Calvin's theology until his pneumatology has been thoroughly explored. But, in our concern for Calvin's Christology, we will sidestep this topic and instead look at Book III for what it will tell us about the work of Christ and, in this particular instance, about the work of Christ in the uniting of believers to himself. For, however much this union through faith is the work of the Spirit, it is equally and completely the work of Christ or, more specifically, the work of Christ as king or head of the Church.

One theme I have maintained throughout our investigation is the dimension of Christ's work by which he not merely has accomplished and established God's covenant with God's Church through his history – what I have called the objective aspect of his work – but also has made the grace and mercy of God thereby manifest to draw the chosen into the covenant through faith – the subjective aspect. So, Calvin now writes that our faith, by which we are united to Christ, rests on God's promises as they have been fulfilled in Christ.[70] Christ does not establish God's kingdom only to passively await our response in faith. He actively seeks that response precisely in the act of the accomplishment of God's mercy among us. In Christ we are confronted with God's gracious promise that makes a claim on our faith.

---

[66] *Inst.* II.vi.2, p. 343 (*OS* 3:322).   [67] With the interposition of the short section on Christ's merit.
[68] *Inst.* III.i.1, p. 537 (*OS* 4:1).   [69] *Inst.* III.i.3–4, pp. 541–542 (*OS* 4:3–6).
[70] See *Inst.* III.ii.30–32, pp. 576–580 (*OS* 4:39–44).

However, Calvin emphasizes equally that this outward manifestation of God's mercy in Christ is futile except that the Spirit bears witness to it within us, thus bringing us to faith: "As has already been clearly explained," Calvin writes, "until our minds become intent upon the Spirit, Christ, so to speak, lies idle because we coldly contemplate him as outside ourselves – indeed, far from us."[71] It is the Spirit who awakens our hearts to the grace of God accomplished in Christ's history, but this work of the Spirit to bring faith is at the same time the work of Christ. Christ as king, the beneficent provider for his people, is the fountain of the Spirit. So, in Book III, Calvin is clear that Christ is the agent whereby the faithful have had the Spirit poured out upon them. Christ was anointed with the Spirit so that he might assemble us into his Church: "[W]e must bear in mind that Christ came endowed with the Holy Spirit in a special way: that is, to separate us from the world and to gather us unto the hope of the eternal inheritance."[72] Though we can say that the Spirit was given to us by the Father (indeed, the Spirit is called the "Spirit of the Father"), we must also understand that the Father "has bestowed the whole fullness of the Spirit upon the Son to be minister and steward of his liberality."[73] The Spirit is the "Spirit of Christ" insofar as Christ is the eternal Word of God joined to the Spirit with the Father; but Calvin emphasizes more strongly the Spirit's relation to Christ as he is the Mediator, since it is only as he can dispense the Spirit that he can complete his work: "To sum up, the Holy Spirit is the bond by which Christ effectually unites us to himself."[74] "Christ, when he illumines us into faith by the power of the Spirit, at the same time so engrafts us into his body that we become partakers of every good."[75] Christ, as king, not only establishes a kingdom for the faithful, a kingdom over which the Father has established him as vice-regent; he also has been made "steward" of the Spirit that, through his dispensation of the Spirit, he might call those whom God has chosen into the fellowship he has created. He is the primary agent in the creation of the Church. He is the giver of spiritual gifts.[76]

---

[71] *Inst.* III.i.3, p. 541 (*OS* 4:5).   [72] *Inst.* III.i.2, p. 538 (*OS* 4:2).   [73] Ibid.
[74] *Inst.* III.i.1, p. 538 (*OS* 4:538).   [75] *Inst.* III.ii.35, p. 583 (*OS* 4:46).
[76] This aspect of Christ's work has not been adequately appreciated by most Calvin commentators. Wendel only gestures at it (see *Calvin*, pp. 239–240), but in Witte this neglect of Calvin's doctrine of Christ as the giver of the Spirit is most apparent. In diatribe against Calvin's neglect of the hypostatic union, Witte complains that, for Calvin, after Christ reconciles us to God, he ascends and leaves the work of "life-giving" to the Holy Spirit. Calvin thereby ignores the Catholic emphasis on Christ as the giver of life (*Die Christologie Calvins*, p. 504).
   Witte has missed Calvin's argument that Christ's ascension is not an abandonment of his work, but a move to gain a better perspective on the management that work requires. Calvin claims that this allows Christ to be involved in the world precisely as the "life-giver," as the one who gives the Spirit to the Church, whereby he protects and blesses the faithful (see *Inst.* II.xvi.14, pp. 522–523

Christ, our brother, and the fellowship of the faithful

Christ, then, unites the faithful to himself, engrafting them into his body through his gift of the Spirit. As I noted at the outset of this chapter, this is a primary soteriological impulse for the incarnation, that Christ might draw the faithful into fellowship with him even as he has fellowship with the Father. That is the point of the covenant history, that God through the ministry of the Mediator might bring fallen humanity into relationship with God. But the primary image that Calvin uses to describe the unity of believers with Christ is the head/body language that he finds in Paul, language that is ambiguous in terms of the nature of the relationship between the faithful and Christ. What kind of unity do believers share with Christ when they are "engrafted" into his body?

Although political language predominates in Calvin's explication of Christ's royal office (in *Inst.* II.xv) – Christ is the king who defeats death and the devil and inaugurates his kingdom – Calvin does not exploit this imagery to describe the ensuing relationship of the believer with Christ. There is little reference to the Church as Christ's commonwealth or to believers as citizens within his kingdom. Likewise, Calvin shies away from a metaphysical characterization of this unity. He will speak at times of our mystical union with Christ, as we dwell in him and he dwells in our hearts.[77] But Wendel helpfully points out that, however much Calvin may invoke this imagery, he is always careful to distance himself from any notion of an essential union or a union between Christ's divine nature and our human nature (as opposed to his own human nature), which this might imply.[78] Such metaphysical language suggests to Calvin a mixing not only of natures but of persons – he calls it "a gross mingling of Christ with believers"[79] – and this violates his sense of the integrity of both natures and persons, which marks his theology throughout. This antipathy for metaphysical understandings of union is evident when Calvin takes up the common notion that Christ "took what is ours in order to give us what is his." Calvin interprets this maxim against its grain, moving away from the metaphysical paradigm of a union and exchange of natures toward a more personal, historical, social paradigm for union. It is a paradigm of fellowship between Christ and his sisters and brothers, introduced at the beginning of this chapter.

[OS 3:501–502]). For Calvin, the work of the Spirit, which has an integrity in its own right, cannot be properly understood except as it is bound up with the work of Christ as king over his Church.
77 See *Inst.* III.xi.10, p. 737 (OS 4:191). 78 See Wendel, *Calvin*, pp. 234–238.
79 *Inst.* III.xi.10, p. 737 (OS 4:192).

When Calvin is explaining the certainty of the believer's faith in Christ, he emphasizes that this certainty has a solidity to it because of the union of the believer with Christ. We are not torn between our vision of Christ's love afar off from us and the vision of our own unrighteousness apart from Christ because Christ has acted to make us participants in him. Calvin continues, then, urging his readers to understand themselves only in their union with Christ: "We ought to hold fast bravely with both hands to that fellowship by which [Christ] has bound himself to us."[80] Insofar as Christ has united himself to us, we share with him not in a metaphysical union of natures or persons, but in a fellowship (*societas*) whereby he shares with us the good things that he won for those who place their faith in him.

Again, in explaining our justification through our unity with Christ (in a section where he refers to our "mystical union" with Christ), Calvin distances himself from Osiander's contention that this union is metaphysical in nature, a union between Christ's divinity and our humanity. Instead, he turns to the notion of fellowship another time: "We do not, therefore, contemplate [Christ] outside ourselves from afar in order that righteousness may be imputed to us, but because we put on Christ and are engrafted into his body . . . For this reason, we glory that we have a fellowship of righteousness with him."[81] That is the work of faith; through our fellowship with Christ it opens to us a share in all that is Christ's, "a partaking in the righteousness of Christ."[82] Calvin's notion of the unity between Christ and the believer is, in the first place, social. It is a relationship established between persons, a benefactor and those who place themselves in fellowship with him through faith, so that they might receive his benefits and be accepted as those who move within his company. His view is not unlike the image we have of Christ, sitting at table with his disciples and asking that they might be one with him even as he is one with the Father.

If we accept this social metaphor as Calvin's primary understanding of the believer's unity with Christ, then we find that it coheres wonderfully with the theme of Christ's brotherhood with believers as the means whereby he establishes this unity (along with his gift of the Spirit). We can recall Calvin's development of Paul's notion of adoption – that we are made children of the Father because Christ has made himself our brother and "[stretched] out his brotherly hand to us."[83] So, in return, Calvin exhorts believers to hold fast with both hands to this fellowship of brotherly affection that Christ has thereby established. Our union with Christ is a personal union.

---

[80] *Inst.* iii.ii.24, p. 570 (*OS* 4:34).　　[81] *Inst.* iii.xi.10, p. 737 (*OS* 4:191).
[82] *Inst.* iii.xi.20, p. 750 (*OS* 4:204), my translation.　　[83] *Comm. John* 3:13, 1.121 (*CO* 47:62).

Christ, our brother, has offered himself to us in love; and, by the power of his Spirit, he has led us to accept that offer and grasp him by faith.[84] This is the point from which Calvin begins his Christology (in *Inst.* II.xii.1). Christ took our nature upon himself, the Son of God becoming the Son of man, so that he might be one with us: "Hence, that holy brotherhood which he commends with his own lips, when he says, 'I am ascending to my Father and your Father, to my God and your God.' "[85] Christ's role as Mediator, or, more specifically, as king and head of the Church, is to so unite God's chosen that he might thereby bring them into union with the Father. This he does by taking on our nature and becoming "the firstborn of many brethren" (Rom. 8:29, cited by Calvin in *Inst.* III.i.1). We, as his sisters and brothers, become God's children. Calvin continually refers to the benefits that Christ bestows upon the faithful, making them "heirs of the kingdom," but surely for Calvin this is the chief benefit, that through Christ the Church is brought into covenant relationship with the Father so that the children of men might become children of God.

Putting on Christ

Finally, Christ brings the faithful into covenant relationship with God, but that is not the end of the story. As we have seen from the beginning of our analysis, God's covenant involves not only the promise of God's grace, fulfilled in Christ, in which we are called to place our faith, but also God's commands, the way of life published in the Law, to which we are to give our obedience. "The object of our regeneration," Calvin tells us, "is to manifest in the life of believers a harmony and agreement between God's righteousness and their obedience, and thus to confirm the adoption that they have received as sons."[86] But this regeneration is accomplished only in and through Christ. On the one hand, Christ leads those admitted into his fellowship into obedience to God's will insofar as he is their king and

---

[84] Again, Calvin speaks on this matter in a multiplicity of ways, and it is possible to read his various discussions of our *koinonia* with Christ in more mystical, essentially participatory terms. See, for example, Gerrish, *Grace and Gratitude*, pp. 73–74, 83f., and 128. The passages from which Gerrish draws (all connected to Calvin's reading of 1 Cor. 1:9) work under the broader image of God and Christ as the fountain of all good, and they reflect one dynamic of Calvin's discussion. But I have chosen to work with a wider collection of passages which orbit around the metaphor of God as Father and Christ as brother – a metaphor more central to Gerrish's thesis (p. 89) and one that is more prevalent and more integral to Calvin's overall theology. It coheres more fully to the covenant as God's chief means of relating to human persons, as well. Calvin himself recognizes these two aspects of our communion with Christ, as is evident in his letter to Peter Martyr Vermigli (*CO* 15:722–723), quoted at length in Gerrish (p. 128).
[85] *Inst.* II. xii.2, p. 465 (*OS* 3:439).   [86] *Inst.* III.vi.1, p. 684 (*OS* 4:146).

pastor. Christ, as our brother and our head, on the other hand, is intimately involved in the righteousness into which we are to live. Through his love he has called us to it and in his life he has modeled it for us, so that we are to put on Christ, patterning our lives after his example and thereby responding faithfully to his love for us. Calvin writes: "For we have been adopted by the Lord with this one condition: that our lives express Christ, the bond of our adoption."[87] God's righteousness is fulfilled in the lives of the faithful insofar as they "express Christ," and, for Calvin, this means that they make Christ's history the pattern for their own. This is a part of Christ's mediatorial work, to serve as an example for believers. Calvin writes: "Scripture shows that God the Father, as he has reconciled us to himself in his Christ, has in him stamped for us the likeness to which he would have us conform." And again: "Christ, through whom we return into favour with God, has been set as an example, whose pattern we ought to express in our lives."[88]

At the heart of regeneration, for Calvin, is repentance, and repentance is constituted by the movements of mortification and vivification, dying to the life of sin and rising to a new life of faith and obedience. But that is to say that the essence of our regeneration is to die and be resurrected with Christ:

> [Mortification and vivification] happen to us by participation in Christ. For if we truly partake in his death, "our old man is crucified by his power, and the body of sin perishes," that the corruption of original nature may no longer thrive. If we share in his resurrection, through it we are raised up into newness of life to correspond to the righteousness of God.[89]

When Christ, as our brother, shares with us what is his, a part of what he shares is his history; indeed, Calvin notes in his commentary on Christ's passion and resurrection (in *Inst.* II.xvi) that we are to die with him and be raised to new life, or, as Paul says: "We were engrafted in the likeness of his death, so that sharing in his resurrection we might walk in newness of life" (Rom. 6:4).[90] We are to become like Christ as a fruit of the fellowship that we share with him. Calvin writes of this fellowship: "Not only does he cleave to us by an indivisible bond of fellowship, but with a wonderful communion, day by day, he grows more and more into one body with us, until he becomes completely one with us."[91] Calvin does not explain what he means by this communion we have with Christ, but it would seem that

---

[87] *Inst.* III.vi.3, p. 687 (*OS* 4:148).   [88] *Inst.* III.vi.3, p. 686 (*OS* 4:148).
[89] *Inst.* III.iii.9, pp. 600–601 (*OS* 4:63).   [90] See *Inst.* II.xvi.7, p. 512; *Inst.* II.xvi.13, pp. 521–522.
[91] *Inst.* III.ii.24, pp. 570–571 (*OS* 4:35).

one aspect of it must involve our increasing unity with Christ through our recapitulation in our own lives of Christ's redemptive narrative, dying and rising with Christ, whereby we come to share the righteousness of God that he has bestowed upon us.

THE ETERNITY OF CHRIST'S KINGDOM

Up to this point we have discussed Calvin's view of Christ's kingdom as a kingdom bound up in history, as a product of God's covenant history with the Church. Thus, this kingdom has its beginning in history, first with God's promise to Abraham, God's anointing of David as king, and God's promise to David that the kingship that sprung from his seed would be everlasting, and then with the coming of Christ and the inauguration of this everlasting kingdom at his ascension. Christ's kingdom, then, appears to be circumscribed at its beginning by God's initiation of the covenant as a response to Adam's fall, though its duration is everlasting, through to God's final judgment of the world. But, in the course of Calvin's writings, there is a countervailing theme that, though it does not belie this earlier reading, certainly nuances it and adds layers of complexity to Calvin's understanding of Christ as Mediator. For Calvin will argue that Christ is the head of the Church and the angels not only within the covenant history, but from the very beginning; as the Eternal Son of God, he is the one by whom all things were made. Moreover, as the head of the Church from the beginning, Christ stands not only as the God by whom the Church was elect and the Mediator through whom this election was worked out, but also as the Beloved in whom we are elect, so that election is bound to Christology in its every dimension. In other words, we will find that there is nothing "before" Christ's headship over creation and the Church. He is the Mediator in all of God's relating to what is not God.

The head of the angels

Calvin in his response to Stancaro initiated his argument with the claim that we can begin to understand Christ's office as Mediator only when we first grasp that he was Mediator from the beginning of creation – that he was head over the Church and the angels, the firstborn of all creation. He goes on to explain that this headship entailed his role both as the one by whom "the angels as well as men were united to God by his grace" and as "the medium between God and creatures, so that the life which was otherwise hidden in God would flow from him."[92] In his second letter, he expands on this, explaining that from the beginning Christ was "the mode of communication from which otherwise hidden source, the grace of God flowed to men."[93] With Adam's fall, Calvin continues, Christ's mediation must also be understood to include his work as expiator, but that does not efface the original function of his office. In light of what we have seen so far in our exploration, we can organize Calvin's point under the rubric of Christ's threefold office. From the beginning, Christ, as God's eternal Son, has executed his office as king or head, whereby he serves as the fountain of God's grace and the source of unity for both humanity and the angels with God. It is only with Adam's fall that he took on an additional role as priest, to reconcile humanity to God, and that he exercised also a second aspect of his royal office, through which he conquers death and the devil and leads a dispersed and fearful humanity back to God.[94] In his letters to the Polish Brethren, then, Calvin articulates a dimension to his understanding of Christ's office as Mediator that has not been explored in detail in this book, not, however, by adding to our understanding of his mediatorial function, but by expanding the realm in which he performed this function from the beginning of the covenant history backwards to the beginning of creation.

We find in the *Institutes* an elaboration of the mediatory involvement of the Son from the beginning of God's work, as the conduit whereby God pours God's grace out upon the world, in the assertion of the Son's involvement in the creation and providential care of the world. In his argument for the full divinity of the Son before the incarnation, Calvin explains that Moses set forth the Word or Son of God as the intermediary between the Father and creation, and he adds that the author of the letter to the Hebrews also teaches that "the world was made through the Son, and that he upholds all things through his powerful Word."[95] This assertion is congruent with his claim in his commentary on John's first chapter, where he argues that Christ, as the eternal Word of the Father, is the source of life and existence for all of creation, both as he brings it into being and as he sustains it.[96] Calvin concludes that we must finally understand these original works of God as thoroughly Trinitarian, that when Jesus proclaims, "My Father and I have worked even to this day" (John 5:17), he indicates

---

[92] Tylanda, "Christ the Mediator," pp. 12–13 (*CO* 9:338).
[93] Tylanda, "Calvin's Second Reply," p. 147 (*CO* 9:350).
[94] In my next chapter I discuss the place of Christ's work as prophet within the threefold office.
[95] *Inst.* 1.xiii.7, p. 129 (*OS* 3:117).
[96] See *Comm. John* 1:4, 1.31–2 (*CO* 47:5); "Deity of Christ," p. 29 (*CO* 47:478–479).

that all of God's work must be understood as the work of the Father and the Son, with the Son serving as the intermediary.[97] In this passage in the *Institutes*, Calvin does not explicitly tie this creative work of the Son as Mediator to his royal office, but the passage, nonetheless, does undergird the argument that Calvin makes in his response to Stancaro, indicating the reality of the Son's mediatory work before the incarnation.

Calvin's commitment to this mediatory understanding of Christ's relationship to creation is brought to focus most clearly in two statements he makes about Christ's relationship to the angels as their head. The angels whom Christ unites in fellowship with God are, of course, not in need of redemption, and their community with Christ extends unbroken back to creation.[98] They, then, serve as an example and test-case of what Christ's relationship to humanity could have been like, had Adam not fallen, and what it can be like, given our redemption in Christ.

In his commentary on the harmony of the Synoptic Gospels, Calvin argues that, when God calls Christ his beloved Son at the time of his baptism, God indicates not only that we, who are reconciled to God in Christ, are loved by God only as we are united to Christ, but also that the angels are loved by and united to God only in and through Christ:

[These words] imply, that the love of God rests on Christ in such a manner, as to diffuse itself from him to us all; and not to us only, but even to the angels themselves. Not that they need reconciliation, for they never were at enmity with God: but even they become perfectly united to God, only by means of their head (Eph. 1:22).[99]

Calvin is clear early on in his thinking that Christ is the Mediator through whom both human persons and angels receive the Father's love and grace as they are united to God through Christ, whether or not they are in need of reconciliation.

Finally, Calvin justifies our appropriation of this discussion under the rubric of Christ's royal office, insofar as he uses just this language of kingship to describe Christ's role over creation before Adam's fall in his debate with Osiander in the *Institutes*. Osiander had argued that Christ was predestined to become incarnate whether or not Adam fell since, as the image of God, he was the model by which all humanity was created. Calvin rejects this argument since Scripture was clear (he felt) that Christ became incarnate

---

[97] *Inst.* I.xiii.7, p. 130 (*OS* 3:118).
[98] The passages that I will explore below stand at some tension with passages from Calvin's sermons which argue for a need, even in unfallen angels, for reconciliation through Christ. See Schreiner, *The Theater of His Glory*, pp. 50–51.
[99] *Comm. Matt.* 3:17, 1.206 (*CO* 45:127). See also *Comm. Matt.* 17:5, 11.314 (*CO* 45:488).

only to redeem a fallen humanity. In response to Osiander's contention that, without the incarnation, Christ could never have served as the Church's head, Calvin points out that he serves as head over the angels, even though he never took on angelic nature. So, too, could he have served as head of the Church simply as the Son of God:

> Osiander shows the same ignorance in saying that if Christ had not been man, men would have been without him as their king. As if the Kingdom of God could not stand had the eternal Son of God – though not endued with human flesh – gathered together angels and men into the fellowship of his heavenly glory and life, and himself held the primacy over all . . . As the angels enjoyed his headship, why could Christ not rule over men also by his divine power, quicken and nourish them like his own body by the secret power of his Spirit until, gathered up into heaven, they might enjoy the same life as the angels.[100]

In his description of Christ's original role in relation to both angels and humanity, Calvin does not resort to language foreign to his description of Christ's royal redemptive office. Instead, he takes up the same understanding of Christ as the king who unites his charges and bestows upon them God's Spirit, so that his mediatory work in creation is not separate from or secondary to his work as Redeemer, but is simply the original instantiation of that work, which was maintained even as his mediatorial role expanded with Adam's fall.[101]

I noted near the beginning of this chapter that Christ's office as king is routinely neglected by commentators on Calvin's thought. The bulk of this chapter has been devoted to developing a more weighty understanding of Calvin's handling of Christ's royal office, underlining Christ's role as the conqueror of death and the agent of our unity with God, but now I can extend this claim even further and argue that Christ as king exercises, perhaps, his primary function as Mediator, the function of uniting humanity and the angels to the Father while serving as a conduit of God's grace. Calvin has identified Christ's priestly office as his primary office in some places, and his justification for this is that without Christ's expiatory sacrifice, a fallen humanity would have been entirely cut off from the blessings which Christ, as king, could have bestowed. That point is well taken. But, seen from another perspective, we must note that, for Calvin, Christ's role as Mediator from the beginning consisted of his work as king and head of the Church, while the need for his sacerdotal work only arose with Adam's fall; and that the primary purpose of the priestly office is to clear the way for God's covenant with God's Church, while in his royal office that covenant

---

[100] *Inst.* II.xii.7, p. 473 (*OS* 3:446).   [101] See Willis, *Catholic Christology*, p. 7.

is consummated as we are united to God and established in righteousness by Christ. Thus, it would seem reasonable to claim a certain primacy for Christ's work as king in Calvin's thought, even though, admittedly, Calvin never explicitly gives it this primacy. This claim receives even more justification if we now extend our investigation a bit farther and examine what Calvin will say of Christ's role in one particular work that encompasses God's creation of and history with the world, the work of election.

Election in Christ

It seems that no account of Calvin's theology could be considered complete until it dealt with his understanding of election, a touchstone of his thinking; and more to our point, it has been more clearly recognized in the last sixty years that Calvin's Christology is intimately related to his doctrine of election, that the two, in fact, are intricately intertwined. Paul Jacobs made this point most forcefully, and the profound influence of his work is reflected both in Wendel's discussion of predestination and in Richard Muller's discussion of Calvin in his book on Christology and the doctrine of election.[102]

Reflection on the relation of Christology and election in Wendel and Muller revolves largely around two points, summarized in this statement by Wendel:

As we have already noted with regard to the relations between redemption and predestination, for Calvin the latter was founded upon Jesus Christ. As it is in him that the promises of salvation find their guarantee, so it is in him that election is sealed. Doubly so, seeing that Christ took part in the decree of election in his capacity as second Person of the Holy Trinity, and that he is also the artisan of this election in his capacity as Mediator.[103]

Christ for Calvin is both the author and the artisan of our election into his kingdom, choosing us in communion with the Father and the Spirit and then working out our salvation in his office as Mediator.

Christ is the artisan of predestination insofar as he in his activity as Mediator – that is, his life, death, and resurrection – accomplishes and manifests the grace of God to God's chosen, decreed from eternity. Muller identifies the doctrine of election as the "causal focus" in Calvin's exposition of our salvation in Christ, and, thus, we can understand Christ's threefold

---

[102] See Paul Jacobs, *Prädestination und Verantwortlichkeit bei Calvin*, Darmstadt: Wissenschaftliche Buchgesellschaft, 1968; Wendel, *Calvin*, pp. 263ff.; Muller, *Christ and the Decree*, pp. 17ff.
[103] Wendel, *Calvin*, p. 274.

redemptive work only in light of this focus.[104] In his discussion of the common substance shared by the two dispensations of God's covenant with the Church (*Inst.* II.x.2), Calvin begins with God's mercy, whence God's gracious call proceeds, and then turns to Christ, the Mediator, in whom that call is effected. Moreover, as Muller points out, Calvin introduces his first specific discussion of Christ as Mediator (in *Inst.* II.xii.1) by tying the necessity of his work to God's eternal decree.[105] We understand Christ's work as Mediator only when we grasp from the outset that this work is conditioned by and revelatory of God's mercy for God's chosen from eternity. Conversely, we must also say that we know of our election only in Christ, through his work as Mediator. We both know of God's gracious choice through Christ's manifestation of that choice in his redemptive activity, and we know that we, in fact, are God's chosen, the elect, as we find ourselves engrafted into Christ. As Jacobs explains, God's eternal decree for our salvation and Christ's realization of that decree are two sides of the same coin – each is rightly grasped only in its relation to the other.[106]

Calvin, though, will say more of the relation between Christ's historical work and God's eternal decree, for not only is Christ the vehicle by which this decree is carried out and made manifest, but he also is the chief example of predestination within the covenant history. To make this point, Calvin takes up Augustine's argument that Christ's human nature was assumed by the divine Word not on the basis of any merit, but purely out of the free, elective grace of God. Calvin writes: "Augustine wisely notes this: namely, that we have in the very head of the church the clearest mirror of free election that we who are among the members may not be troubled about it; and that he was not made Son of God by righteous living but was freely given such honor so that he might afterward share his gifts with others."[107] If election is the alternative to merit, then we must understand that even Christ was elect and did not merit his role as Mediator, by which he shared this elective grace with the chosen. Moreover, as Muller helpfully points out, Calvin follows the example of Bonaventure and Scotus before him and understands Christ's predestination to his office as Mediator not simply in relation to his human nature *in abstractio*, but to his person in its wholeness.[108] Christ was chosen Mediator as the God–man. The foundation of the accomplishment of God's elective grace in the chosen is God's election of Christ in both his divinity and his humanity to be the medium through which God's grace would flow to the Church. Such a

---

[104] Muller, *Christ and the Decree*, p. 23.   [105] Ibid., p. 28.   [106] Jacobs, *Prädestination*, p. 73.
[107] *Inst.* III.xxii.1, p. 933 (*OS* 4:380).   [108] Muller, *Christ and the Decree*, p. 37.

view involves the subordination of the Son to the eternal decree – it is the Son who has assumed human nature, who is chosen by God – and this subordination is integral to his kenosis in his incarnation.

This raises the question, though, of whether for Calvin Christ is finally subordinate to God's decree, merely serving as the means to the end of God's election established in eternity apart from him, or whether Christ stands with or before the decree, so that the decree in some sense depends upon him as much as it serves as the causal explanation for his office. Muller responds at this point, drawing on Jacobs, that we must grasp that Calvin sets Christ forth not only as the agent of the decree, but also as its Author.[109] For not only has Calvin told us that any reference to the activity of God presumes the unitive action of the undivided Trinity – so that to say that we are predestined by God is to say that we are chosen by Father, Son, and Holy Spirit – but he also specifically identifies Christ as the Author of election along with the Father. Calvin writes: "Meanwhile, although Christ interposes himself as Mediator, he claims for himself, in common with the Father, the right to choose";[110] and, later: "Christ makes himself the Author of election."[111] In this light, we see that Christ, as the eternal Son, stands before the decree and co-determines it with the Father and the Spirit, just as much as he is subordinated to the decree in his office as Mediator. Muller, then, reprises the two relations of Christ to the decree that we found in Wendel: "The Son as God stands behind the decree while the Son as Mediator is the executor of the decree."[112] For Muller this dual relationship is a reflection of the *extra-calvinisticum*, reflecting his dual roles as the eternal Son and as the incarnate Christ.

But is this recourse to the role of the Son with the Father and the Spirit in the decision of election an adequate response to the concern voiced in our previous question? Have we yet answered whether, for Calvin, Christology is finally subordinated to election or not, and if we have, what is the answer? For it seems fair to argue that, for Calvin, Christology concerns principally Christ's role as Mediator; indeed, that is the thesis that has guided all our efforts. That is not to say that it concerns only Christ's work in the incarnation, for as we have seen, he is active as Mediator not only through the covenant history, but also at creation as God's eternal Son. Thus, to confine Calvin's Christology to Christ's work as Mediator is not to narrowly define it, but it would seem to exclude his work as the Author of election; for in his role as Author of election, he stands not between God and humanity,

---

[109] Ibid., pp. 35–38. See Jacobs, *Prädestination*, pp. 74ff. for a far more complete discussion.
[110] *Inst.* III.xxii.7, p. 940 (*OS* 4:387).   [111] Ibid., p. 941 (*OS* 4:387).
[112] Muller, *Christ and the Decree*, pp. 37–38.

but on the side of the Electing God, over against the elect. In the above quotation, for example, Calvin himself distinguishes these two functions, speaking on the one hand of Christ interposing himself as Mediator between humanity and the Father, and on the other of his claim of the right to choose along with the Father. If we accept this distinction, then we are still left with a mediatorial Christology that finally serves a purely functional purpose in subordination to God's eternal election, even if that election is determined by the undivided Trinity. Election, then, and not Christ's mediation, would seem to stand as the prime instantiation of God's grace toward humanity, even though such election is only complete as it is enacted by Christ. This is not, however, a conclusion that Calvin would be satisfied with, I believe, and so he will have more to say on this matter.

When Muller develops his argument about Christ's role as Author of election in response to the question of Calvin's subordination of Christology to the decree, he takes his point to be a proper summary of Jacobs' claim that, for Calvin, "Christ is election itself."[113] Jacobs makes this statement in the context of a discussion of two of Calvin's sermons in which Calvin describes Christ not as the Author of election, but as "le vray registre," the book of life into which God has written the chosen.[114] That is, we are elected in Christ, even before we come to the history of salvation in which that election is worked out, and this is why Christ can be called "election itself." He not only mediates the salvation that flows from our election; he mediates this election in the first place.

Jacobs's point is grounded most clearly in the *Institutes*. Calvin, commenting upon Paul's statement in Ephesians that "[God] chose us in [Christ] before the foundation of the world" (Eph. 1:4), writes: "it is just as if he said: since among all the offspring of Adam, the Heavenly Father found nothing worthy of his election, he turned his eyes upon his Anointed, to choose from that body as members those whom he was to take into the fellowship of life."[115] For Calvin, it is not that we are chosen by God and, on the basis of that choice, engrafted into Christ's body; we are too lowly, even in an unfallen state, to merit God's favor. Rather, God looked upon our head, and predestined the chosen to life only as they were members of Christ. Christ is election itself, then, insofar as he is the head of the body. We are chosen by God only in and through him. This is just another way of making the point of the previous section, that it is only in Christ that both humanity and the angels are loved by God. Christ mediates God's love and

---

[113] Jacobs, *Prädestination*, p. 77. See Muller, *Christ and the Decree*, pp. 35–36.
[114] Jacobs, *Prädestination*, p. 76, from Sermon on Eph. 1:3ff. (*CO* 51:268–269).
[115] *Inst.* III.xxii.1, p. 933 (*OS* 4:381).

eternally gracious choice from the very beginning. Thus, we cannot finally subordinate Christology to election. Christ's work as Mediator begins with our very election, and the history of his mediation, insofar as it is tied to our election, is, thus, founded on this primal mediatory work. This is the point made earlier in this chapter. We must understand God's love for us in Christ in two ways. On the one hand, in the history of the covenant, he enacts and manifests that love in his threefold office of prophet, priest, and king; but, on the other hand, we are loved by God in Christ, our head, from eternity in a manner that we cannot understand, and this love is the foundation of the covenant history.[116]

Thus, finally, if we are to take up Jacobs' notion of the Trinitarian foundation of Calvin's doctrine of election, we can see it in its relation to the undivided work of the three Trinitarian persons in the Authorship of election; but Calvin also depicts this divine activity in terms of the Father's election of the Church in the Son, who is his Anointed. In this second sense, we see that the Son mediates between the Father and his chosen from the very beginning, and so we must speak of the subordination of the Son to the Father even here. The kenosis of the Son begins, for Calvin, not with his incarnation, but with the initiation of God's economy for the creation and salvation of the world. We are created in the Son. We are loved in the Son. We are chosen in the Son. Finally, we are redeemed in the Son. He is our head and king from before the foundation of the world, and all of God's activity toward us can be understood in relation to this headship.

CHRISTOLOGY IN THE *INSTITUTES*

I must, however, qualify this last statement and note that, although these doctrines can be understood and exposited Christologically for Calvin, this does not mean that they all must be thus exposited. For example, in the *Institutes*, Calvin clearly develops his doctrines of creation and providence with little explicit Christological reference. Moreover, in his development of his doctrine of predestination, although there is a Christological aspect to this doctrine, it certainly should not be argued that Christology dominates Calvin's discussion. In making these connections between Calvin's

---

[116] There is an obvious circularity to Calvin's position. He says both that we are engrafted into Christ's body on the basis of our eternal election and that we are elect by God insofar as we are found to be members of Christ's body. This circularity derives, in part, from Calvin's hesitation to speculate extensively into matters beyond our comprehension, and so he relies on Scripture's witness to both of these claims. There is, as well, a certain Christocentrism in this circularity, evident in the twofold testimony of Scripture, understanding election primarily in its relationship to Christ – how we are engrafted into him and how we are elect in him.

Christology and the other doctrines that he develops within his theology, I need to be clear that, in the first place, this book is focused on Calvin's Christology, and not on his overall theology, so that when I discuss the relationship between Christology and the doctrine of Creation, for example, I do so not to argue that Calvin's doctrine of Creation is finally Christological, but to indicate that Calvin's Christology, in one of its dimensions, involves his understanding of creation.

I also hope to suggest an outline of the relationship between Calvin's Christology and his overall theology, as it is captured in the *Institutes*. The disconnection between the Christological dimension of Calvin's doctrines of creation and providence and his non-Christological development of these doctrines within the *Institutes* provides an opportunity to explore this relationship in some of its lineaments, in some ways anticipating arguments in the following chapters. What we see in this disconnection, first of all, is the manner in which Calvin's theology, as it is developed in the *Institutes*, is not systematically Christological. In other words, Calvin does not begin the *Institutes* with the axiom of Christ's mediatorial role in all of God's work – an axiom which I do believe that he holds – and then construct a theology on the basis of this axiom, spinning out the doctrinal implications that it entails. Rather, Calvin organizes the *Institutes* largely around the narrative of Scripture, so that, just as Scripture describes God's creation and providential care of the world (chiefly in Genesis 1 and 2) as the work of "God," so, too, does Calvin describe this work as "God's." He does, however, inform us that when we read "God," we must understand God as Trinity, so that this work proceeds from the Father through the mediation of the Son. Again, Calvin's *Institutes* are not systematically Christological, however significant Christology may be within his theology, overall.

Second, however, we must note that his theology is Christologically saturated – that he does find a place for the mediatorial work of the Son in every aspect of his theology, not only throughout his doctrine of redemption, but also in his doctrines of creation, providence, and Scripture, whether or not he chooses to explore this work of the Son in his development of any particular doctrine. In other words, although he does not develop his doctrine of creation Christologically, he would surely reject any notion of creation that systematically excluded the mediatorial work of the Son from this divine endeavor. This means that we cannot place Calvin's doctrine of Creation, and the knowledge of God that can be derived therefrom, alongside his Christology as a non-Christological alternative to the knowledge of God that we have in Christ. For Calvin creation is the work of the one Mediator between God and humanity, the Son of God who took on flesh and revealed

God ever more clearly in Jesus. Calvin does not develop his doctrine of creation Christologically, but that does not mean that it is a non-Christological doctrine.

Finally, I would argue that Calvin does not develop his doctrines of creation and providence Christologically because of the specific nature of the Christocentric focus of the *Institutes* that I will explain in the next chapter – that Calvin in the *Institutes* intends to direct his readers to find God and their salvation in Christ, that is, in his history as the incarnate one who was crucified, resurrected, and ascended into heaven. This is the historical focus of Calvin's Christology that I have returned to throughout this book. To develop his doctrines of creation and providence Christologically, however, would be to divert his readers from this focus on Christ's Gospel history and would suggest that we can find Christ, and thus God, equally well in creation. That is not a path that Calvin wishes to take. In the *Institutes*, Calvin introduces creation as an avenue to the knowledge of God, not to embrace this avenue, but to indicate how, through sin, we have blockaded it, necessitating the coming of Christ as Mediator. Again, Calvin explores the knowledge of God that can be had through God's creation not to provide an alternative source of revelation, not even Christological revelation, alongside the knowledge revealed in Christ and his history, but to convict us of the seriousness of our sin, whereby we have cut ourselves off from this lesser knowledge of God, driving us to Christ as he is presented in the Gospel, for there we find God as God is fully with us in Christ. I return to this last point in my discussion of the *extra-calvinisticum* in chapter 6.

CHAPTER 5

Christ as prophet

We saw in chapter 2 that Calvin understood the office of the prophets to revolve around their roles as interpreters of the Law, that consists of both the doctrine of life and the covenant of grace.[1] Calvin describes Christ's role in the Gospels as prophet or teacher of the Church along these same lines. In his doctrine Christ taught both the principles of a pious life and the Gospel of the salvation that he would accomplish, and thereby he established God's truth in the midst of God's Church. Calvin calls Christ God's "ambassador and interpreter,"[2] for he would make God's ways plain to God's chosen, illuminating both God's gracious initiative in himself toward God's Church and God's requirements of the Church in response. As a considerable amount of all four Gospels consists of Christ's teaching, there is no shortage of material from which Calvin could work to develop his understanding of this office. But ultimately, his thinking on this topic can be summarized largely under the rubrics drawn from Calvin's understanding of the Old Testament prophets – that Christ's teaching revolves around his exposition and proclamation of the doctrine of life and covenant of grace, and that this office is subordinated by Calvin to Christ's royal and sacerdotal roles.

The first half of this chapter will take up Calvin's exposition of this office, but, in the course of our discussion, we will find that Calvin understands all teachers in the Church to have a place in Christ's teaching office, and Calvin himself would be included among these teachers. Thus, in the second half of this chapter, we will look at the general shape of Calvin's teaching in the *Institutes* to measure it against the standard he offers for all the Church's teachers – that they, like Paul, know nothing but Christ, and him crucified. This second discussion will open up the question not only of the Christocentric form and content of the *Institutes*, but also of Calvin's understanding of God's revelation of Godself as it is centered in Christ.

---

[1] See above, p. 66f.   [2] *Comm. John* 3:32, 1.137 (*CO* 47.73).

CHRIST'S PROPHETIC OFFICE IN THE GOSPEL COMMENTARIES

Interpreter of the Law

Although Christ's teaching can be found scattered throughout the Gospels, Calvin argues that a useful summary of his doctrine is located in Matthew's sermon on the mount and the related sermon on the plain in Luke's Gospel. In these sermons we find a compendium of Christ's exposition of the "doctrine of life," which Calvin characterizes quite simply as his explanation and clarification of the Law given by Moses. Christ says that he has come to fulfill the Law, not abolish it, and Calvin takes this to mean that Christ quickens the Law with his Spirit so that it might not remain merely a dead letter with no power in the hearts of its hearers. Christ would not change the Law, since, for Calvin, "[the Law] is the eternal rule of a devout and holy life, and must, therefore, be as unchangeable, as the justice of God, which it embraced, is constant and uniform."[3] Later, he writes: "That the doctrine of the law not only commences, but brings to perfection a holy life may be inferred from a single fact, that it requires a perfect love of God and of our neighbor (Deut. 6:5, Lev. 19:18)."[4] Thus, Christ does not in any way correct the Law, but is its "faithful expounder, that we may know what is the nature of the law, what is its object, and what is its extent."[5]

Within Christ's expansive interpretation of Moses' Law in the two sermons, Calvin highlights one basic thrust of Christ's teaching: that true happiness is not to be found in the things of this world, but in God's heavenly kingdom. This notion is not novel with Christ; Calvin is clear elsewhere that the Church of the Old Testament was led to place their faith in heavenly blessings, not earthly ones. But this teaching is, nonetheless, significant for Calvin within the context of the Gospels, inasmuch as through it Christ begins to lay the groundwork necessary to prepare his followers to bear the cross, whereby we are conformed to the example that Christ has set for us (a central theme of the Christian life, as Calvin explains it in the *Institutes* III.viii). Christ in his teaching, then, leads the Church into an imitation of him as its Head. It is this teaching that makes such imitation possible. "The only consolation," Calvin writes, "which mitigates and even sweetens the bitterness of the cross and of all afflictions, is the conviction that we are happy in the midst of miseries: for our patience is blessed by

---

[3] *Comm. Matt.* 5:17, 1.277 (*CO* 45.171).   [4] *Comm. Matt.* 5:21, 1.283 (*CO* 45.174).
[5] Ibid., 1.283–284 (*CO* 45.175).

the Lord."[6] We are willing to bear our cross, following in Christ's footsteps, only because Christ has taught us the benefits of this course of life.

Preacher of the Gospel

Insofar, then, as Christ explains and enlivens the Law for his disciples, he fulfills one aspect of his prophetic office, leading the Church more deeply into the doctrine of life; but, within the context of Calvin's broader Christological project, the more significant aspect of Christ's teaching office is his testimony to that covenant of grace that he fulfills through his work as priest and as Head of the Church. When Calvin discusses the distinctions between the Synoptic Gospels and John, he observes that John's Gospel contained far more of Christ's teaching than do the Synoptics. At first glance, Calvin's vision on this point appears a little distorted. Given the large number of parables, the sermons on the mount and the plain, and numerous other discourses of Christ in all three Synoptics, it would seem that they could equally be said to devote extended space to Christ's teaching, especially if one allowed for the cumulative effect of the teaching in all three. However, when Calvin distinguishes John's Gospel for the teaching that it contains, he focuses not on Jesus' teaching in general, but on his teaching specifically about his office toward us, that in him God manifests God's love and God's power to save. "John dwells more largely," Calvin writes, "on the doctrine by which the office of Christ, together with the power of his death and resurrection is unfolded."[7] And within John's text, it is Christ in his role as teacher who sets this doctrine forth. Calvin, then, singles John's Gospel out not simply for the preponderance of teaching found therein, but for John's presentation of Christ's concentrated exposition of the Gospel, of the meaning and significance of his gracious mission into the world to renew God's covenant. This concentration stands in contrast to so much of the teaching of Christ in the Synoptics, which is oriented more around the doctrine of life. The teaching of Christ that interests Calvin in John's Gospel (which seems to make it, therefore, the teaching that most interests Calvin overall) is Christ's teaching about himself insofar as he is the fulfillment of God's covenant of grace, insofar, that is, as he reconciles and reunites us to God as our priest and our Head.

This activity of Christ's, teaching the Gospel, is important for Calvin, because through it we come to enjoy the benefits that Christ would bestow

---

[6] *Comm. Matt.* 5:2, 1.260 (*CO* 45.161).   [7] *Comm. John, Arg.*, 1.21 (*CO* 47.VII).

upon us in his role as priest and Head. Through Christ's teaching, in other words, we gain access to the salvation he won for us in his death and resurrection. Calvin makes this point in his comments on John 8:31ff. ("Jesus said, 'If you continue in my word . . . you shall know the truth, and the truth shall make you free' "). Christ, Calvin explains, claims for the Gospel that he preaches title to God's truth, and the fruit of this truth is our freedom. The Gospel, that is, produces freedom in God's chosen: "All men feel and acknowledge that slavery is a very wretched state; and since the Gospel delivers us from it, it follows that we derive from the Gospel the treasure of a blessed life."[8] Now, what does Calvin mean when he says that the Gospel delivers us from slavery and into freedom?

On the one hand, he seems to be referring to what Christ accomplishes through his royal and sacerdotal offices. We are free insofar as Christ has delivered us from Satan, sin, and death, insofar as we are adopted children of God through him, insofar as he is our deliverer. The Gospel, in the first place, is the history of what Christ has done, whereby we have been restored to covenant relationship with God. But Calvin also, and perhaps more pointedly, means by "Gospel" the doctrine taught by Christ that explains this history. We need knowledge of the Gospel, Calvin tells us. We must understand whereby we are delivered so that we can place our faith in this deliverance. The Gospel must not only be enacted by Christ, but must also be taught by him so that we can know to entrust ourselves to him. We are made free by the Gospel insofar as through its teaching – its presentation of Christ's history and its explanation of what that history means for us – we believe in Christ and through this belief are ingrafted into his body and become his members. Only thus are we regenerated by the Spirit and made free.[9] Christ, through his office as teacher of the Gospel, leads us to place our faith in his work as priest and as head of the Church – as teacher he explains in detail the love and power of God to save that he has manifested in those offices – and the fruit of this faith is that we are renewed by the Spirit so that we can obey God's Law and follow the doctrine of life that Christ expounds.

Christ's office as prophet or teacher, thus, stands distinct from, but in a complementary relationship to, his offices as priest and as Head of the Church. Calvin highlights this distinction in his comments on the application of Isaiah's words to Jesus ("The Spirit of the Lord is upon me . . . he hath sent me to preach the gospel" [Luke 4:18]). Calvin writes:

---

[8] *Comm. John* 8:32, 1.342 (*CO* 47.202).   [9] See *Comm. John* 8:32–36, 1.342–345 (*CO* 47.201–204).

It is certain that what is here related belongs properly to Christ alone, for two reasons: first, because he alone was endued with the fullness of the Spirit, to be the witness and ambassador of our reconciliation to God (and, for this reason, Paul assigns peculiarly to him what belongs to all ministers of the Gospel, namely, that he "came and preached peace to them which were afar off and to them that were nigh"); secondly, because he alone, by the power of his Spirit, performs and grants all the benefits that are here promised.[10]

Christ as priest and Head performs or accomplishes God's covenant whereby we are forgiven and blessed, and he has manifested God's love therein, while Christ as teacher bears witness to and explains this accomplishment and this love and thereby leads us into faith in it.[11] This latter task is no less central to the renewal of the covenant relationship, but it rests on the former. On the one hand, Christ can only preach reconciliation as he first reconciles the Church to God, but, on the other hand, that reconciliation is only effective as he gathers us into his body; and though our unity in Christ is accomplished as he is our Head, we are gathered to him as he is our teacher, as he preaches peace to those who are far off and those who are near.

Shepherd among shepherds

A corollary distinction between Christ's offices as priest and Head and his office as teacher is that ministers in the Church have been called by God to continue in Christ's teaching office since the Gospel will always need to be proclaimed and truthfully explained in order that believers might be drawn to Christ in faith, while Christ, alone, serves as priest and head of the Church. Calvin's inclination to understand Christ's sharing of his teaching office with his ministers in the Church is most strikingly revealed in his commentary on John 10, the Good Shepherd passage, where Jesus contrasts his faithful care for his flock with the wanton treatment that they receive from the hirelings, that is, those appointed by God who neglect their duty. Calvin defines this role of "shepherding" the Church largely in terms of the teaching office – the hirelings are those who teach false doctrine, while the good shepherds are those who lead us straight to Christ since he is "the principal point of all spiritual doctrine, on which souls are fed."[12] Most

---

[10] *Comm. Luke* 4:17, 1.228 (*CO* 45.141).
[11] As priest and king, Christ manifests God's love as he enacts it; but we, being slow students, would not grasp the magnitude or significance of this love unless Christ, as teacher, led us through a detailed exposition of its many dimensions.
[12] *Comm John* 10:7, 1.397 (*CO* 47.238).

typically, the Good Shepherd pericope has been read with reference to the distinction between Jesus' care of the Church and that of the bad priests and pharisees in Jesus' time, but Calvin reads it more broadly and includes with Christ all faithful teachers, down to the present day, among those who are good shepherds. As the sheep are called to heed the Good Shepherd, so Calvin tells the faithful that they are to listen to "Christ or his instructor"; when it is said that the sheep know the shepherd's voice, Calvin claims that Christ speaks here of all shepherds, that "God should be heard speaking by them."[13] The ministers of the Church teach the Gospel to the faithful with Christ. They share in his teaching office.

But they share only in his teaching office. Later in the passage Christ explains that, though the thieves have come to destroy the sheep: "I am come that they may have life" (John 10:10). As Calvin now must address the sense in which Christ is the Good Shepherd who gives life, he contrasts Christ's role as both teacher and Head of the Church with the minister's role of mere teacher:

Indeed, there is no other to whom this honor and title [of shepherd] strictly belongs; for, as to all the faithful *shepherds* of the Church, it is he who raises them up, endows them with the necessary qualifications, governs them by his Spirit, and works by them; and therefore, they do not prevent him from being the only Governor of his Church, or from holding the distinction of being the only *Shepherd* . . . They are masters and teachers in such a manner as not to interfere with his authority as a Master.[14]

Ministers are teachers in the Church, but Christ alone is Governor; he alone calls them and equips them with the necessary gifts of the Spirit. Likewise, when Christ states that the Good Shepherd lays down his life for the sheep (John 10:11), Calvin argues that many in the Church have been good shepherds in this sense, dying martyrs' deaths for the good of their flock. But their deaths must be distinguished from Christ's: "He laid down his life as the price of satisfaction, shed his blood to cleanse our souls, offered his body as a propitiatory sacrifice, to reconcile the Father to us. Nothing of all this can exist in ministers of the Gospel, all of whom need to be cleansed."[15] Christ shares his role as teacher of the Gospel, by which the Church is directed to Christ's saving work, but Christ alone accomplishes the Gospel in which believers are saved.

This, then, is the shape of Christ's teaching office that emerges from Calvin's reading of the Gospel accounts of Christ's history. We find this

---

[13] *Comm. John* 10:4, 1.396 (*CO* 47.237); see also *Comm John* 10:1, 1.395 (*CO* 47.236).
[14] *Comm. John* 10:10, 1.401–402 (*CO* 47.240).   [15] *Comm. John* 10:11, 1.403–404 (*CO* 47.242).

same general pattern in Calvin's teaching in the *Institutes*, although Calvin will place the emphases in different places in this more dogmatic work. If we now turn to this latter source, we can not only discern these peculiar accents, but we can also add depth and nuance to our understanding of this office within Calvin's Christological thinking through an engagement of J. F. Jansen's thorough but somewhat misdirected explication of the same.

CHRIST'S PROPHETIC OFFICE IN THE *INSTITUTES*

In his chapter in the *Institutes* on Christ's threefold office (II.xv), Calvin moves quickly, almost seamlessly, from his introduction of the chapter to a discussion of Christ's office as prophet to the Church. Calvin's explication of this office revolves around three central points. First, he contends that an expectation of a Messianic teacher who would bring to God's people a perfect doctrine suffuses the Old Testament witness to God's covenant history. God had always provided God's people with an unbroken line of prophets, Calvin reminds us, so that they would never be without sufficient teaching about God's commandments and God's promise of salvation; but a primary task of these prophets was to direct the people to the coming Messiah, who would be a "messenger or interpreter of great counsel."[16] Although Israel always had prophets among them, they were led to hope for a Messianic prophet, for the Christ. Second, he argues that implicit in this title, "Christ" or "Messiah" or "Anointed," is a reference to the prophetic as well as the royal and priestly offices; as Isaiah writes: "The spirit of the Lord Jehovah is upon me, because Jehovah has anointed me to preach to the humble" (Isa. 61:1–2). "We see," Calvin continues, "that he was anointed by the Spirit to be herald and witness of the Father's grace."[17] The anointing of God's Mediator was an anointing to be a prophet as much as to be a priest or king. Finally, Calvin notes that Christ receives this prophetic anointing not only for the sake of his own teaching ministry, but also as the Head of all God's appointed prophets and teachers, "that the power of the Spirit might be present in the continuing preaching of the Gospel."[18] But that is not to say that those who are called to be teachers after Christ should add to his teaching. Because Christ has brought a perfect and complete doctrine, any supplement to this doctrine would detract not only from Christ's authority, but from Christ himself. He is

[16] *Inst.* II.xv.1, p. 495 (*OS* 3:472). Calvin here conflates Isa. 9:6 with Isa. 28:29 and Jer. 32:19.
[17] *Inst.* II.xv.2, p. 496 (*OS* 3:473).   [18] Ibid.

this perfect Gospel teaching – as Paul says, "I decided to know nothing precious . . . except Jesus Christ and him crucified" (1 Cor. 2:2) – thus, "it is not lawful to go beyond the simplicity of this Gospel."[19] Calvin concludes, "[T]he prophetic dignity in Christ leads us to know that in the sum of doctrine as he has given it to us all parts of perfect wisdom are contained."[20]

Calvin's discussion of this office is decidedly brief, and it is seldom echoed elsewhere in the Christological sections of the *Institutes*. For example, Calvin mentions Christ's work as teacher neither in his originating discussion of the necessity of the God–human (II.xii) nor in his exposition of the Creed (II.xvi). We are, thus, again presented with the question of the relation of this office to the previous two. J. F. Jansen explores this question within the context of the *Institutes*, and he concludes that Calvin conceived of Christ's salvific work originally in terms of his twofold office of priest and king, that the inclusion of the prophetic office alongside these other two was a late addition, and that Calvin never successfully integrated this third office into his overall Christological schema.[21] Jansen outlines the development of Calvin's doctrine of Christ's office, showing that in the early editions of the *Institutes* and in various catechisms Calvin spoke only of Christ's twofold office of priest and king; it is only with the 1545 edition of the *Institutes* and a catechism from this same time that he incorporates Christ's prophetic office into his formulation of this doctrine.

Jansen argues that this shift is precipitated neither by outside sources – there are witnesses from within the tradition that attest to both the twofold and the threefold office – nor by exegetical concerns – throughout his commentaries Calvin continues to discuss Christ's redemptive work only in terms of his priesthood and his kingship, even after he has switched to the threefold formula in his more dogmatic works. Therefore, Jansen offers two separate reasons for Calvin's adoption of this new formula. On the one hand, Jansen feels that Calvin sought a manner to dogmatically express Christ's revelatory role within God's salvific economy alongside his redemptive work as king and priest, leading him to take up the prophetic office as an expression of this role. On the other hand, Jansen contends, Calvin needed a means to validate the ministerial order of the Reformed movement; by emphasizing both Christ's prophetic or teaching office and its relation to the teaching office within the Church, Calvin had a bulwark from which he could defend the Reformed order from the Anabaptists on the one side, who rejected all orders, and from Rome on the other, who

---

[19] Ibid. [20] Ibid.
[21] J. F. Jansen, *Calvin's Doctrine of the Work of Christ* (London: James Clark & Co., 1956), pp. 39–59.

rejected the Reformed order as an innovation outside of the ecclesiastical tradition.

However, Jansen continues, Calvin never successfully melds this three-fold formulation into his theology – Calvin continues in both the *Institutes* and in his commentaries to speak of the salvation accomplished in Christ in terms of his priestly and kingly work. In fact, Jansen claims, the threefold formulation betrays elements of Calvin's Christology more fundamental to his overall thought. Jansen believes that Calvin allocates the function of revelation to Christ's teaching office and that this move on Calvin's part belies his general tendency to speak of the revelatory character of Christ's work in relation to his redemptive work overall. Revelation "permeates" his priestly and kingly offices, Jansen will say, rather than existing alongside them,[22] insofar as Christ revealed God as he revealed God's will and love for God's chosen in his redemption of the world. Jansen thus feels that Calvin misdirects his readers when he turns them from Christ's redemptive work in his history to find revelation only in his teaching.

Likewise, Jansen argues that an essential aspect of Calvin's teaching about Christ's priestly and kingly offices is that through these offices he "gives himself to all believers."[23] For Jansen, this means that Christ became king and priest in order to make his people "kings and priests unto God"; through his work, his kingship and priesthood are poured out onto all believers so that they might share in these ministries. But, in Calvin's discussion of the prophetic office, he is clear that only a few are given the spirit of teaching to follow after Christ as leaders of the Church in this way. This violates the inclusive nature of the relation between Christ and his chosen, as Jansen understands Calvin's teaching, in his gift of his official work to them.

Jansen's work is regularly cited by Calvin scholars in their discussion of Calvin's teaching about Christ's threefold office, largely because his book has been the most complete recent treatment of this topic. But there is seldom any support for his conclusions offered in these citations. Few are willing to dismiss the threefold formulation that Jansen attacks. In light of the understanding of Calvin's Christology that I have developed thus far, however, I think we can cultivate a more nuanced view of both Jansen's work and Calvin's understanding of Christ's prophetic office if we pursue Jansen's claims in some detail. His observations about the nature of Christ's revelation, the incongruence of Calvin's treatment of Christ's priestly and kingly offices with relation to his treatment of the prophetic office, and the relation of Christ's prophetic office to the ministerial order of the Church

---

[22] Jansen, *Work of Christ*, p. 58.   [23] Ibid., p. 50.

are on the mark. But Jansen never grasps what Calvin finally wanted to say about Christ's prophetic office, chiefly, that it deals more with Christ's explanation of or teaching about his salvific work, in order that we may grasp its significance, than it does with revelation as a category unto itself. Thus, Jansen ill negotiates Calvin's handling of Christ's prophetic office as it is related to his offices as priest and king, to his understanding of revelation, and to the teaching office within the Church. The task for this section, then, will be to flesh out these three relations so that we might understand not only how this office fits into Calvin's Christology, but also how it shapes that Christology and its place within Calvin's overall theology, given that Calvin, as a teacher in the Church, shares this ministry with Christ.

The messianic significance of perfect doctrine

Jansen centers his thesis on his contention that Christ's prophetic office is not for Calvin a Messianic office, whatever else Calvin will say about it. Jansen complains, most literally, that the office of prophet does not involve an anointing as does the office of priest or king.[24] Jansen's point is that there is essentially no example of a prophet's anointing with oil within either the Old or New Testament, but he evidently chooses to ignore Calvin's interpretation in the *Institutes* and in his commentaries on Isaiah and Luke of the Messianic passage from Isaiah 61 ("The Spirit of the Lord is upon me because the Lord has anointed me to preach to the humble"). Calvin understands this passage to refer to just such a Messianic anointing of God's chosen prophet. Christ's prophetic office is founded upon this passage and this anointing for Calvin, as are the calls of all God's prophets and teachers.

Jansen's concern, more broadly, is that there is for Calvin a fundamental distinction between Christ's royal and sacerdotal work, whereby he has worked out our salvation, and his prophetic office. Jansen's conclusions on this point correspond to what we have seen in our study thus far. Consistently throughout the *Institutes* and his commentaries on the Old and New Testaments, Calvin explains the redemption enacted by Christ in terms of his kingly and priestly roles. The Church has been restored to covenant relationship with God insofar as it has been reconciled to God through Christ's work as priest and reunited to God through Christ's work as king or Head of the Church.[25]

This centrality of the royal and sacerdotal offices does not eliminate Christ's prophetic office from God's covenant history. We have equally

---

[24] Ibid., p. 74. [25] See *Comm. Ps.* 78:69–70, III.280 (*CO* 31:744–746).

seen thus far that the role of the prophets was to interpret God's Law, explaining for God's people both the doctrine of life and the covenant of grace to lead them into a deeper participation in each of these. This participation is essential to the covenant relationship. Indeed, it is, from the human side, the heart of the relationship. Thus, as we saw at the beginning of this chapter, Christ's teaching office in this sense is vital to his redemptive work, for through his perfect doctrine he makes clear for God's people the meaning and significance of his Gospel history so that they may know the salvation that he has accomplished and thereby place their faith in him. We understand Christ's prophetic office in the context of Calvin's theology, then, when we grasp both the manner in which this office is distinct from his kingship and his priesthood, and the manner in which it is related to them. Christ as king and priest reconciles the Church with God, manifesting God's love and mercy for the Church in this reconciliation; Christ as prophet opens this way of reconciliation to the Church through his explication of its sense and significance so that God's chosen might live into it.[26]

Therefore, we should accept Calvin's categorization of Christ's prophetic office with these other two as a Messianic office, for through this office Christ, as Mediator, brings God's covenant to fruition. Through his teaching Christ leads God's chosen to place their faith in God, and he guides them into full obedience to God through his clarification of the doctrine of life. It is telling that Jansen gives little space in his explication of Christ's prophetic office to Christ's role in that office as teacher of the Law. This is an indication that he misses the broader covenantal context that shapes Calvin's thinking on these matters. Within the context of the covenant history in the Old Testament, it is clear that God's prophets are as essential to the life of the people in covenant with God as are the priests and kings, for it is the prophets who call the people to obedience and hold out to them the promise of the Messiah in whom they are to place their faith and hope. God's covenant can be said to be truly and robustly established in the Church only when the Church has responded to its accomplishment with such faith and obedience. Christ, therefore, as the fulfillment of this covenant history, not only must redeem the Church from its sin and defeat its enemies; he must also offer to the Church the

---

[26] Jansen seems not to understand the significance of this connection for Calvin. He complains that elevating Christ's prophetic office to stand beside his royal and sacerdotal offices is to equate "knowledge-about-redemption with redemption, itself" (*Work of Christ*, p. 109). But that is exactly Calvin's point – an aspect of Christ's redemptive work is to bring us to full and true knowledge of that work so that we can place our faith in him.

perfect doctrine out of which its true faith and heartfelt obedience might emerge.

The ambassador of God

Given this interpretation of Christ's prophetic office, that thereby he is the Church's teacher, making plain the sense and significance of God's covenantal will to God's people, we can agree with Jansen that Christ's revelatory function should not be organized under the rubric of this office. But then we must object that Calvin never claimed it to be. For Calvin, Christ is revelatory as the image of God, insofar as we see God's love, mercy, and will for our salvation worked out in Christ's redemptive history. Christ reveals God in the whole of his work, so that it would be improper to consign this revelation to any one aspect of that work. This notion of revelation is fundamental to Calvin's Christology, and we shall explore it further in the next section of this chapter. What is important for our present discussion is that Calvin's notion of Christ's revelation is not particularly dogmatic in nature. Christ is not the image of God because he reveals to the Church true doctrine about God. This is the notion of revelation that Calvin wants to reject from the very beginning of the *Institutes*. Christ reveals God as he reveals how God is for us so that we will embrace and obey God as our loving Parent.[27] Christ does this in the first place as he has covered our sins through his sacrifice, defeated our enemies, bestowed God's grace upon us, and united us to God as our Head and king.

Christ's prophetic office, then, in relation to this revelation is not to give the revelation, but to explain it. Christ is to make plain who he is and what he has done among us so that we might see, understand, and be grasped by the love of God evident in his history. Christ is the interpreter of God's revelation. In this sense, the relationship of Christ's teaching office to his royal and sacerdotal offices is similar to the relationship between Scripture and creation that Calvin describes in the first book of the *Institutes*. There, Calvin explains that Scripture supplements God's revelation of Godself in creation as Author of the universe so that we might see and understand God as Creator in our ignorance and blindness. Calvin writes: "This, therefore, is a special gift, where God, to instruct the church, not merely uses mute teachers but also opens his own most hallowed lips."[28] Just as Scripture explains God's revelation of Godself in creation,

---

[27] Jansen, *Work of Christ*, p. 102.   [28] *Inst.* I.vi.1, p. 70 (*OS* 3:60–61).

so Christ in his teaching office has "opened his most hallowed lips" to instruct the Church concerning the mute witness of his redemptive activity toward us.

Insofar as God has first promised and then provided such an interpreter, such a conveyor of perfect doctrine without whom the Church would be blind to or ignorant of the purpose and effect of Christ's royal and sacerdotal work, Christ in his prophetic office is also a manifestation of God's love to the Church. God is merciful when God provides the Church with a true prophet as well as a true priest and king. In this sense we can say that Christ, as prophet, is not only the interpreter of revelation, but also revelation itself – even as he is revelation itself in his work as priest and king – for also in this work the Church discovers God's salvific will for it.

When Calvin is describing Christ's teaching office in his commentary on John's Gospel, he calls Christ God's "ambassador."[29] He is the one who "preaches peace to those who are far off and those who are near" (Isa. 61:1ff.; Luke 4:18ff.). Christ is the one sent by God to explain God's ways to a people far off, so that they might understand God and God's will for them and thereby come into covenant with God, even as Christ as king and priest is accomplishing that will among them. Jansen in the end acknowledges the importance of Christ's teaching office – he writes in Calvin's words, "The prophet 'is one who interprets and administers revelation,'" and thus, he explains, the prophet is one who brings a redemptive word.[30] But, insofar as the prophet's word is redemptive, he concludes, the prophet is ultimately exercising a kingly or priestly function. For Jansen, Christ's prophetic work should finally be absorbed into the work of his other two offices because there is an intimate connection between the three.

Of course, Jansen is correct that there is an intimate relationship among Christ's three offices. He is true prophet, true priest, and true king only because he is truly all three. But we must be mindful of Calvin's intentionality in defining Christ's office in threefold rather than in twofold terms. If the prophet's word is a redemptive word, as Jansen claims, then this would seem to support, not negate, Calvin's claim for the Messianic character of this office. And indeed, it would seem that Calvin elevates Christ's prophetic office alongside of his priesthood and kingship to emphasize the import of the word. It is not enough for Christ to accomplish our salvation on God's behalf; that salvation must also be proclaimed. Christ, as God's ambassador, has been charged with that proclamation. He brings his royal and sacerdotal work to fulfillment through this proclamation, and so this

---

[29] *Comm. John* 3:32, 1.137 (*CO* 47.73).   [30] Jansen, *Work of Christ*, p. 98, from *Comm. 1 Cor.* 14:6.

proclamation equally serves a Messianic role and is vital to the life of the Church.

Christ's teaching office in the Church

Indeed, Calvin underlines this significance of the prophetic office of Christ when he emphasizes its continuance in the teaching office of the Church. Through their exposition of the Gospel and their interpretation of God's Law, pastors and teachers persistently place God's grace in Christ before the eyes of the faithful and call them to live their lives in response to this grace in obedience to God. Through the continuance of Christ's prophetic office, Christ maintains a lively presence in the Church. As Calvin notes, Christ is "clothed" in his Gospel, and although he is referring here to the biblical narrative, it is clear that he would include the preaching of the Church as some of his outer garments.[31]

Jansen is critical of Calvin's linkage of Christ's office to a particular ministerial office in this way because he feels that it belies Calvin's more significant insistence on the share Christ gives to all believers in these redemptive ministries. In fact, Jansen calls this the essential meaning of Christ's redemptive offices – "[Christ] is king and priest that his people may be 'kings and priests unto God.' "[32] Jansen reminds us here that Christ, as king, has equipped his saints with all spiritual gifts so that they may fight with him under the cross throughout the course of their lives.[33] Christians share in Christ's battle with sin and the devil. Likewise, Calvin instructs his readers that they have been sanctified in Christ so that they are priests in him in order that they may "offer [themselves] and [their] all to God and freely enter the heavenly sanctuary that the sacrifices of prayers and praise that [they] bring may be acceptable and sweet-smelling before God."[34] Insofar as Jansen has recalled for us this important element in Calvin's teaching, his point is helpful.

But he is surely wrong to label this the "essential meaning" of Christ's Messianic office. Christ has taken on his threefold office in order to restore us to covenant relationship with God. He does so as priest by taking away our sin and making us worthy to stand before God. He does so as king by defeating our enemies once and for all, by bestowing upon us God's grace, and by uniting us to God. Believers clearly play no role in any of these activities except to receive the grace poured out from them by faith.

---

[31] *Inst.* III.ii.6, p. 548 (*OS* 4:13).   [32] Jansen, *Work of Christ*, p. 50.
[33] *Inst.* II.xv.4, pp. 498–499 (*OS* 3:475–476).   [34] *Inst.* II.xv.6, p. 502 (*OS* 3:481).

Christ may give us the spiritual graces to fight alongside of him, but we are soldiers under him, not kings; and we may be able to offer prayer and praise to God in God's heavenly sanctuary, but we do so only as we are sanctified by Christ, our great High Priest. Calvin's emphasis in his teaching on the redemptive office of Christ is not that we share in these offices in any significant way, but that Christ alone can serve as our priest and king, Christ alone is the Mediator between God and the Church, so that we must entrust ourselves to his gracious mediation.

The distinctive mark of Christ's prophetic office, then, is that believers do have some share in it, insofar as God has called teachers for God's Church. Calvin is able to allow for this exception precisely because the prophetic office differs in nature from the other two; Christ as priest and king accomplishes our salvation, whereas Christ as prophet interprets and proclaims this salvation. The former happened once and for all in Christ, while the latter must continually occur in the Church so that God's chosen will be repeatedly called to return to the source of their life in Christ. The participation of the Church's ministers in Christ's prophetic office does not detract from his position as the sole Mediator because they are in their doctrine to turn people to Christ; and they have been called by God because this ministry is required throughout the life of the Church.

Calvin as teacher

Finally, we must remind ourselves that Calvin, as a theologian, shares in this teaching office as well, and this will open a second front to our discussion. For, indeed, if we are to trust that Calvin is true in practice to his own theology, then we must trust that his writings, and in particular his *Institutes*, are structured by his conception of this office to which he has been called by Christ, his Head. What does this mean? Most generally, Calvin has informed us that God's teachers are to instruct the Church in the doctrine of life and the covenant of grace. That is, they are to proclaim and interpret for the chosen both God's commands, to which the faithful are to give their obedience, and God's promises to nourish the Church's faith.

In the *Institutes* Calvin completes the first of these two tasks chiefly, we should suppose, in the chapters on his general understanding of God's Law, its uses, and purposes (*Inst.* ii.vii) and on his exposition of the Ten Commandments (*Inst.* ii.viii). In the former of these chapters, he informs his readers that the Law is intended not only to convict them of their unrighteousness and to constrain lawless folk, but also, and more importantly, that it is "the best instrument for [believers] to learn more thoroughly each day the nature of the Lord's will to which they aspire, and to confirm them in the understanding of it."[35] In his exposition of the commandments, then, he pursues in detail the will of God that is expressed therein, for insofar as we keep these commandments in all of their aspects, we will "express the image of God, as it were, in [our] own lives," since God has depicted God's righteous character in them.[36] Calvin, thus, in his instruction to believers concerning God's law, has laid a groundwork for the obedience that God's righteousness requires.

We should notice that Calvin takes up this subject again, in another key, when he turns to the sanctification of the believer in Christ. In Christ, Calvin insists, believers are not only forgiven, but are also brought to a certain newness or holiness of life by faith through their repentance.[37] This repentance consists of their mortification, in which they share in Christ's death, and their vivification, in which they share in his resurrection. Calvin then devotes several chapters (*Inst.* III.vi–viii) to an exploration of the Christian life, shaped as it is by this movement, which he entitles "bearing one's cross." Beyond the particular content of any of these chapters in the *Institutes* is the movement Calvin makes within them, from a construal of Christian righteousness in terms of God's law to its construal in terms of the Christian's conformity to Christ's life. Calvin, on the one hand, takes very seriously God's revelation of God's righteous will in the Law and believes this to be a helpful and necessary guide for the Christian life. On the other hand, Calvin will not give the Law the last word on this matter, reorienting his readers, as he does, to Christ as the pattern by whom they are remolded into the image of God. We find in Calvin, ultimately, a certain Christocentrism in his treatment of this subject, and we should not be surprised that this concern shapes his teaching.

In his brief discussion of Christ's prophetic office in the *Institutes*, Calvin notes that the Church's teachers have not been authorized to imagine any new doctrine, but are to instruct believers in the "simplicity of Christ's Gospel." As Paul writes, they are to know only "Christ and him crucified." Christ stands at the center of the Church's doctrine. We found Calvin making this same point in his exposition of the Good Shepherd passage. There he contrasted the hirelings who teach false doctrine with the good shepherds or teachers who lead their flock straight to Christ, because "the principal point of all spiritual doctrine, on which souls are fed, is Christ."[38] This is what we find Calvin doing, then, in his teaching on the righteousness

---

[35] *Inst.* II.vii.12, p. 360 (*OS* 3:337).   [36] *Inst.* II.viii.51, p. 415 (*OS* 3:390).
[37] See *Inst.* III.iii.1, pp. 592–593 (*OS* 4:55).   [38] *Comm. John* 10:7, 1.397 (*CO* 47.238).

to which Christians have been called. He does provide his teaching with a foundation in the exposition of the Law, but he finally turns the believer to Christ, and him crucified, as the pattern and source of the life that God demands and in which God offers fulfillment.

I emphasize Calvin's Christocentrism in his instruction about God's doctrine of life to ask whether we should not, then, expect and be disappointed if we do not find this same thing in his discussion of the covenant of grace? On the basis of all that he has written about Christ as the one Mediator between God and humanity and about Christ's teaching office, through which Christ informs his chosen of the meaning and significance of who he is and what he has done – an office in which Calvin shares – is Calvin not obligated to place Christ and his history firmly at the center of his *Institutes* – a text in which he claims to instruct those who desire it "in the doctrine of salvation"[39] – and to orient everything else he has to say in this text around Christ and the redemption that he has accomplished? Must not Christ be, if not the methodological or systematic center, the formal and material center of his teaching? Calvin's answer to these questions would be an unqualified "yes," and, in the section that follows, I explore the manner in which the structure of Calvin's Christology that we have discovered thus far, ordered as it is around Christ's threefold office of the Mediator within the context of God's covenant history with God's Church, facilitates and is determined by this fundamental, Christocentric conviction at the heart of Calvin's thinking about God.

CHRIST AS THE OBJECT OF FAITH

When Calvin introduces the categories of Christ's threefold office in the *Institutes* (II.xv), he makes the distinction between orthodox theology and that of the heretics who know Christ "in name only, but not in reality."[40] Heretics will say that Christ is the Redeemer, but they neither understand nor teach in what manner he redeems – they have no firm grip on what it is that Christ does, and Christ's activity, for Calvin, is his reality – and so they lead their followers astray. Calvin intends to guard against this error through his explanation of Christ's threefold office, for this is the "firm basis for salvation in Christ." To know Christ not merely in name, but in his power and dignity, is to know that he is priest, prophet, and king; and indeed, Calvin tells us, we must know together with these Messianic titles

---

[39] *Inst.*, "Subject Matter of the Present Work," p. 7.   [40] *Inst.* II.xv.1, p. 494 (*OS* 3:471).

their "purpose and use" because they are cold and ineffectual if they are left devoid of content.

What does that mean, though, to say that our knowledge of Christ's office is "cold and ineffectual" unless it is complete in this way? It means that it is vital that we know the details through which Christ's work is for us so that we will both possess the truth of his work and be moved by this truth to faith. Calvin is continuing here a theme with which he began the *Institutes*, that our knowledge of God cannot remain disinterested, but should lead us into a pious relationship with God. So here he is arguing that Christians require a proper knowledge of Christ's offices – a knowledge not only of the titles that are applied to Christ, but also the content of these titles that he enacted in his ministry – so that this knowledge of Christ and his work will be effective in our lives.

We have spent this and the previous two chapters examining the content that Calvin provides for Christ's threefold office, developing just such a proper and complete knowledge of Christ as Calvin recommends. One thing that we have found, beyond any particular details of this content, is that there is an intimate relationship between Christ's threefold office in Calvin and Christ's Gospel history. The threefold office is, in fact, simply a manner of explicating that history to lay out the salvation that Christ has accomplished in it. I have already discussed how Calvin's use of the rubric of the threefold office in his Christology is historically grounded in God's covenant history with Israel – insofar as Christ is the Mediator of God's covenant with God's people, we find in him the fulfillment of the offices through which God's covenant was realized with God's Church from the very beginning. But now we also see the historical rootedness of the threefold office in its relationship to the Gospel history. On the one hand, we see that the Gospel history, especially as it is summarized in the Creed, was the venue through which Calvin could develop the detailed reality of Christ's threefold office in the *Institutes*. Under the guidance of Christ's teaching, we see his kingship and his priesthood worked out by attending to the history of his passion, death, resurrection and ascension. It is there in his history that he fulfills his role as Mediator of the covenant. On the other hand, we can say that the threefold office operates as a helpful template for the exegesis of Christ's history. We grasp our salvation in Christ and his Gospel in all of its detail through the lens of the threefold office. We see that the history of Christ is his history precisely and completely as prophet, priest, and king. Thus, the doctrine of the threefold office helps us to hear and appropriate Christ's history in a way that moves us to faith in Christ, thereby engrafting us into his history.

Indeed, what must strike any reader, beyond any particular detail of the content exhibited in the preceding sections, is its sheer diversity and breadth. According to Calvin, Christ redeems God's people insofar as he interprets God's Law, unites God's people, bears their judgment, defeats their enemies, leads them into a right understanding of his work, pours out his Spirit upon them, models for them a right way of living, covers their sin, and the list could go on. This, for Calvin, is Christ's reality worked out in his Gospel, encompassing every dimension of our redemption from sin into new life with God. Calvin is able to develop his understanding of the salvific implications of Christ's history in this detail and breadth only under the rubric of the threefold office; it provides the categories with which Calvin is able to explore all the dimensions of Christ's work explained in this book up to now. In fact, given the thoroughness with which Calvin is able to develop his picture of Christ's work as Mediator within his Gospel history under the rubric of the threefold office, it seems evident that his use of this formula is tied up with his desire to develop for his reader just such a complete picture of Christ's Gospel history. This is the true knowledge of Christ's reality that Christians require.

Why is it important that Calvin in his Christology reflect the breadth and diversity of Christ's ministry? How, in other words, does Calvin's development of Christ's history under the rubric of the threefold office further his Christological project, apart from any particular detail of that history that it accentuates? The answer to this is twofold. On the one hand, this breadth of Christ's office highlights the richness of God's grace offered in Christ and his Gospel, drawing God's chosen to Christ in faith. On the other hand, on the basis of this breadth, Calvin is able to construe the entirety of God's salvific relationship with God's chosen in relation to Christ's history so that the chosen are directed only to Christ for faith. In other words, through his use of the threefold office to develop his variegated picture of Christ's ministry, Calvin is able to focus his readers on Christ and his history as the foundation and goal of their faith. Let us examine these points in a little more detail.

The richness of grace in Christ

First, given this broad sense of Christ's redemptive activity in his Gospel that Calvin develops under the rubric of Christ's threefold office, Calvin can say that Christ's activities are all of these activities outlined above. We cannot, therefore, focus our conversation about these activities on any of their aspects at the expense of the others. More particularly, we cannot focus our conversation about Christ's activity completely, or even largely, on Christ's work as priest, whereby he has atoned for our sins, while ignoring his royal or prophetic office. Whatever Calvin will say about this one aspect of Christ's threefold office – and, as we have seen, he will say a great deal – it is only one aspect of that office. Christ redeems humanity because he has removed the barrier of sin by which we are estranged from God through his obedience and death, but this redemption is effective only as he also conquers the powers that would separate us from God, unites us through our fellowship with him to God, and teaches us the significance of this mission that he has from God.

I emphasize this breadth of Christ's work in Calvin, in part, as a corrective to the narrow interpretations of that work found in many of Calvin's commentators – as I mentioned in the previous chapter, some commentators will note Calvin's commitment to Christ's threefold office, but their discussions of Christ's office inevitably neglect his royal and prophetic work and focus solely on his work of priestly atonement. Calvin's development of this doctrine simply will not allow such a constricted interpretation. Indeed, Calvin, in arguing for Christ's threefold office, is pushing for an expansion of our grasp of the dimensions of Christ's work, not allowing theologians, such as Stancaro, to limit Christ's work to his priestly sacrifice. This expansion is vital to Calvin, for it invites Calvin's readers into a richer, more complex view of Christ's reality, and this returns us to where we began this discussion – Calvin's concern that Christ's reality be presented in a manner that moves his readers into a relationship of faith in Christ.

For Calvin, Christ is as Christ is for us. That is what it means to equate Christ's reality with his threefold office worked out in his history. Thus, we understand what is important about Christ and he has a claim on our faith insofar as we grasp what he has done in that history to change our reality – to save us by renewing our relationship with God. Calvin, therefore, is not content to allow Christ's work to be restricted to his atonement for human sin because doing so would diminish Christ. By neglecting all that he does as king and prophet, it curtails his impact on our lives and thereby lessens his claim on our faith. Calvin instead deliberately develops a more comprehensive and diverse picture of Christ's work, accenting the multitude of ways in which he acts to realize our covenant relationship with God, in order that we might be gripped by this emergent picture of his history and attach ourselves to this one whose salvation so encompasses us. That Christ's activity is all of this activity means that we can expect to find wisdom and mercy and security and strength and all manner of spiritual gifts in Christ – that, for Calvin, is his reality into which we have been invited through his ministry among us. Proper knowledge of Christ under the category of his threefold office means in the first place, then, that we will find an abundance of God's blessings in Christ and his Gospel history.

The totality of grace in Christ

The corollary for Calvin to the fact that Christ's activity is all of this activity is that all of this activity is likewise Christ's. We cannot talk about atonement, God's Law, righteousness, election, God's mercy, or the out-pouring of the Spirit without in the same breath mentioning Christ, for all of these are enacted, manifest, and understood in and through his threefold office worked out in his history. Every dimension of God's relationship with God's Church involves Christ intimately because Christ is the Mediator of that relationship. This means not only that we understand those aspects of redemption that Calvin discusses in Book II of the *Institutes* in relation to Christ's work, but also all that he discusses in Book III. Christian faith, sanctification, justification, election, and even the work of the Spirit, insofar as Christ is the steward of the Spirit, are founded on Christ's work. Calvin takes seriously Bernard's admonition that "every discourse in which [Christ's] name is not spoken is without savor."[41] Indeed, it is not enough for Calvin that Christ's mere name be spoken in every discourse, but that his name be accompanied by his reality, that is his threefold office worked out in his Gospel, for he in his history is the moving force behind every aspect of the realization of God's salvific will for God's Church. A proper and complete knowledge of Christ means, in the second place, then, the knowledge that all that must be accomplished for our salvation is accomplished in Christ and his history, so that we find the totality of God's blessings only as we look for them in Christ; and, indeed, it makes no sense to seek these blessings apart from him.

When these two conclusions about Christ's history are taken together, so that we see that the grand sweep of the Christian life, constituted by the working out of God's redemptive will, is realized in that history's details, then we can say that for Calvin there is a certain Christocentrism to his theological project and to the spiritual or religious project that he recommends to the believer in the *Institutes*. Calvin's intent in the *Institutes* is consistently to direct his readers to Christ and his history as the catalyst for their faith. This Christocentrism is encapsulated by Calvin in his summary

---

[41] *Inst.* II.xvi.1, p. 504 (*OS* 3:482–483) from Bernard, Sermons on the Song of Songs, xv.6 (J. P. Migne, *Patrologiae cursus completus, series Latina*, 183.340f.; trans. S. J. Eales, *Life and Work of St Bernard*, IV.83f.)

of his exegesis of the Creed (*Inst.* ii.xvi.19), where he rehearses a distillation of the Gospel and the "rich store of every kind of good" that is made available to Christians through it. In this distillation Calvin is directing believers to Christ and his history because they will find God's grace fully and completely available in them. Calvin writes:

We see that our whole salvation and all its parts are comprehended in Christ. We should therefore take care not to derive the least portion of it from anywhere else. If we seek salvation, we are taught by the very name of Jesus that it is "of him." If we seek any other gifts of the Spirit, they will be found in his anointing. If we seek strength, it lies in his dominion; if purity, in his conception; if gentleness, it appears in his birth. For by his birth he was made like us in all respects that he might learn to feel our pain. If we seek redemption, it lies in his passion; if acquittal, in his condemnation; if remission of the curse, in his cross; if satisfaction, in his sacrifice; if purification, in his blood; if reconciliation, in his descent into hell; if mortification of the flesh, in his tomb; if newness of life, in his resurrection; if immortality, in the same; if inheritance of the Heavenly Kingdom, in his entrance into heaven; if protection, if security, if abundant supply of all blessings, in his Kingdom; if untroubled expectation of judgment, in the power given to him to judge. In short, since rich store of every kind of good abounds in him, let us drink our fill from this fountain, and from no other. Some men, not content with him alone, are borne hither and thither from one hope to another; even if they concern themselves chiefly with him, they nevertheless stray from the right way in turning some part of their thinking in another direction. Yet, such distrust cannot creep in where men have once for all truly known the abundance of his blessings.[42]

This paragraph exposes the heart of Calvin's Christology, that "the whole of our salvation and all of its parts are comprehended in Christ," and that this comprehension should be exhibited through the narration of Christ's history, the Gospel of his threefold ministry worked out from his birth to his final coming. I would argue that, in fact, this paragraph, as the culmination of Calvin's exploration of Christ's Gospel summarized in the Creed, stands at the very center of his *Institutes*, demanding the undivided attention of its readers. All that comes before it is preparation – both the knowledge of God, our Creator, that was obscured with Adam's fall so that we can know this God only as the one before whom we stand condemned without a Mediator, and the knowledge of the Mediator in the Old Testament covenant history, that serves to set the stage for this Mediator's coming. Likewise, all that follows this Christological center serves our incorporation into Christ's Gospel history, as we, through Christ's out-pouring of the Spirit, are justified through our incorporation into his righteous fellowship and sanctified as we conform our lives to his through our mortification

---

[42] *Inst.* ii.xvi.19, pp. 527–528 (*OS* 3:507–508).

and vivification, our death and resurrection with him. Calvin here near the end of the most specifically Christological section of the *Institutes* clearly centers his readers on the knowledge of Christ, and this knowledge most particularly as it is given through his history, seen under the rubric of Christ's threefold office.

Christ as the image of God

Calvin will make a further claim, though, for this true knowledge of Christ gained through his Gospel history. For in this Gospel, insofar as Christ has realized God's eternal, merciful will for God's chosen, engrafting them into his body and thereby bringing them into covenant fellowship with God, Christ has revealed God to God's people as merciful Father. Thus, Christ in his history is God's lively image in God's relationship with God's Church.[43]

One of Calvin's favorite epithets for Christ is: "God manifest in the flesh." This is, obviously, a simple definition of who Christ is, encompassing, as it does, his two natures in his one person; and it also serves as a basis for understanding Christ's office more broadly construed – Christ is able to be priest, king, and prophet because he is both God and human. Both of these senses of the term will be explored in the next chapter, but, between the narrow, definitional sense of this phrase and its broader, enabling sense, there is, for Calvin, a particular function of Christ hereby expressed. It points to Christ's role as the one who reveals God, who is the Father's "lively image." Calvin writes:

But since, when we wish to rise to God, all our senses immediately fail, Christ is placed before our eyes as a lively image of the invisible God. There is no reason, therefore, why we should toil to no purpose in exploring the secrets of heaven, since God provides for our weakness by showing himself to be near in the person of Christ . . . whenever the inquiry relates to the government of the world, to our own condition, to the heavenly guardianship of our salvation, let us learn to direct our eyes to Christ alone, as all power is committed to him (Matt. 28:18), and in his face God the Father, who would otherwise have been hidden and at a distance, appears to us so that the unveiled majesty of God does not swallow us up by its inconceivable brightness.[44]

---

[43] Randall Zachman, in his article "Jesus Christ as the Image of God in Calvin's Theology" (*Calvin Theological Journal* 25:1 [Apr. 1990], 45–62) argues that Christ as the image of God stands at the center of Calvin's Christology. But this notion is better seen as an implication of Calvin's Christology, derived from its center in Christ's salvific history. We can understand how Christ is God's image only as we first grasp his revelation of God's mercy in his history in his threefold office. Zachman attends to Christ's threefold office, as well, such that our differences seem to revolve more around our emphases; see also his discussion in *Assurance of Faith*, pp. 159–173.

[44] *Comm. John* 5:22, 1.201 (*CO* 47.114).

Calvin is impressed by the distance between God and God's creation. As he writes in the *Institutes*, even without sin, humanity is "too lowly" to reach God without a Mediator.[45] He expresses this distance alternately as God's hiddenness and God's overwhelming brightness. God in God's essence is too distant to be discovered by creaturely endeavors, so that if God were to appear in God's glory, humanity would be "swallowed up" by it. Therefore, we can know God only through the mediation of God's Son. Calvin writes: "[A]s God dwells in inaccessible light, he cannot be known but in Christ, who is his lively image."[46] Accommodating himself to us, he has placed himself between the Father and us so that he might elevate us to the knowledge of the Father.[47] "Whoever aspires to know God and does not begin with Christ, must wander in a labyrinth. For it is not without good reason that Christ is called the image of the Father."[48] Calvin is impressed by the distance between God and God's creation, but in Christ, as Calvin is quoted above, God has "shown himself near," God has made Godself present through God's lively image, and so the Church should turn its attention to this image to learn of God.[49]

Indeed, there was a sense in which God was known to the Church in the Old Testament, as was illustrated in the second chapter, but finally, for Calvin, in comparison with the knowledge of God that was given to the Church in Jesus Christ, God was known to Israel only as God was concealed in God's glory, as if behind a veil. On the one hand, the knowledge of God given in the covenant history was given through shadows and figures, Calvin says, while we perceive God openly in the face of Christ; and on the other hand, he contends, whenever Israel wished to know God, "they always turned their eyes toward Christ," by attending to his promised manifestation.[50] This presence of God in Christ, so that God is known

---

[45] *Inst.* II.xii.1, p. 465 (*OS* 3:438).   [46] *Comm. John* 1:18, 1.53–54 (*CO* 47:19).

[47] See *Comm. John* 14:28, II.102 (*CO* 47:336).   [48] *Comm. John* 8:19, 1.329 (*CO* 47:195).

[49] Calvin's use of the term "image" for Christ could be confusing, since the term typically refers to that which is a copy of the thing imaged, or a representation at least one remove from the thing represented, while Calvin is clear that Christ does not merely represent God to God's people, but actually is God. Calvin's use draws on the relationship of the Son as the image of the Father that Calvin derives from his reading of Hebrews 1:3 (see *Comm. Heb.* 1:3, pp. 35ff. [*CO* 55:11–12] and *Comm. John* 1:18, 1.54 [*CO* 47:19]). The Son, then, is the one who makes God known, in the first place through Creation, in whose structure God's wisdom and will are represented. In this case, Creation is the representation – the revelation at second hand – but the Son is the one who is called the image of God's purpose, for he, who is truly God, is the one who mediates this revelation. In Christ, however, representation and true presence come together. Christ represents God's merciful will to God's Church in his history, but he does not represent God at second hand. He is prophet, priest, and king only as he is truly and completely God. "God's infinite goodness, wisdom and power are clearly manifested in him," because "full Divinity dwells in him and displays its power" (*Comm. John* 14:10, II.87 [*CO* 47:326]).

[50] *Comm. John* 1:18, 1.55 (*CO* 47:20), my translation.

in Christ's face, is the radical departure of the New Testament toward which even those in the Old Testament turned, for it is only through this presence that we can truly know God and so come into covenant relation with God.

Having argued for the revelation of God in Christ, the lively image, I must make equally clear that for Calvin this revelation is not a straight-forward matter. As I explained at the end of chapter 1, it is not, in the first place, that God's essence is revealed in Christ. God's essence remains inscrutable, according to Calvin. Rather, it is that God's "goodness, wisdom, and power" are made known in Christ, and they are made known in and through Christ's threefold office as Mediator. Christ is the lively image of the Father insofar as he is priest, king, and prophet toward us. In the grace that he works out in the fulfillment of these offices, he manifests God and God's love for us. Therefore, as we have seen in our exploration of Calvin's exposition of Christ's triple office toward us, what is accomplished in Christ's various activities is not only the grace specific to each office, but the revelation of God that stands as a corollary to all of Christ's particular work. This is why I argued earlier in this chapter that Christ, through his teaching, does not reveal God per se, but rather explains and clarifies that revelation that was manifest in all of Christ's mediatorial work.

Christology, revelation, and the Institutes

This notion of Christ as the revelation of God moves to the center of our understanding of Calvin's theology when we take up the expression of that theology found in the *Institutes*. If we return to the broader historical context for Calvin's Christology, the renewal of God's covenant relationship with God's Church, then within the *Institutes*, we could argue, this relationship is discussed under the rubric of knowledge: We find ourselves in proper relationship with God insofar as we possess a true, pious knowledge of God as both Creator and loving Father, and of ourselves as God's creatures owing God faith and obedience. Before Adam's fall, creation itself was to lead us to this pious knowledge. "The natural order," Calvin tells us, "was that the frame of the universe should be the school in which we were to learn piety, and from it pass over to eternal life and perfect felicity."[51] Through God's creative will and providential care, mediated through the work of the Son, we were to come to a full appreciation of and devotion to God in God's mercy; but, with Adam's fall, though we still may know God as

---

[51] *Inst.* II.vi.1, p. 341 (*OS* 3:320).

Creator, we have lost any sense of God as loving Father and encounter in our knowledge of God, apart from the Mediator, only God's curse:

This curse, while it seizes and envelops innocent creatures through our fault, must overwhelm our souls with despair. For even if God wills to manifest his fatherly favour to us in many ways, yet we cannot by contemplating the universe infer that he is Father. Rather, conscience presses us within and shows in our sin just cause for his disowning us and not regarding or recognizing us as his sons.[52]

A redemptive knowledge of God, then, would be a knowledge in which we would recover our knowledge of God in God's love and mercy – knowledge of God as our loving Parent.[53]

Much has been written in the past century on the knowledge of God in Calvin's theology, particularly as this knowledge is mediated both through creation and through Christ. I will neither reprise nor resolve this debate. Rather, I want to focus on only one point within it. Calvin does distinguish between two modes of our knowledge of God in the *Institutes*, knowledge of God as Creator and as Redeemer, and these two modalities of knowing are operative for him even after the Fall. He, for example, discusses the knowledge of God as Creator possessed by the Patriarchs, apart from their knowledge of the Mediator, a knowledge that separated them from the idolaters of their generation.[54] Creation, as seen through the spectacles of Scripture, is the medium of this more general knowledge, mediated by the Son, but this more general knowledge no longer includes the knowledge of God as Father. We can no longer know God in God's mercy, for we in our sin are instead surrounded by only guilt and curse. After the Fall, then, we can know God truly and completely only in Christ. Calvin writes: "Therefore, since we have fallen from life into death, the whole knowledge of God the Creator that we have discussed would be useless unless faith also followed, setting forth for us God our Father in Christ."[55] And again: "Therefore, although the preaching of the cross does not agree with our human inclination, if we desire to return to God our Author and Maker, from whom we have been estranged, in order that he may again begin to be our Father, we ought nevertheless to embrace it humbly."[56] This is the basis on which Calvin denominates Christ as the Father's image – that in him, God's mercy is enacted in the world and thereby manifest.

To say that Christ is God's image, making God in God's mercy manifest, will involve two things in the *Institutes*. First, it means that God, who is invisible and inaccessible in God's eternity, is visible in the face of God's

---

[52] Ibid. [53] See Gerrish, *Grace and Gratitude*, esp. p. 59. [54] *Inst.* i.vi.i, p. 70 (*OS* 3:61).
[55] *Inst.* ii.vi.i, p. 341 (*OS* 3:320). [56] Ibid.

Son: "In this sense Irenaeus writes that the Father, himself infinite, becomes finite in the Son, for he has accommodated himself to our little measure, lest our minds be overwhelmed by the immensity of his glory."[57] Christ addresses the problem of human finitude. Second, and more importantly, Calvin will emphasize that Christ makes God manifest because we through sin are cut off from any knowledge of God's mercy. Christ takes a human form, therefore, in order that in him God's love might dwell with us and touch us. Calvin introduced his Christology proper (*Inst.* II.xii) with this thought, and clearly much of what we saw in our examination of Christ's threefold office is directed to this second problem of our ignorance of God's love on account of our alienation from God. Christ, then, serves as God's image in both of these ways, and he does so insofar as he enacts God's grace in our midst. Calvin writes: "For this purpose the Father laid up with his only-begotten Son all that he had to reveal himself in Christ so that Christ, by communicating his Father's benefits, might express the true image of his glory."[58]

Again Calvin does not speak of Christ revealing God in God's essence. The divine nature is inscrutable even in the incarnation. Rather, in and through his threefold office, Christ reveals God's merciful will through his accomplishment of that will in his history. Through Christ's history the invisible God has become visible among us, accommodating Godself to our weakness. Through his history God's mercy has touched us so that we might turn and know and embrace God as Father. This, in some sense, is just a reprise of our discussion of the relationship of predestination and Christology – that Christ in his history has realized God's eternal will in the world's history, and that he has thereby revealed God's will to God's chosen. My point here, then, is simply that one implication of the relationship between these two doctrines is Christ's reality as the image of God. He in his history is the concretization and manifestation of God's eternal will in the world, and through our knowledge of God's merciful will, we come to know God as Father.

If this is the case, if we know God through Christ's history among us, then Calvin's delineating of Christ's history under the rubric of the threefold office, as we observed above, is vital to our knowledge of God. For, just as this categorization of Christ's history allows Calvin to develop his picture of Christ in his reality more expansively, so, too, does it provide such an expansive vision of God's mercy revealed in Christ. To neglect Christ's work in any of its details would be to lessen our knowledge of God's mercy seen

---

[57] *Inst.* II.vi.4, p. 347 (*OS* 3:325–326).   [58] *Inst.* III.ii.1, p. 544 (*OS* 4:8).

therein, and this would diminish our true knowledge of God as Father, on which our relationship with God should be built. So, again, I want to underline the importance of the breadth of knowledge found in Calvin's picture of Christ's threefold office, for this breadth gives the true scope of God's grace active among God's people.

Moreover, Calvin will also emphasize that his contention that Christ is God's image means that we should look only to Christ to find knowledge of God. Calvin is critical of scholastic theologians who simply identify God as the object of faith. Calvin will admit this principle, but only if it is qualified by the fact that we know God truly, that is, as God is merciful toward God's chosen, only in Christ. Calvin writes: "In fact, when faith is discussed in the schools, they call God simply the object of faith, and by fleeting speculations, as we have elsewhere stated, lead miserable souls astray rather than direct them to a definite goal. For since 'God dwells in inaccessible light' (1 Tim. 6:15) Christ must become our intermediary."[59] And again: "It is true that faith looks to one God. But this must also be added, 'To know Jesus Christ whom he has sent' (John 17:3)."[60]

Calvin accepts that the end of Christian life is relationship with God – faith in God, that is, through a true knowledge of God; but, given the fullness of God's mercy that has been made manifest in Christ, he is arguing that this faith, relationship, and knowledge are consummated only in and through Christ. Calvin's purpose here is the same as in his summation of Christ's Gospel with which we ended the previous section ("We see that the whole of our salvation . . ."), that we must direct our attention wholly to Christ – not only do we find the totality of our salvation worked out in his history, but in that history we also find the revelation of God, insofar as Christ's salvation is the fulfillment of God's eternal will for us.

---

[59] *Inst.* III.ii.1, p. 543 (*OS* 4:7).   [60] *Inst.* III.ii.1, pp. 543–544 (*OS* 4:8).

CHAPTER 6

The person of the Mediator

Jesus said: "You believe in God, believe also in me" (John 14:1). It is "wonderful," Calvin comments, that Christ would place faith in the Father before faith in himself, against the expected logic. Since Christ is the lively image of the Father who has descended to us that we may ascend to the Father, he continues, it would have made more sense if Christ had argued that the disciples "ought to believe in God since they had believed in Christ."[1] We come to God having begun with Christ. But Christ was pushing toward a different conclusion:

> For all acknowledge that we ought to believe in God, and this is an admitted principle to which all assent without contradiction; and yet there is scarce one in a hundred who actually believes it, not only because the naked majesty of God is at too great a distance from us, but also because Satan interposes clouds of every description to hinder us from contemplating God. The consequence is, that our faith, seeking God in his heavenly glory and inaccessible light, vanishes away.[2]

Christ begins his final instructions to his disciples in John's Gospel in the same place that Calvin began his *Institutes*, with the sense inherent in all persons that we are called to faith in God, but that we are cut off from God both by our finitude and by the barriers that Satan can erect because of sin.[3] Therefore, Calvin would say, our faith fails until it is restored through the knowledge of God that we gain in Christ:

> Christ, therefore, holds himself out as the goal to which our faith ought to be directed, and by means of which it will easily find that on which it can rest; for he is the true Immanuel, who answers us within, as soon as we seek him by faith. It is one of the leading articles of our faith, that our faith ought to be directed to Christ alone, that it may not wander through long windings; and that it ought to be fixed on him, that it may not waver in the midst of temptations.[4]

---

[1] *Comm. John* 14:1, 11.80 (*CO* 47:321).   [2] Ibid.   [3] See *Inst.* i.iii, pp. 45–47 (*OS* 3:39–40).
[4] *Comm. John* 14:1, 11.81 (*CO* 47:321–322), translation emended.

Christ's purpose in beginning with faith in God, to Calvin's mind, is to drive his disciples to himself. Given their need of God, they must see that God is available only in Christ and that they will be securely bound to God only as they attach themselves to Christ. In other words, although God is ultimately the end of faith, Christ stands at the center of faith. He is not merely faith's temporary object to be moved past once faith finds God through him; rather, he is faith's focus, so that there is knowledge of God only as that knowledge remains in him. He is the Mediator, not because he is a means to God, but because he is the Medium through whom faith in God can be realized and without whom we are left to wend our way through an insoluble labyrinth. He is Immanuel, God with us.

Christ is the Mediator of faith, for Calvin, and he is so precisely in his threefold office of priest, king, and prophet. Christ has removed from us the burden of sin and shown us God's love. Christ has united us to God and revealed the grace with which God would bless us. And Christ has led us into faith in God, explaining to us the significance of what he has done so that faith might grasp the Good News of his work among us. In his threefold office, Christ has revealed the power and wisdom of God whereby God has redeemed us out of sin and taken us into relationship with Godself. The burden of the preceding three chapters has been to show how Christ enacts his mediatorial office and thereby draws God's chosen through faith into relationship with God.

However, this emphasis on Christ's office is not Calvin's only or final word on this matter, for he claims that we cannot rightly understand our relationship with God renewed in Christ except as we also see that Christ can carry out his threefold office because he is Immanuel. Christ is worthy of our faith, he is a fit focus for faith, because he is God. Only thus does he exhibit God's power to save. But that power is exhibited to us and available for our faith only insofar as he is with us – insofar as he has accommodated himself to our lowly condition and become human. Calvin writes:

[E]ver since Christ was manifested to the world, heretics have attempted by various contrivances . . . to overturn sometimes his human and sometimes his Divine nature, that either he might not have full power to save us, or we might not have ready access to him. Now as the hour of his death was already approaching, the Lord himself intended to attest his divinity, that all the godly might boldly rely on him; for if he had been only man, we would have had no right either to glory in him, or to expect salvation from him . . . For as the weakness of the flesh, by which he approached to us, gives us confidence, that we may not hesitate to draw near to him, so if that weakness alone were before our eyes, it would rather fill us with fear and despair than excite proper confidence.[5]

---

[5] *Comm. Matt.* 22:42, iii.67 (*CO* 45:617).

We find confidence in Christ first because he has become our brother and invited us to draw near – we are not overwhelmed either by his glory or by our own sinfulness as he has come to us in his humanity. But when we approach him, we find in him the power of God to save, we find in him the presence of the God who has embraced us, so that we also need not fear that Satan, death, or our sinfulness will separate us from God.

In the preceding passage, the emphasis is placed on Christ's assertion of his divinity; Christ was not among us simply as another human too weak to save us, but he wielded the power of God. Elsewhere, Calvin emphasizes the importance of Christ's humanity – that we can only find God's power to save in Christ's weakness. So Calvin likens the relationship between Christ's two natures to that of a fountain and the channel by which that fountain pours itself out. God's righteousness, and the life that it yields, "flows from God alone."[6] The eternal Word of God – that is, Christ's divinity – is its source; but Christ's humanity plays an equal role in our salvation, serving as the channel by which that life and righteousness are conveyed to the Church.

We shall not attain the full manifestation of [God's righteousness] anywhere else than in the flesh of Christ; for in it was accomplished the redemption of man, in it a sacrifice was offered to atone for sins, and an obedience yielded to God to reconcile him to us; it was also filled with the sanctification of the Spirit, and at length, having vanquished death, it was received into the heavenly glory. It follows, therefore, that all the parts of life have been placed in it, that no man may have reason to complain that he is deprived of life, as if it were placed in concealment or at a distance.[7]

Righteousness and life, our relationship with God, are only available to us in Christ, as he is God manifest in the flesh. We are lost if we look for them anywhere else.

Calvin emphasizes this point because he perceives that human persons recoil from God's presence in this fleshly form. We reject Christ's weakness and suffering because it would require of us that same form of life, or because it would require us to accept that we can know God only as God has accommodated Godself to us. We prefer to move past Christ and know God in God's glory, in God's eternal divinity, apart from God's manifestation in Christ. For Calvin, this is folly: "Proud men are ashamed of Christ's humiliation, and, therefore, they fly to God's incomprehensible Divinity. But faith will never reach heaven unless it submit to Christ, who appears to be a low and contemptible God, and will never be firm if it does not seek a

---

[6] *Comm. John* 6:51, 1.262 (*CO* 47:152).   [7] Ibid., 1.262–263 (*CO* 47:152–153).

foundation in the weakness of Christ."[8] God is only known in Christ, our brother, in Christ crucified, in Christ in his full humanity, however much this may offend.

In this final chapter of our exploration of Calvin's Christology, I take up Calvin's understanding of Christ's person. We come to this topic at the end of our discussion so that we might investigate it only in the light of what I have said of Calvin's view of Christ's office. For Calvin, there is no purpose to the knowledge of who Christ is apart from what he does. But to understand Calvin's doctrine of Christ's person in relation to his doctrine of Christ's office is not to imply that the former is finally subordinated to the latter, that it serves a merely functional purpose, asserting that Christ's person consists of two distinct but united natures only in order to enable Christ in his office as Mediator. Rather, the relationship between these two doctrines is more organic. On the one hand, Christ's identity as the God–human is the foundation on which his office is built: it is the necessary presupposition for his history as the Mediator. On the other hand, that office and history do not lead us away from Christ in his person but to him, insofar as they direct us both to find God in him – as his divinity is made accessible to us through his humanity – and to be united to God through him – as we are engrafted into his body by faith. For Calvin, Christ's person and office are two sides of the same coin, so that, just as we must understand Christ's person functionally, so, too, must we understand his office personally. That is what it means to say that Christ is the Mediator: it is to tie person and office inextricably together.

In this chapter, I examine Calvin's doctrine of Christ's person in its relationship to his doctrine of Christ's office, looking first to his broader concept of Christ's *persona* – what Calvin understands this term to mean and how he deploys it in his Christology – to discover the fit between these two doctrines. Calvin, in other words, utilizes this concept not in opposition to or apart from his concept of Christ's office and history, but in direct connection to it. When Calvin speaks of "the person and office of the Mediator," he is identifying the same reality under its two aspects. After I make this more general point I take up Calvin's discussion of Christ's identity as the God–human in his one person, looking first to the intimations of this identity that Calvin finds throughout the witness of the Old Testament to Christ and then to the revelation of this identity in the Gospels. All of this will set the stage for a discussion of the nuts and bolts of Calvin's exposition of the doctrine of Christ's two natures in one

---

[8] *Comm. John* 14:1, 11.81 (*CO* 47:322).

person, as it is found in the *Institutes*, with an eye not only to this exposition's
theological orthodoxy, but also to its theological power in setting forth
Christ's reality as Immanuel, God with us.

To grasp Calvin's understanding of Christ's person, we must first explore
his understanding of the word *persona*, for we will find that Calvin typically
uses the word not only in a manner unrelated to the psychological coloring
with which we might shade it today, but also in a manner differently related
to the medieval theological use of the term in its concern for metaphysical
definition. Boethius' definition of *persona* as "an individual substance of
a rational nature" orients the sense of this term around a concern for the
substantial self.[9] When we speak of *personae* under this construal of the term,
we are concerned with their essence, abstracted from and preliminary to
our understanding of their engagement with the world. But, in the classical
Latin to which Calvin was committed, *persona* designated principally one's
role or character in a play or one's role or office within the fabric of society –
not the role, character, or office that one simply filled, but that which one
was, for one's role, character, or office defined one's significance within the
outworking of the greater whole. *Persona* in this classical sense was focused
primarily on one's activity within the surrounding economy, and then, only
secondarily, on one's status as a substantial self or personage who fills this
role.[10]

The medieval and classical traditions were married in Calvin, who was
heir to both, for he was concerned to articulate a sense of Christ's person
that attended both to his role or activity as Mediator within history, God's
drama of salvation, and to the metaphysics of Christ's person as the God–
human, on which this activity was founded and through which it was
consummated. The term is not purely functional in Calvin's usage – there
is no role apart from the actor who creates it – but it also is not purely
metaphysical – he wishes to talk about persons insofar as they fulfill their
respective roles in the drama of God's history. There is a tension, in other
words, in his use of the term, whereby he incorporates both the dynamic
element of the activity of the person, to which the identity of the person is

---

[9] *De Duabus naturis* 3 Pl 64.
[10] See Jill Raitt, "Calvin's Use of *Persona*," in *Calvinus ecclesiae Genevensis custos: International Congress
for Calvin Research*, Wilhelm Neuser, ed. (New York: Lang, 1984), pp. 276–277, 282–283, and Lewis
and Short's *Latin Dictionary*, edited by Charlton T. Lewis and Charles Short (Oxford: The Clarendon
Press, 1879), pp. 1355–1356.

directed, and the ontic element of the identity of the person in which the activity of the person is grounded. But there is a coherence to his use of the term within this tension as each use refers to the other within the context of the history that they create.

Jill Raitt, in her excellent article on Calvin's notion of *persona*, outlines three principal uses of the term in Calvin, two of which concern us here.[11] Raitt first notes that Calvin does not rely on any traditional theological or philosophical definition of *persona* – disregarding, for example, Boethius' definition of a person – and that he offers no specific definition of his own under which his various uses could be catalogued.[12] Instead, Raitt explains, we find various uses of *persona* in Calvin, uses that can be broken down into three categories: as an office or role, as a "somebody," and with reference to the Trinity. I will argue elsewhere that Calvin's use of *persona* with reference to the doctrine of the Trinity is *sui generis*; it is a technical term in this context that shares little or no meaning with the more common usage referring to actors on the world's stage. As Calvin explains, quoting from Hilary, whatever we say about God's eternal reality beyond the "natural names" of Father, Son, and Spirit "is beyond the meaning of language, above the reach of sense, above the capacity of understanding."[13] Thus, his third, Trinitarian use of the term has little bearing on his more general understanding of the term. But, if we attend to his other two uses – *persona* as a role and as a somebody – we can find some unifying sense within them precisely at their intersection. Moreover, in this integrative sense, we see most clearly the truth of Raitt's conclusion about Calvin's understanding of this term, that by it he is designating not "a static mode of being, but rather a dynamic mode of acting."[14] This conclusion falls in line with the supposition stated at the outset of this chapter, that Calvin's understanding of Christ's person can come fully to light only in the context of his understanding of Christ's office.

Persona *as an office or role*

We find Calvin's use of *persona* to mean "office" or "role" in his Christological statements, and it appears to be his most general use of the term. For

---

[11] Raitt, "Calvin's Use of *Persona*," pp. 273–287.
[12] He does use language reminiscent of Richard of St. Victor within the context of a discussion of the Trinity, but, as Calvin treats the Trinitarian use of the term as a genus of its own, this definition plays no role in Calvin's general use of the term. See *Inst.* I.xiii.6, p. 128 (*OS* 3:116).
[13] *Inst.* I.xiii.5, p. 127 (*OS* 3:115).   [14] Raitt, "Calvin's Use of *Persona*," p. 286.

example, this usage is evident in Calvin's Genesis commentary when he is discussing Melchizedek's dual role as priest and king. Calvin writes:

That [Melchizedek] received Abram and his companions as guests belonged to his royalty; but the benediction pertained especially to his sacerdotal office. Therefore, the words of Moses ought to be thus connected: Melchizedek, king of Salem, brought forth bread and wine; and seeing he was the priest of God, he blessed Abram; thus to each *persona* is distinctly attributed what is its own.[15]

We find a similar use in his explanation of the *persona* sustained by the Jewish priests in their role as expiators of the people's sins; and, again, Raitt notes a comparable use from Calvin's commentary on Galatians in his contention that Paul rightfully corrected Peter by virtue of the apostolic *persona* that he bore.[16] In these instances, we see that Melchizedek, the priest, and Paul play out a certain role or function in a certain capacity. Indeed, their *persona* is defined essentially by this role.

However, as Raitt notes, this way of phrasing the matter is incomplete, for it does not "convey the personal dynamic behind the 'office.' "[17] These offices or roles are not simply carried out by Paul, the priest, or Melchizedek, but they are filled by them, or embodied, or personned. There is apostleship, priesthood, and kingship, we might say, only as there are apostles, priests, and kings. Our understanding of and relationship to these roles are intimately tied up with the personages who fill them, insofar as these roles imply not merely a particular activity, but also a personal presence as a dimension of this activity. Thus, when *persona* is used in its sense of role or office, it nonetheless refers us to the "someone," the personage who fills this role.

With regard to Christ, we find a similar usage in Calvin's commentary on John. Christ speaks "in the *persona* of Mediator or Minister when he says he teaches only what he has received from the Father."[18] Here to say that Christ speaks in the *persona* of Mediator clearly refers to an office that he fulfills or a role that he plays – Christ's statement that he teaches what he has received from the Father should be understood in relation to his subordinate role as the Mediator, and not as he is the eternal Son and Wisdom of God, coequal with the Father. Christ should be understood in this context in terms of the function that he serves in the covenant history – as the Mediator of the covenant who conveys God's truth to humanity. But, as with the previous

---

[15] *Comm. Gen.* 14:18, 1.387 (*CO* 23:200).
[16] *Comm. Luke* 1:23, 1.29 (*CO* 45:22); Raitt, "Calvin's Use of *Persona*," p. 282, from *Comm. Gal.* 2:11 (*CO* 50:191).
[17] Raitt, "Calvin's Use of *Persona*," p. 282.
[18] *Comm. John* 17:8, (*CO* 47:379), from Raitt, "Calvin's Use of *Persona*," p. 282.

instances, this functionalism does not so thoroughly dominate Calvin's use of the term as to obscure entirely the personal dynamic that pervades it. Christ does not merely play the part of the Mediator for Calvin; he is the Mediator, and this office or role has its particular color and shape insofar as it is personned by Christ. It is not insignificant to Calvin's understanding of Christ's office that the one who mediates God's wisdom and truth is, himself, in his divinity, the very presence of that Wisdom and Truth, only veiled in his human nature so that we might receive it. Calvin uses the term *persona* in the sense of office or role, but he deliberately chooses this term and not simply "office" to bear this sense. He thereby insinuates into his meaning the personal dynamic required for the fulfillment of this office. The office of Mediator is not simply occupied by Christ, he is saying, but it is fulfilled or embodied in Christ.

We encounter this usage also in Calvin's comments on Luke's statement that Christ, after his childhood incident in the Temple, was "subject to" his parents (Luke 2:51). Calvin writes:

Though this subjection, on the part of Christ, arose from no necessity which he could not have avoided, yet, as he had taken upon him human nature on the condition of being subject to parents, and had assumed the *persona* both of a man and of a servant – with respect to the office of Redeemer, this was his lawful condition.[19]

Again, *persona* in this instance bears the sense of role; it was not inappropriate that Christ be subject to his parents, for he was playing the role of a man. He was among us not in his divine glory, but as a servant. Calvin accents here Christ's position within the salvific economy that runs, in some sense, counter to his eternal identity, but we also must say that this role or *persona* was grounded precisely in Christ's identity. Christ did not merely take on the role of a man; he assumed a human nature and actually became that role. This *persona* was his functionally, but also substantially.

Calvin, thus, uses the term *persona* in this sense of office or role, a sense that corresponds to the theme I have developed throughout this essay – that we must understand Christ and who he is in terms of what he does within the context of the covenant history. Christ bears the *persona* of the Mediator because that is the office he fulfills – that is the purpose for which the Father sent him. In this sense, the term is functionally oriented, but this functionalism is not divorced from an emphasis on Christ as a someone or personage; rather, it directs us to it insofar as Christ fulfills his *persona* only as he embodies it and gives it substantial reality. Again, Christ does not

---

[19] *Comm. Luke* 2:51, 1.172 (*CO* 45:107).

merely act as Mediator; he is the Mediator. This, then, is one dimension of the meaning that *persona* bears for Calvin.

Persona *as a personage or somebody*

Calvin also uses the term *persona* to refer quite directly to a someone or a personage. Raitt notes that in the Latin version of the 1559 *Institutes* Calvin writes of our knowledge of God not only as the founder of the universe, but also "in the person of the Mediator as the Redeemer"[20] – an ambiguous use of *persona*, calling to mind both the office and the personage of Christ. In the French 1560 version, however, he writes that we come to know God as Redeemer, "in the person of our Lord Jesus Christ" (*"en la personne de nostre seigneur Iesus Christ"*), presenting Christ in his substantial self as the center of our knowledge of God's redemptive will.[21] Jesus is the someone through whom we are brought to a saving faith in God. In this case, *persona* refers not directly to Christ's office, but to his personage; yet it does so in a context that bears on his office – our focus is placed not simply on Christ's person, but on his person insofar as he is the one who redeems us. Calvin does not wish to speak of Christ's person except in this connection.

We find this same usage in Calvin's Matthew commentary: "For whenever we contemplate the one person of Christ as God–human, we ought to hold it for certain that, if we are united to Christ by faith, we possess God."[22] Again, the focus is on Christ in his substantial identity, and there is a direct linkage of Christ's personage with his office of uniting humanity to God. Just as Calvin's use of *persona* to mean "office" or "role" implies as well the one who personned that role, so, too, we see that Calvin's use of *persona* to mean a someone speaks of that someone in connection to their office or activity. A *persona* is not simply a someone, but a someone who is doing something, fulfilling an office or carrying out a role. Thus, we understand who they are to some degree in terms of what they do or what role they play. These two senses of *persona* are bound together in Calvin's mind, each functioning within the orbit of the other.

We also see in the above passage that when Calvin uses *persona* to mean Christ's personage, he often specifies Christ's identity in his *persona* as the God–human. To know Christ in his substantial self is to know that he is both human and divine. But this definition of Christ's identity in terms of his two natures is not divorced from the linkage of personage and office

---

[20] *Inst.* I.vi.1, p. 71 (*OS* 3:61).   [21] Raitt, "Calvin's Use of *Persona*," p. 280.
[22] *Comm. Matt.* 1:23, I.106 (*CO* 45:69).

that I thus far have illustrated; rather, it plays into that linkage, insofar as Christ's identity as the God–human underwrites his activity as Mediator. We see this relationship in the above passage where Calvin's definition of Christ's identity ("Whenever we contemplate the one person of Christ as God–human") is tied directly to his understanding of his office – that, insofar as we are united to Christ in his humanity, we possess God in his divinity. Christ can unite us to God because he is the God–human, but his identity as the God–human has significance for us because through it, we are united to God. Activity and identity depend upon each other, and they intersect in Christ's *persona*.

This analysis of the interlocking senses in which Calvin uses this term returns us to Raitt's conclusion that, for Calvin, *persona* is never used "to designate a static mode of being, but rather a dynamic mode of acting." This is to say that Calvin is less concerned with an idea of *persona* focused on the ontology of personhood, than with the mutual relationship between a person and their activity, so that the person cannot and should not be understood apart from their work – that, indeed, this work is in some sense the *raison d'être* for the person. Thus, we are discussing Calvin's doctrine of Christ's person only in the light of his understanding of Christ's office because we can only grasp the full implication of who Christ is in light of what he has done. Indeed, who he is, that is, the Mediator, is simply a restatement of what he has done. His identity is in one sense dynamically defined.

That is not to say that Calvin relegates a concern for the substantial self of a person to the periphery of his discussion because any understanding of this substantial self is only derivative of the person's activity. As we have also seen, the role or office that is one's *persona* is reliant on and grounded in one's substantial self through which that *persona* is embodied or personned. Inasmuch as Calvin's notion of the person is dynamically defined, so, too, we want to say that his notion of activity is personally defined. There is no office of king, priest, or apostle apart from those who realize these offices. So, in terms of our understanding of Calvin's Christology, we must understand that Christ's office as Mediator is fundamentally personal. He does not simply occupy his office; he is his office, especially as his activity as the Mediator is grounded in and shaped by his identity as the God–human. Calvin's notion of Christ's person is not such that we are to move past his person to the activity whereby he restores our relationship with God. Rather, we are to find that restored relationship in him, as he embodies this activity and becomes the focal point of our faith. In other words, we are to consider neither who he is apart from what he does nor what he does apart from who he is, for these two realities are, in fact, the one reality of the *persona Christi*. There obviously is not a univocal sense in which Calvin uses the term *persona*, but there nonetheless appears to be a coherent and theologically significant coalescence of sense around the twinned usage of office and personage, activity and identity, illustrated above.

The significance of Calvin's use of persona

It is this coalescence of sense that ties Calvin's notion of *persona* so closely to his understanding of Christ's office as the Mediator within God's covenant history. In the first place, Calvin orients his use of this term toward its context within the covenant history. He is interested in "dynamic modes of acting," and the fundamental dynamism of Calvin's Christology is the dynamism of history. Thus, we should expand our sense of *persona* as role or office to include the vital sense that this office or role that Christ fulfills in his *persona* is an office or role within the drama of God's history. Christ's *persona* is in some sense scripted by God, the Author of history, so that through his *persona* he both enacts and manifests God's grace in the world. To state the case in this way is to pick up on the classical sense of *persona* as the character one sustains within a drama or within an economy or society. Christ, who is God's eternal Son, plays the role of the Mediator, he takes up this *persona*, so that he might restore the covenant relationship between God and humanity, both establishing God's covenant with God's Church and drawing God's chosen into this reestablished relationship. Having said this, we must understand that this *persona* is not a role that Christ plays apart from his identity, a mere superficiality to be cast aside when his performance is completed; rather, we have seen that Christ takes up the *persona* precisely by making it his identity, assuming a human nature so that, as the God–human, he is able to embody and fulfill this office that he has accepted.

We also see that, just as *persona* is in some sense historically defined for Calvin, so, too, is Calvin's understanding of history, or at least of God's covenant history, personally defined, especially as that history is fulfilled in Christ's Gospel history. In his discussion of the Gospel Calvin wants to virtually identify person and history so that we neither understand nor embrace either without the other. In his sermon on the deity of Christ, Calvin equates Christ's history with his person, arguing that the substance of Christ's Gospel history is "comprehended in the Person of the Son of God."[23] And we find this same language echoed in Calvin's summary of

---

[23] "Deity of Christ," p. 14 (*CO* 47:466).

his exegesis of the Creed, quoted in the last chapter, where he writes: "We see that our whole salvation and all its parts are comprehended in Christ," and then he goes on to spell out this comprehension through a rehearsal of Christ's history. The Gospel history is a personal history insofar as it is simply and only Christ's history – he is the one who was obedient, who suffered, who defeated death, who rose again, and who poured out God's spirit. It is the history of Christ's *persona* as priest, prophet, and king, but it is also a personal history insofar as it presents Christ in his personage, in his substantial self as God manifest in the flesh, and it presents him so that we might be bound to his person, engrafted into his body through faith. Calvin does not finally call on Christians to place their faith in Christ's history or office, in the function he fulfills; rather, he calls on them to place their faith in Christ himself – in his person – because of the office he fulfills. Through the faith that he in his office elicits, we are to attach ourselves to him, who is the presence of God with us, and thereby be brought into renewed relationship with God.

We must understand Calvin's use of *persona*, then, as the intersection of activity and identity in Christ so that we can properly balance an emphasis on the functional dimension of Calvin's Christology with the personal dimension illustrated here. To say that Calvin favors his doctrine of Christ's office over his doctrine of Christ's person is not to say that the latter is finally subordinate to the former to the extent that its significance falls away. Rather, it is simply to say that we must understand the significance of the latter in terms of the former, not so that we are directed to Christ's person to explore the metaphysical implications of the hypostatic union, but so that as we find God's grace enacted and manifest in him, we might bind ourselves to him by faith and thereby be reunited with God as our Father. That, of course, does not mean that Calvin had nothing to say about Christ's identity as the God–human and the unity of distinct natures in his person; rather, it is to say that as we turn now to his discussion of Christ as the God–human, we must always keep in mind its context, Christ's salvific office toward us.

TESTIMONY TO CHRIST'S *PERSONA* IN CALVIN'S COMMENTARIES

In chapter 2, I examined Calvin's Christological interpretation of God's covenant history with God's Church under the rubric of the threefold office of priest, king, and prophet, through which that history was realized. That discussion has formed the backbone of this book, but there is another strand of Christological witness for Calvin in the Old Testament narration of God's relationship with Israel, a strand that testifies to *who* the promised Mediator will be – Immanuel, God with us. In his explication of this other strand of the Old Testament's witness to Christ, Calvin begins to develop the essential themes that run throughout his discussion of Christ's person, that in Christ we have to do not only with God's power to save, but also with God's very presence, and that in Christ we who are alienated from God have access to this presence of which we are afraid. Thus, we begin our consideration of Calvin's understanding of Christ's personal reality as the God–human with an examination of Calvin's handling of three Old Testament passages, through which he makes this case.

In his commentary on Isaiah 7:14 ("Behold, a virgin shall conceive . . . and his name shall be called, 'Immanuel' "), Calvin argues that Isaiah's prophecy of the child, Immanuel, refers directly and exclusively to Christ, the promised Messiah, and not to a child contemporary to Isaiah and Ahaz. This makes sense in the context of a prophecy related to imminent deliverance of Jerusalem because the prophet wanted to recall for the people God's fundamental covenantal promise, that God will send a Redeemer, on which all of God's particular promises to God's people are built. Not only are all the particular promises subsumed under this one great promise as foretastes of its blessing, but they are possible only in light of the promised Mediator, in that there is a covenant relation between God and the Church only in him.[24]

When Calvin continues, though, to consider the name Immanuel, "God with us," he turns to a new topic – who this Messiah will be. The Jews, he tells us, contend that Hezekiah is the one promised by Isaiah since God delivered Israel by his hand, and that he is "God with us" because "He who is the servant of God represents his person." Calvin rejects this argument, pointing out that this name is extraordinary. It promises not merely God's power displayed through one of God's servants, but God's presence with us, God's relationship to us. Even the greatest deliverers of the nation – he takes Moses and Joshua as his examples – were never so denominated. Only Christ is God with us, for he is the Son of God clothed with our flesh. He, thus, is a Messiah set apart from all other servants in Israel's history.[25]

In the commentary, Calvin develops from this prophecy the doctrine of the Incarnation. That Christ is Immanuel indicates his deity,[26] while the prophet's testimony to his human activity, for instance, his eating butter and honey (Isa. 7:15), proves his human nature.[27] To say that he is God

---

[24] *Comm. Isaiah* 7:14, 1.244–246 (*CO* 36:154–155).   [25] Ibid., 1.248–249 (*CO* 36:157).
[26] Ibid., 1.248 (*CO* 36:157).   [27] Ibid., 1.249 (*CO* 36:158).

with us is to say that he is God united to us in the person of Christ. Calvin's discussion of this passage thus introduces us to an idea that he dwells on at more length elsewhere in his Old Testament commentaries, that the promised Mediator of the covenant is not one who will merely do the work of God, exhibiting God's power; rather, in doing this work, he will also mediate the presence of God. In his exegesis of other passages, he adds the second point, that Christ will mediate this presence in a form accommodated to our human weakness.

God's accommodated presence

Throughout the Old Testament narrative, whenever there is a heavenly presence that affects the movement of the story – the appearance of angels to Abraham or Joshua, the burning bush, or the fire that went before Israel as they fled from Egypt[28] – Calvin argues that God is present in the story through Christ, the Mediator, before he has taken flesh. The account of the burning bush (Exod. 3:1ff.) is emblematic of such stories, and it is adequately representative of Calvin's explication of these phenomena. In the story, God presents Godself to Moses in the form of an angel to communicate with him. Calvin agrees with "the ancient teachers of the Church" that this angel is the eternal Son of God in his office as Mediator, for the saints never had "any communication with God except through the promised Mediator."[29]

In some sense, this is only a further development of Calvin's notion of the office of the Mediator, an extension, perhaps, of his office as prophet – Christ is the one through whom God communicates with the Church. But in this instance, Calvin wants to emphasize that Christ bears this office not in or through someone else (the priests, kings, or prophets of the Old Testament); rather, he himself has come down and taken created form.[30] He has done so because Christ's immediate presence is necessary here in a way that it is not in God's other communications. In the angelic appearances, God does not merely communicate information, but God makes Godself present as a part of that communication. Christ, as the Mediator, is the one in whom God can effectively present Godself to God's chosen.

The story of the burning bush is the story of the renewal of the covenant, which had fallen into disregard over the years durng which Israel had been enslaved in Egypt. A premise behind Calvin's explanation of the story is that God desires to be present to Moses as God recalls the covenant relationship

---

[28] Gen. 18:1ff.; Exod. 3:1ff.; Exod. 14:19.   [29] *Comm. Exod.* 3:2, 1.61 (*CO* 24:35–36).
[30] Calvin notes elsewhere that in these angelic appearances it is only the form of humanity that Christ takes in distinction from his Incarnation, where he takes a human body and nature. *Comm. Gen.* 18:16, 1.478 (*CO* 23:256).

that God had begun with Abraham before. God does not transact God's covenant with Israel from afar – God's presence in the tabernacle and then the temple attests to God's desire to be near to God's people – and so, God presents Godself to Moses to call Moses to be a minister of the covenant. But God cannot present Godself in God's essence, for God's glory would be too great for Moses to bear. God must accommodate Godself to Moses' capacity, "[assuming] a visible form, that he might be seen by Moses . . . as the infirmity of the human mind could comprehend him." [31] It is through the Mediator that God makes this accommodation; as Calvin writes in the commentary, it is in this "character" or *persona* that God makes Godself known.[32]

God manifest . . .

This notion of Christ making God present in an accommodated form is developed more completely in Calvin's exposition of the dream of Jacob's ladder (Gen. 27:12ff.), wherein God promises this presence in Christ as a sign of the covenant. In Genesis, we are told that Jacob has the dream of a ladder extending from heaven to earth, and that God then appears above the ladder and, addressing Jacob, renews his covenant with him. In Calvin's final analysis of the dream, the purpose of the ladder vision is to ratify the covenant, "illustrating" God's spoken word and thereby adding clarity and authority to it.[33] The vision is able to illustrate the covenant by offering a picture of the Mediator, in whom the covenant is secured. Calvin focuses his interpretive work here on the manner in which Christ secures the covenant not through his threefold office, but through his personal reality as the presence of God to the Church, by which he overcomes humanity's alienation from God.

Calvin argues in his interpretation of Jacob's dream that the ladder is a sign of Christ as the Mediator, the foundation of the covenant, insofar as he is "the eternal image of the Father, in which he [the Father] manifested himself to the holy patriarchs."[34] In the vision, God promises that God will be present to the Church, with a presence similar, Calvin explains, to that of the angelic appearances mediated by Christ. In making this case, Calvin begins by reminding us of humanity's alienation from God – that by sin not only do we cut ourselves off from God's original attempt to draw us to

---

[31] *Comm. Exod.* 3:2, 1.60–61 (*CO* 24:35).
[32] See Battles, "God was Accommodating Himself to Human Capacity," pp. 19ff., for more on the notion of accommodation in Calvin.
[33] *Comm. Gen.* 28:12–13, 11.113–114 (*CO* 23:390–392).   [34] *Comm. Gen.* 28:12, 11.112 (*CO* 23:391).

Godself through creation, but we also flee from God's presence, regarding God "as adverse to us."[35] Sin separates humanity from God not only by initially breaking our relationship with God, but also by instilling within us a fear of God that springs from the guilt produced by our sin. Therefore, Christ is required to connect heaven and earth; that is, God and humanity: "[H]e is the only Mediator who reaches from heaven down to earth: he, it is, through whom the fullness of all celestial blessings flows down to us, and through whom we, in turn, ascend to God."[36] Christ reunites humanity with God by serving as a conduit for God's grace and as the pathway by which we may return to God from our forsakenness.[37]

In many ways, this is merely an expansion of what Calvin has told us of Christ's office as head of the Church; we receive God's grace through Christ and Christ leads us to God. But Calvin also wants to emphasize an additional point in his exposition of this text. In the dream, we are told that Jacob saw God seated on the ladder. This indicates that the fullness of deity dwells in Christ (Calvin writes), and this is significant: "For although all power is committed even to his human nature by the Father, he still would not truly sustain our faith, unless he were God manifested in the flesh."[38] Christ mediates between God and humanity not simply as Christ exercises power on God's behalf – that is, as Christ blesses us – but as he makes God present to us – as he is Immanuel. Only thus does he sustain our faith. Calvin offers no explanation why the divine manifestation in Christ is necessary for faith, but his logic becomes apparent given his preceding points. Christ was necessary, he had told us, because of our alienation from God, because we were afraid to approach God. So Christ brings God near to us in an accommodated form; he makes God manifest to us so that we might not only be blessed by God but also turn to God, putting aside our fear and alienation.

In his exposition of Jacob's dream, then, Calvin informs us that the exercise of power does not fully describe Christ's mediation. We found above Calvin making this same point in his discussion of Isaiah 7. Many have been called to be servants of God through the exercise of divine power, but the one who is to be the only Mediator between God and the Church does not merely wield such power, even in a greater degree. Rather, he is God with us in a form that we can comprehend and of which we will not be afraid. (Again, this picks up a theme that emerged in the discussion of the burning bush passage.) If we now turn to Calvin's discussion of

---

[35] Ibid., II.113 (*CO* 23:391). [36] Ibid., translation emended.
[37] Ibid. [38] Ibid.

Christ's person in the Gospels, we find that, from Calvin's perspective, Christ enacted his identity in his history in a manner congruent with the truth of this identity, that he so revealed his humanity that his disciples would be encouraged to draw near to be grasped by the reality of his divinity. In this way, Calvin tells us, Christ was God manifest in the flesh.

God manifest in the flesh

In the prelude to the story of Christ walking on the water Matthew tells us that Jesus sent his disciples out in a boat while he went up on to the mountain to pray (Matt. 14:23ff.). Why, Calvin asks, did Jesus send his disciples out into danger and devote himself to prayer? He answers:

[I]n discharging all the parts of his office as Mediator, [Christ] showed himself to be God and man, and exhibited proofs of both natures as opportunities arose. Though he had all things at his disposal, he showed himself to be a man by praying; and this he did not hypocritically, but manifested sincere and human affection toward us. In this manner his Divine majesty was for a time concealed, but was afterwards displayed at the proper time.[39]

In Calvin's reading of the Gospels, especially the Synoptics, there are incidents through which Christ gives evidence of both his divine and human natures so that his followers might recognize fully who he is. Thus, in the above example, he demonstrates his human nature by praying, indicating both his need of God and his affection toward those for whom he prays. Later in the story, Christ walks on the water, a miracle, and thereby displays his divine power.

There are many instances in which Calvin understands Christ's divinity to have cloaked itself so that his humanity might manifest itself fully. Calvin understands Luke's report that the young Christ "grew and was invigorated in his spirit" (Luke 2:40) as a development in which Christ's divinity was in repose so that it might be apparent that he shared the weakness of human ignorance and, thus, suffered under the full burden of our humanity.[40] In the same place, he quotes approvingly Irenaeus' comment that Christ's divinity was quiescent in his suffering on the cross so that his humanity was revealed in his death. Likewise, when Christ laments with compassion over doomed Jerusalem (Luke 19:41ff.), Calvin tells the reader that his divinity rested that his humanity might be seen in this very human feeling.[41]

---

[39] *Comm. Matt.* 14:23, II.237–238 (*CO* 45:440–441).
[40] See *Comm. Luke* 2:40, I.165–167 (*CO* 45:103–104).   [41] *Comm. Luke* 19:41, II.453–454 (*CO* 45:576).

Conversely, Calvin finds opportunities to speak of the revelation of Christ's divinity as it was displayed in his miracles. Writing of the feeding of the five thousand, Calvin says that this miracle "had given ample evidence that Christ possessed divine power to assist his followers."[42] This is merely an example of the general principle that Calvin sets forth in his commentary on John 15:24 ("If I had not done among them the works. . . ."): "Under the word *works* Christ includes, in my opinion, all the proofs that he gave of his Divine glory; for by miracles, and by the power of the Holy Spirit, and by other demonstrations, he clearly proved that he was the Son of God."[43] Among the works that Calvin highlights from Christ's ministry, the transfiguration holds a special place. The disciples did not understand this event at the time, he opines, but after Christ's resurrection, they understood it to demonstrate that Christ "continued to retain his divinity entire, though it was concealed under the veil of the flesh."[44] The resurrection, of course, for Calvin is the most striking proof of Christ's divine glory. There, he says, Christ "exerted the power of his Spirit, and proved himself to be the Son of God."[45]

In these two types of texts, then – in stories in which Christ acts or is spoken of in a particularly human manner and in stories in which Christ works miraculous wonders – Calvin argues that Christ's two natures are each revealed. Indeed, that is the central point both of the historical incidents underlying these particular stories and of the record of these incidents in the Gospels – that Christ's followers, both those who lived with him and those who read of him, might perceive his two natures and understand his true identity. However, it is also clear that as Calvin reads the Gospels, the appropriation of this identity by Christ's followers was not a straightforward matter. Although he gave evidence of his divine power in all of his miracles, those who surrounded him were slow on the uptake, so that who he was was only gradually revealed through the course of his story. It was, in fact, only with his resurrection and ascension to the Father that his disciples fully grasped the character of this one who had lived and died among them. This gradual recognition of Christ's divinity was not an accident of Christ's story for Calvin, but, rather, it was intrinsic to the soteriological dimension of his identity, that through Christ's humanity we are drawn near to a divinity of which we are afraid because of sin.

Calvin is clear throughout his Gospel commentaries that few, if any, fully recognized Christ's divinity. The centurion who believed that Christ could

---

[42] *Comm. Matt.* 14:24, II.239 (*CO* 45:441). [43] *Comm. John* 15:24, II.128 (*CO* 47:352).
[44] *Comm. Matt.* 17:9, II.317 (*CO* 45:490). [45] *Comm. Matt.* 28:1, III.338 (*CO* 45:792).

heal his servant from a distance called Christ "Lord," but Calvin claims that this did not mean that the centurion recognized Christ's divinity because almost none were aware of this at the time. Rather, the centurion only saw in Christ the power of God to do miracles – a power that had been possessed by others in Israel's past.[46] Likewise, at the end of the story of Jesus walking on the water, when he had again manifested his divine power, Matthew tells us that those in the boat approached Christ "and worshipped him, saying, 'Truly thou art the Son of God' " (Matt. 14:33). Here Calvin acknowledges a recognition of Jesus' identity, not only by his disciples but also by the sailors in the boat; yet, again, he qualifies it, arguing that "Son of God" served in this instance more as a title for the Messiah than as a recognition of Christ's divine reality.[47]

It is only when Calvin comes to Peter's confession that Jesus is the Christ that Calvin acknowledges that some might have recognized his divinity during his earthly ministry. When Matthew has Peter declare in this pericope that Jesus is the Son of the Living God, Calvin explains that Peter grasped that the Godhead uniquely "inhabited" Christ's flesh.[48] This was a recognition of Christ's divinity, that he not merely manifested God's power, but that God dwelt in him. However, in his comments on the transfiguration story that follows Peter's confession, Calvin argues that the disciples' understanding of this divine indwelling remained incomplete until it was sealed by his resurrection.[49]

For Calvin, it was only when Christ was resurrected that his glory was fully evident, so that his divinity was recognized and acknowledged by his disciples. When Christ appeared to his disciples a final time (Matt. 28:16ff.), according to Matthew's account, the disciples worshipped him. Matthew mentions that some doubted, but Calvin assures the reader that their doubt was overcome when Christ "made a more familiar approach to them," and they all worshipped him, "because the splendor of his divine glory was manifest."[50] At the end of the story, Christ in the full splendor of his divinity was revealed to his disciples, and here they recognized him with no ambiguity, but note that the disciples were able to recognize Christ's divinity and worship him here only *because he was able to make himself familiar to them*. He drew near in an accustomed way. They grasped his divinity only because they first had established an intimacy of relationship

---

[46] *Comm. Matt.* 8:8, 1.381 (*CO* 45:236). Calvin's commentary on this passage is interesting in the attention which Calvin devotes to the question of the centurion's knowledge. Calvin worked through his solution in some detail, indicating that he obviously had a theological stake in his conclusion, that Christ's divinity was not yet evident to those who surrounded him.
[47] *Comm. Matt.* 14:33, 11.242–243 (*CO* 45:444).   [48] Ibid.
[49] *Comm. Matt.* 17:9, 11.317 (*CO* 45:490).   [50] *Comm. Matt.* 28:17, 111.381 (*CO* 45:820).

with Christ, whom they knew in his humanity, and this allowed him to draw near.

Calvin makes this point even more clearly in the story of Jesus' post-resurrection appearance to Thomas. When Thomas saw Jesus, he declared him "My Lord and my God" (John 20:28). Calvin tells us that he thereby began by acknowledging Christ's role as Mediator, calling him "Lord," and progressed to a confession of Christ's eternal divinity. This is not an unnatural progression, Calvin writes:

> That our faith may arrive at the eternal Divinity of Christ we must begin with that knowledge that is nearer and more easily acquired. Thus, it has been justly said by some that by Christ man we are conducted to Christ God, because our faith makes such gradual progress that, perceiving Christ on earth, born in a stable and hanging on a cross, it rises to the glory of his resurrection, and, proceeding onwards comes at length to his eternal life and power, in which his Divine Majesty is gloriously displayed.[51]

Throughout the Gospels, by Calvin's understanding, Christ consistently revealed his divinity, primarily through his miracles; but his followers were never able to fully grasp their sense, even when they were aware of the divine power that they evinced. They only came to finally understand who he was with the glory of his resurrection, but that does not mean that the earlier stages of Christ's history were for naught. For in his ministry and death, Christ's followers saw and embraced Christ in his humanity; they were drawn to Christ, their brother, and he became familiar to them. It is this familiarity along with their awareness of the divine power they had seen working in him throughout his history that allowed them finally to recognize him in his divinity. They moved from Christ man, as Calvin says, to Christ God. Beyond the manner in which Christ's identity empowers him in his activity – that is, as his identity as the God–human allows him to carry out the threefold office of the Mediator – this, for Calvin, is the point of Christ's personal reality: that through his humanity we are led into relationship with his divinity. This is a theme that winds its way throughout his biblical commentaries, as we have just seen, and it is also the theme with which he introduces his Christology in the *Institutes*.

"HOPE THAT GOD MIGHT DWELL WITH US"

Calvin begins the most explicitly Christological section of the *Institutes* with a discussion of the human predicament, that we are so estranged from God that we are in need of an intermediary who is both human and

---

[51] *Comm. John* 20:28, ii.277 (*CO* 47:444).

divine.[52] In making this case, Calvin first identifies human fear before God as a product of our fall and estrangement, that must be addressed if the divine–human relationship is to be restored. Indeed, it is because of this fear, Calvin opines, that no one who was simply human could have served as such an intermediary because all of humanity was "terrified at the sight of God." Thus, God chose to descend to us in such a way that, as the "divinity [of the Son] and our human nature by mutual connection [grew] together," he became Immanuel, God with us. Calvin's point is not that our reunion with God was effected simply through the hypostatic union but that through his taking on our human nature, God could then draw sufficiently near "for us to hope that God might dwell with us." Indeed, that is why Paul describes the Mediator as "the *man*, Jesus Christ" (1 Tim. 2:5, "There is one Mediator between God and man, the man Jesus Christ"). Calvin writes:

[Paul] could have said "God" or he could at least have omitted the word "man" just as he did the word "God." But because the Spirit speaking through his mouth knew our weakness, at the right moment he used a most appropriate remedy to meet it: he set the Son of God familiarly among us as one of ourselves. Therefore, lest anyone be troubled about where to seek the Mediator . . . the Spirit called him "man," thus teaching us that he is near us, indeed touches us, since he is our flesh.[53]

When Calvin sets out to describe Christ's office as Mediator, he begins with our estrangement from fellowship with God, a fellowship in which we dare not hope because we in our sin perceive that we have cut ourselves off from God – we are like Adam hiding in the garden, fleeing from God's approach. So Christ, for Calvin, is the one in whom God has drawn near and touched us. In Christ, God is with us so that we know that God can sympathize with our condition – Calvin quotes the passage from Hebrews: "We have not a high priest who is unable to sympathize with our weaknesses . . ." (Heb. 4:15). Calvin begins his exposition of the Mediator's office, then, with humanity's need for God's graceful proximity so that we might dare to turn to God and find God in our abysmal state.

Muller helpfully notes that Calvin, by starting with the human predicament of broken relationship and the divine intention to heal this brokenness as the conditions that together necessitated the coming of the God–human, has inverted the typical order of doctrine, so that "the function of mediation becomes determinative, and the person of Christ must be considered in and

---

through his office."[54] Calvin, in other words, begins with humanity's need of a Mediator and orients his discussion of the identity of the Mediator around the demands of his office – thus, the shape of this book. But note that, in this introduction to his Christology, focus on Christ's office does not mean moving Christ's person to the periphery; or rather, it helps the discussion of his person to be rightly centered. For it is only through the unique person of Christ as the God–human that we are brought near to the God from whom we are estranged. Indeed, it is only through the person of Christ that we are brought into intimate relationship with God, so that Christ's person, for Calvin, serves not simply as the ground for his activity as the Mediator of the covenant history but also as the goal of this activity, that through his work as priest, king, and prophet, we are led into fellowship with God as we have fellowship with Christ.

With this statement of the intersection between identity and activity in Christ's *persona* as the introduction to his Christology in the *Institutes*, Calvin has laid out a context into which his discussion of the metaphysical reality of Christ's *persona* must be fit. Christ's identity as the God–human must always be understood in its relation to his activity as the Mediator. Thus, when Calvin turns to his explication of the metaphysical reality of Christ's identity as the God–human, he has a twofold purpose in mind: (1) to warrant the actuality of each aspect of his identity – his divinity, humanity, and their distinct unity in his person, and (2) to mark the role of each of these in his mediatorial work. So Calvin first devotes a discussion to Christ's divinity (1.xiii.11–13) and to his humanity (11.xiii), arguing for the reality of each of these natures in Christ, over against the teaching of the anti-Trinitarians (who rejected Christ's divinity) on the one hand, and Menno Simons (who, Calvin thought, rejected the true humanity of Christ) on the other. The basis of Calvin's argument is the manner in which Christ's identity is revealed by his activity – his divinity in his miracles and his humanity in his suffering, to state it briefly. But, in making this argument, he also identifies the manner in which each nature is necessary for his overall activity as the Mediator – he can defeat death, for example, only as he first suffers it. In other words, in his discussion of each nature, Calvin demonstrates not only Christ's divinity and humanity, but also the significance of this reality for our salvation.

Having spoken of the reality of each nature in isolation from the other, Calvin then discusses their union with each other in Christ's one person. Calvin's intention behind this discussion is to balance the demands for

---

[54] Muller, *Christ and the Decree*, p. 28.

the unity of the two natures with the demands for their distinction, an intention evident in his definition of Christ's person – "For we affirm [Christ's] divinity so joined and united with his humanity that each retains its distinctive nature unimpaired, and yet these two natures constitute one person"[55] – and in his whole-hearted rejection of both the Nestorian and Eutychian heresies.

The bulk of the chapter, however, is devoted to a defense of the distinction of natures, an emphasis that has provoked commentators such as Wendel to comment: "[w]hat mattered above all to Calvin was to avoid anything that might be interpreted as a confusion of the divinity with the humanity, even at the centre of the personality of Christ."[56] Now, to state that Calvin wishes to avoid anything by which the natures of Christ would be confused is simply to argue that Calvin is thoroughly Chalcedonian, but clearly the gist of Wendel's remarks is that Calvin evinces far more concern in the *Institutes* for the distinction of natures than he does for the equally Chalcedonian concern for their unity.

What Wendel and others have missed, though, is the context for Calvin's focus on the distinction of the natures in the *Institutes*, that is, his battle with Servetus. I mentioned above that Calvin orients his discussions of Christ's humanity and divinity around his rejection of the teaching of Simons and the anti-Trinitarians. So, too, his discussion of the unity of the natures in Christ's person is oriented around his rejection of Servetus' teaching that Christ was not constituted by the hypostatic union of the divine nature in the person of the Word and an assumed human nature, but that (in Calvin's words) he is "a figment compounded from God's essence, spirit, flesh, and three uncreated elements."[57] Servetus' doctrine was a threat to the reality and distinctiveness of the natures in Christ, and so Calvin devoted a great deal of space toward its rejection.

This is not to say, however, that Calvin allots little or no attention to the unity of the two natures in Christ within the attack on Servetus. For along with his rejection of Servetus' teaching, Calvin was forced to defend his own theology from Servetus' accusation of Nestorianism – that Calvin's teaching left God with two sons, the eternal Word and the incarnate Christ. Thus, within his explanation of the distinction of natures in Christ, Calvin also sets forth briefly his understanding of the foundation of their unity in the assumption of a human nature by the eternal Word.

[55] *Inst.* II.xiv.1, p. 482 (*OS* 3:458).
[56] Wendel, *Calvin*, pp. 220, 222. Wendel's critique is rooted in the conviction that Calvin is overconcerned to protect Christ's divinity from contamination by his humanity, a conviction that we will explore below.
[57] *Inst.* II.xiv.5, p. 487 (*OS* 3:464).

Moreover, Calvin offers a broader resource for developing his understanding of Christ's unity earlier in the chapter, directing his readers to Christ's office as Mediator as the focal point for this unity. After beginning his chapter on Christ's unity with the definition of that unity offered above, Calvin notes that Scripture speaks of Christ in four separate ways:

[T]hey sometimes attribute to him what must be referred solely to his humanity, sometimes what belongs uniquely to his divinity; and sometimes what embraces both natures but fits neither alone. And they so earnestly express this union of the two natures that is in Christ as sometimes to interchange them. This figure of speech is called by the ancient writers "the communicating of properties."[58]

The first two ways apply to what Calvin says of each nature in isolation, and the last way refers to the *communicatio idiomata*; but it is the third way that concerns us now, insofar as it expresses the union of natures in Christ. These passages, Calvin explains, "comprehend both natures at once," but they comprehend them through their reference to Christ's reality as the Mediator, not through any overt reference to the natures themselves.[59] They describe Christ as the "light of the world" (John 9:5, 8:12), the "good shepherd" (John 10:11), the "only door" (John 10:9), and the "true vine" (John 15:1). They describe him as the One who reveals God to the world and leads God's chosen back into relationship with God, and the implication of Calvin's argument is that we can understand these activities of Christ only as we first grasp in him the union of his humanity and his divinity. For Calvin, Christ's unity is established and developed not through an exploration of the metaphysical mechanics of this unity, but through the relation of the unity of natures in Christ to his office as Mediator – the confluence of identity and activity of which I have spoken. Calvin, then, has devoted no small space to Christ's unity in the *Institutes*, for it seems that this unity in Christ's person is manifest anywhere in which his office is set forth and explained. Our task is to examine what Calvin has to say about each of Christ's two natures and their distinction from and union with one another; but we shall be mindful always to hold in the forefront of our discussion the relation between these topics and Christ's office as Mediator, for only then do we obtain a true sense of Calvin's argument.

Christ's divinity

The first and most obvious point to make about Calvin's discussion of Christ's divinity is that it is conducted under a method of indirection. God's

---

[58] *Inst.* II.xiv.1, pp. 482–483 (*OS* 3:459).   [59] *Inst.* II.xiv.3, p. 484 (*OS* 3:460–461).

essence or nature for Calvin is inscrutable, beyond the capacity of human knowledge or perception. God is the one who dwells in light inaccessible. Calvin insists that this is no less the case for God's nature as it dwells in Christ than it is for God's nature in eternity: "Christ, so far as regards his hidden Divinity, is not better known to us than the Father."[60] But that does not mean that we have no knowledge of Christ's divinity; rather, this inscrutability directs us to find evidence for this divinity in our experience of his work among us, in God's "infinite goodness, wisdom, and power," which are clearly manifest in Christ. We are to look to Christ's work to gain true knowledge of Christ as the one who is God with us.

Calvin develops his argument for Christ's divinity (*Inst.* I.xiii.7–13) along these lines through an exposition of the activity of God that we find in Christ. Christ manifests God's authority insofar as he forgives sins and has been made judge over all the world. Christ manifests God's power through his miracles, through the salvation, righteousness, and life that dwell in him. Christ manifests God's glory in that he has been made the center of the Church's faith and adoration. Indeed, Calvin claims, the divinity of Christ is evident not simply in his work as God incarnate, but also in the salvation that he visited upon the Church of the Old Testament, appearing to them as God's angel, and even in his creation and preservation of the world, insofar as he is the eternal Word of God. In all of these, we experience the power of God in Christ, and this experience is matched by the testimony of both the prophets, who promised that God would be present and active in God's Mediator, and the apostles, who proclaimed that they had found God in Christ.

For Calvin, our knowledge of Christ's divinity is a knowledge of recognition in a double sense. We recognize in Christ those qualities that had been attributed in the Old Testament to God in a singular sense. God would judge the world. God would lead captivity captive (Ps. 68:18). God forgives sins (Isa. 43:25). In the knowledge of God we should glory (Jer. 9:24). We know God in Christ because of God's testimony to Godself given to God's Church from the beginning. But this knowledge, in itself, could be disinterested – a matter of merely noting that what was promised in one text was fulfilled in another. More significant for Calvin, then, is our recognition of Christ's divinity in our experience of Christ, the "practical knowledge" that is more certain than any "idle speculation." It is in this practical knowledge, Calvin concludes, that "the pious mind perceives the very presence of God, and almost touches him, when it feels

---

[60] *Comm. John* 14:10, II.87 (*CO* 47:326).

itself quickened, illumined, preserved, justified, and sanctified."[61] In Christ and his history, we have found life in every sense of the word; and on the basis of that gift of life, we can and must conclude not simply that God works through him, but that the fullness of deity dwells within him. It is from that fullness that he has blessed us.

This connection between the fullness of deity that dwells in Christ and the blessing that we receive from Christ is vital to Calvin's understanding of Christ's divine nature. It has too often been commented that Calvin's chief concern in his Christology is to exalt Christ's divinity at the expense of its connection with his humanity. So Wendel speaks of Calvin's "unilateral interest in the divine nature and its exaltation," arguing that Calvin begins his Christology with a broader theological preoccupation concerning the immutability and incommunicability of the divine nature and derives all else that he says from this first principle.[62] This contention against Calvin can take divergent forms. Wendel argues that Calvin maintains a constant vigil to allow nothing about the hypostatic union to "diminish the divinity [in Christ] or divest it of any privileges."[63] He must, therefore, protect the divinity from the humanity, guarding it against any contamination.[64] In other words, for Christ to be fully divine, he must be in some sense cut off from humanity so that his divinity maintains its "privileges" or attributes. Van Buren, on the other hand, focuses on the sense in which Calvin seemingly "reserves" Christ's divine essence insofar as it is inscrutable in its transcendence, so that we are left to know Christ's divinity only in his activity toward us. Van Buren then asks if, in the light of this reservation, Christ is not something less than "a full gift of God to us."[65] Is Christ in his transcendence, from Calvin's point of view, not simply shielded from contamination by his relationship with humanity, but in fact unavailable in some essential ways to humanity, so that we would not want to say that God is present in God's fullness to us in Christ? The crux of both arguments is that Calvin in his concern for and articulation of Christ's divine transcendence has isolated God from humanity, even in Christ, and thus jeopardized the salvific implications of the hypostatic union. From their perspective, the implication of Calvin's teaching on Christ's divinity is that in Christ, God is something less than with us.

Given this brief exposition of Calvin's doctrine of Christ's divine nature, several comments in response to this critique seem in order. First, we should affirm the basis of this critique, that Calvin does emphasize the reality of

---

[61] *Inst.* I.xiii.13, p. 138 (*OS* 3:127). [62] Wendel, *Calvin*, p. 224. [63] Ibid., p. 223.
[64] See ibid., p. 220. [65] Van Buren, *Christ in Our Place*, p. 12.

the divine transcendence in Christ – that Christ is God in all of God's inscrutability and with all of God's privileges or attributes. But, *pace* Van Buren, this is not to withhold God in some sense from humanity; it is to say that Christ is fully and completely God with us. Christ is God in all of God's Godness, inscrutability and privileges included. For Christ to be anything less would mean for him to be not really God at all. However, we must quickly add that Calvin emphasizes the fullness and transcendence of the Godhead in Christ not out of a "unilateral interest in the Divine nature and its exaltation," but out of his attention to our salvation. The salvation that Christ works out in his history depends both on Christ's divine power to save – his power to forgive sins, raise to life, and make righteous – and on the divine presence within him, through which we are brought into fellowship with God. Moreover, our faith in Christ depends on our knowledge of that divine presence and power.[66] For Calvin, Christ has that power and presence and we are assured of it only as we recognize that the fullness of deity dwells in Christ – again, that fullness in all of its inscrutability and with all of its privileges. Thus, Calvin insists on the divine transcendence in Christ not out of a concern to protect Christ's divinity, but out of his concern for Christ's salvific work among us. Finally, the result of this concern is not to ensconce Christ and his divinity in this transcendence so that the Divine dwells only far from humanity in its pitiful and fallen state. Rather, Calvin insists that in Christ, God in God's merciful power has drawn near, so that we "perceive the very presence of God, and almost touch him." The upshot of Calvin's discussion of Christ's divine nature is not that God is not really with us, but that it is really God who is with us, even as God had promised from the beginning of God's covenant history with God's Church.

Christ's humanity

When Calvin turns to the issue of Christ's humanity, he specifies from the start that he will consider the issue only in its connection with Christ's work as Mediator. He writes: "It remains, then, for us [having proven Christ's divinity] to see how, clothed with our flesh he fulfilled the office of Mediator."[67] Calvin has already made the point (in II.xii) that Christ assumed a human nature to fulfill this office, and so we can understand his human nature only in its light. Calvin develops his argument both in terms of God's promises in the Old Testament – the Mediator was to be

---

[66] See *Comm. Matt.* 22:42, III.67 (*CO* 45:617).   [67] *Inst.* II.xiii.1, p. 474 (*OS* 3:447).

a descendent of Abraham and of the line of David – and in terms of the Gospel witness to Christ's human experience – that he was "subject to hunger, thirst, cold, and other infirmities of our nature";[68] but the core of his argument for Christ's human nature is found in his assertion that in Hebrews ("Christ shared in flesh and blood . . ." [Heb. 2:14]) "Christ is clearly declared to be comrade and partner in the same nature with us."[69] For Calvin, it is not the simple fact of Christ's human nature that is significant, but the fellowship or brotherhood that he thereby established between himself and humanity. That fellowship was and is the basis of his fulfillment of God's promise to Abraham – the basis of his threefold office as Mediator. Through that fellowship, Christ suffered the infirmities of our nature so that we would have a high priest who could sympathize with us (Heb. 4:15).[70] Christ "had to be made like his brethren . . . so that he might be a merciful and faithful intercessor" (Heb. 2:17).[71] It was only as Christ was our comrade in our mortality that he might "through death destroy him who had the power of death" (Heb. 2:14).[72] Likewise, he could serve as the conduit of God's Spirit because we were united to him as a body to its head through our fellowship of nature. This fellowship of nature that Christ instantiated through his incarnation is not, of course, the sole condition of our union with him. We must also, through the power of the Spirit, respond to him in faith. But it is only on the basis of our shared humanity, our shared infirmity, that we, who were terrified before God, dare approach Christ so that we might find the presence, power, and mercy of God manifest in him. Calvin's argument for Christ's human nature, then, begins with Scripture's testimony to that human nature in the history of the promise and in the narration of Christ's human experience among us, but it focuses this testimony through the lens of Christ's office as Mediator, leaving a picture centered on Christ's brotherhood with humanity. Without Christ's true humanity, Calvin is saying, there is no true bond between us, and the covenant relationship that God promised would be left unfulfilled.

One conclusion to be drawn from this analysis is the absolute centrality of Christ's human nature to Calvin's conception of his person and work. Christ's "clothing himself with our flesh" is the fundamental basis of his "fulfilling of his office of Mediator." This is important to note, for a corollary to the critique of Calvin's handling of Christ's divinity, voiced in the last section, is the claim that Calvin takes Christ's human nature too lightly, that it is, at most, only of instrumental value for his work. So Wendel

[68] *Inst.* ii.xiii.1, p. 475 (*OS* 3:448).   [69] *Inst.* ii.xiii.2, p. 477 (*OS* 3:452).
[70] *Inst.* ii.xiii.1, p. 475 (*OS* 3:448).   [71] Ibid.   [72] Ibid.

quotes Dominice's earlier conclusion: "this human nature of the Christ has value for [Calvin] only by its union with the Divine nature."[73] Under this type of critique, Christ's humanity appears to be merely a tool of his divinity, through which he can be obedient, suffer, and die; but its value does not endure past this use. Willis has already noted the peculiar nature of Dominice's worry in that Calvin, in line with orthodox thinking, must maintain that there is no human nature of Christ apart from its union with the divine nature of the Word. No one sensitive to the Nestorian heresy would wish to speak of an independent human nature in Christ, so, of course, Calvin's understanding of Christ's human nature is bound up with its relation to his divinity.

In terms of our discussion, however, this does not limit the human nature of Christ to an instrumental role in Calvin's Christology. Yes, Christ is able to do many things through his humanity – be obedient, suffer, die, and serve as the fountain of God's Spirit, but the foundation of all that Christ does through his humanity is who he is in his humanity – he is our brother. His activity has meaning only as he is our brother, and it is only in this brotherhood that Christ in his divinity can reunite us to God. This fellowship of nature, the brotherhood, that Christ establishes through his incarnation is in many ways the pivot on which Calvin's Christology turns. It is through this fellowship that God is revealed, that the covenant is fulfilled, and that God's chosen are adopted into God's family. In one sense, Calvin's Christology is a Christology of the brotherhood of Christ.

The distinction of natures and the extra-calvinisticum

What, then, do we make of the claim that Calvin's emphasis on the distinction of the two natures in Christ distorts his discussion of their unity? This question is, in fact, three questions: concerning the actuality of this emphasis in Calvin, concerning the purpose of this emphasis, and concerning the relation of Calvin's teaching on the distinction of the natures to his teaching on their unity in Christ's *persona*. In this section, we take up these first two questions but reserve the last for our next section. To begin to grasp Calvin's thought about this matter, though, we must first understand that there are two contexts or debates that shape his teaching on it, so that we understand what he writes only when we place it within the context for which it was written.

---

[73] Dominice, *L'Humanité de Jésus*, p. 48, from Wendel, *Calvin*, p. 225.

On the one hand, much of Calvin's teaching on the distinction of natures in the *Institutes* is in response to Servetus' claim that Christ is constituted not by the union of the divine nature of the person of the Word and the human nature of his assumed flesh, but by a mixture of divine and human elements such that he became Son of God in reality only at the time of his birth. In this context, the debate centers on whether there are distinct natures in Christ and is of a piece with the Trinitarian controversy over the eternity and divinity of Christ as the Word or Son of God. The central question of Calvin's debate with Servetus appears to be whether there was in reality a second person of the Trinity, the Eternal Word and Son of God, before the incarnation. Insofar as there was, then this Son of God had and maintained a distinct divine nature even when he assumed a human nature at his incarnation.[74]

On the other hand, Calvin also expresses his teaching on the distinction in what came to be known as the *extra-calvinisticum* (in *Inst.* ii.xiii.4). Here Calvin argues that though Christ's divinity is united to his humanity and is fully present therein, it nonetheless is not contained by that humanity in its finitude, but is ubiquitously present outside (*extra*) it. In other words, the natures of Christ remain distinct, so that his divine nature retains its infinity and his human nature its finitude. Our understanding of this doctrine is shaped by the debate between Lutheran and Reformed theologians over the *extra*. Lutherans maintained that subsequent to his incarnation Christ's divinity was nowhere present outside of his humanity, but that there was an exchange of attributes between the two natures, so that the human nature could be ubiquitously present with the divine. From the Reformed perspective, this teaching about the unity of natures obscured their distinction and threatened the integrity of the natures – a ubiquitous human nature is no human nature at all. In the context of this debate, Calvin's teaching on the distinction of natures in Christ centers on the question not of the reality of Christ's two natures – the Lutherans were of one mind with Calvin against Servetus – but of the manner in which these natures did or did not share attributes in and through this unity. The central question, at least from Calvin's point of view, is whether or not Christ is ubiquitous in his human nature.

It is clear from both of these contexts that Calvin wished to emphasize the distinction of natures in Christ. As he states in his general definition of Christ's person (ii.xiv.1), "Christ's divinity [is] so joined and united to

---

[74] Calvin's explanation of Servetus' position in the *Institutes* (ii.xiv.5, 8) forms the basis of the summary just given.

his humanity that each retains its distinctive nature unimpaired," but the purpose of his stress on this distinctiveness varies widely with the context, so that we can understand how this teaching fits into the overall pattern of his Christology only as we understand these multiple purposes. The general opinion regarding Calvin's teaching about the distinction of natures is that he maintains it largely out of his devotion to protecting Christ's divinity from diminution by his humanity, a critique that I have discussed above.[75] Thus, he must protect it from confusion with Christ's humanity, even in the hypostatic union. Moreover, the doctrine of the *extra-calvinisticum* is portrayed as Calvin's definitive teaching on the distinction of natures, in which Calvin begins with his commitment to the immutability of the divine nature and derives his Christology therefrom. These points are, in a sense, correct, but only as they are placed in their proper contexts, for they belong to divergent contexts.

In his debate with Servetus, Calvin is intent on maintaining the reality and distinction of Christ's divinity in the Incarnation. We should note, however, that his dedication to this point springs not from any desire to protect his divinity from his humanity, but from his wish to argue that he was truly divine in the first place – that he was the real and eternal second person of the Trinity who had taken on flesh. His concern, in other words, was not the effect of the hypostatic union on Christ's divinity, but the original reality of his divinity preceding this union. Moreover, in making this argument, Calvin is equally concerned with the reality of Christ's human nature in the hypostatic union, for Servetus seemingly robs Christ of both in his claim that Christ consists instead of a melange of elements.[76] Thus, in this context, we can grant that Calvin is concerned for Christ's divinity, but only as we admit an equal concern for the reality of his humanity. We should note as well not only that he does not introduce the concept of the *extra-calvinisticum* into this discussion, but also that his primary debate partners over this latter doctrine would have been in full accord with his teaching on the distinction of natures against Servetus.

When we turn to Calvin's doctrine of the *extra-calvinisticum* and the later debate that sprang from this doctrine, however, we see that Calvin's concern was not so much the integrity of Christ's divinity – this was assumed on the part of all orthodox thinkers – but the integrity of his humanity. Calvin's mention of the *extra-calvinisticum* in the *Institutes* is brief, and

---

[75] See, for example, Wendel, *Calvin*, p. 220.   [76] See *Inst.* II.xiv.8, p. 493 (*OS* 3:470–471).

occurs at the conclusion of his discussion of Christ's human nature. Calvin had been arguing against the claim of Menno Simons that Christ was not truly human. Simons argued that it was disgraceful to believe that Christ, as the eternal Word of God, had so united himself to a human nature that he permitted himself to be contained by and born of the virgin's womb. Calvin countered, on the one hand, that there is nothing a priori contaminating in human generation or birth – the viciousness of the act was an accidental quality derived from the Fall. Since Christ was sanctified in his conception by the Holy Spirit, he was immune to this contagion. On the other hand, Calvin notes that to say that Christ in his divinity was joined to his human nature in the virgin's womb does not mean that he was contained therein, for he continued to dwell in heaven and throughout the earth in his ubiquitous being as the Word of God. Calvin writes: "Here is something marvelous: the Son of God descended from heaven in such a way that, without leaving heaven, he willed to be borne in the virgin's womb, to go about the earth, and to hang upon the cross; yet he continuously filled the world even as he had done from the beginning."[77] This is the doctrine that was later labeled the *extra-calvinisticum*; and as Willis has helpfully explained, Calvin stood with the majority of patristic and medieval theologians in making this case.[78] When Calvin employs this doctrine and the distinction of natures that it implies at this point in the *Institutes*, he is arguing not for the purity of Christ's divine nature, but for the reality of his human nature. That Christ is divine does not prevent him from assuming our flesh, he is claiming, because he can maintain his divinity and all of its attributes even as he is incarnate.

Lutheran theologians, however, objected to Calvin's claim in the *extra-calvinisticum*, not because of the narrower point he is making in the *Institutes*, that Christ's divinity is not diminished by his incarnation, but because of the broader implications of this doctrine – that it makes it possible to speak of Christ in his divine nature as God's Eternal Word apart from his being as the incarnate Christ subsequent to his incarnation. They were concerned by the possibility of speaking of a *Logos asarkos*, a Christ outside of his flesh, once he had taken flesh and so defined himself principally and essentially as God with us. Their claim, then, in relation to Christ's two natures was not that Christ's humanity contained and therefore limited his

---

[77] See Menno Simons, *On the Incarnation of Our Lord*, in *Complete Works of Menno Simons*, J. C. Werger, ed., L. Verduin, trans. (Scottsdale, PA: Herald Press, 1956), pp. 783–943. *Inst.* II.xiii.4, p. 481 (*OS* 3:458).
[78] See Willis, *Catholic Christology*, ch. 2, pp. 26–60.

divinity, but that his humanity, so joined to his divinity, contained it only insofar as it took on the attributes of his divinity and participated in his infinitude. As one theologian later expressed it, his humanity could never have this infinitude "according to itself, subjectively, formally, or inherently," but possessed it as it was communicated to it by the Word above or against its nature.[79] For Calvin, this Lutheran notion of an exchange of attributes (*communicatio idiomata*) contradicted a proper doctrine of the distinction of Christ's natures because it threatened the reality of his human nature. Again, a ubiquitous human nature is no human nature at all.

We must recognize that, within this debate, Calvin's concern was not with simple speculation over the nature of Christ's humanity, for what was said of his human nature had bearing in Calvin's mind on our understanding of and participation in his salvific history. The central facet of Calvin's doctrine of Christ's humanity is that through it he shared in our infirmities and became in every way, apart from sin, our brother. It was only through this fellowship of brotherhood that he could fulfill his office as Mediator and redeem us, and it was only through this fellowship of brotherhood that we dared to approach Christ and attach ourselves to him in faith. From Calvin's perspective, then, the Lutheran teaching on the *communicatio idiomata* destroyed this fellowship, for Christ in his humanity was no longer like us; he no longer shared in our infirmities and weaknesses, insofar as he possessed, through this exchange, the power of the divine nature.

We can thus see that, although a proper understanding of Christ's divine nature did underlie Calvin's teaching on the distinction of the natures in his debate with Servetus, within the debate over the *extra-calvinisticum*, it was his concern for the integrity of Christ's human nature, in light of the vital role Christ's humanity played in his construal of Christ's salvific activity, which guided his thinking. But what of the Lutheran concern that Calvin's approach in some sense divides Christ or holds up a second Christ, a Christ outside of his flesh, to faith? Does Calvin threaten the unity of Christ and thereby turn Christians away from the incarnate Christ as sole image of God, the one through whom alone they can know God in the truth of God's being? In answer to this question, we can say with assurance that at least within the context of Calvin's theology, this should not be a concern, for Calvin directs Christians nowhere other than to the *persona* of the Mediator, Christ in the unity of his two natures, to find and unite themselves to God as God has revealed Godself in God's love and mercy.

---

[79] Martin Chemnitz in I. A. Dorner, *History of the Development of the Doctrine of the Person of Christ*, trans. D. W. Simon, II, 2 (Edinburgh: T. & T. Clark, 1866), pp. 199–205, in Willis, *Catholic Christology*, p. II.

Calvin is clear that "we shall not attain a full manifestation of God's righteousness anywhere else than in the flesh of Christ," and he complains of those who "ashamed of Christ's humiliation . . . fly to God's incomprehensible Divinity." He concludes: "[F]aith will never reach heaven unless it submit to Christ, who appears to be a low and contemptible God, and will never be firm if it does not seek a foundation in the weakness of Christ."[80] Calvin does not argue for the ubiquity of Christ's divinity outside of his humanity to in any way turn believers to this divinity apart from his humanity. Indeed, as I noted in chapter 4, though Calvin maintains that Christ, as God's Eternal Word, is central to God's creation and providential care of the world, he never develops either of these doctrines Christologically; to do so would divert his readers' attention from Christ in his incarnation. Calvin is maintaining in his doctrine of the *extra-calvinisticum* that, just as we have to do with one who is really our brother in Christ, so, too, are we related through this brotherhood to one who is really God; but we are only related to God in and through the incarnate Christ, Christ as he is God manifest in the flesh. So Calvin begins his summary of Christ's history at the end of his discussion of the Creed: "We see that our whole salvation and all its parts are comprehended in Christ. We should therefore take care not to derive the least portion of it from anywhere else."[81]

The unity of natures in Christ's person

Calvin's teaching on the distinction of natures in Christ, then, should not be understood in contrast or in contradiction to his teaching on Christ's unity – he in no way intended to divert our attention from the unity of the natures in Christ's one person to either nature in separation from the other. Whatever Calvin writes about the distinction of natures in Christ is directed to his concern for Christ's office, executed in his *persona* as the Mediator, the God–human. Thus, this emphasis on distinction must be understood within the context of his teaching on Christ's unity; his claim is never simply that Christ's two natures are distinct, but that they are distinct within their unity by which they make up the one Christ. Calvin's teachings on the distinction and unity of natures in Christ must be taken together.

The close connection between these two notions in Calvin's thinking is evident in his introduction to the topic in the *Institutes* (II.xiv.1). There

---

[80] *Comm. John* 6:51, 1.262–263 (*CO* 47:152) and *Comm. John* 14:1, 11.81 (*CO* 47:322).
[81] *Inst.* II.xvi.19, p. 527 (*OS* 3:507–508).

Calvin first defines the relation of the natures in Christ's person in terms of both unity and distinction ("For we affirm his divinity so joined and united with his humanity that each retains its distinctive nature unimpaired, and yet these two natures constitute the one Christ"), and then he introduces the simile of the relationship of body and soul in a human person as the means by which to best understand this ontological reality of Christ's *persona*. Just as a body and soul are united to make one person while each maintains its own properties – our souls remain immortal, for example, and our bodies mortal – so, too, do Christ's divinity and humanity make one person while each nature retains its own properties. Through this simile, Calvin is in no sense trying to explain the mechanics of this relationship of union and distinction of the natures in Christ; he is only maintaining that such a union and distinction are not unreasonable. Calvin calls the relationship of the two natures in Christ a "great mystery"; it is not so much to be explained as to be gestured at through similes or other devices. This is how he understands the *communicatio idiomata*.

This is a term, he explains, that patristic writers used with reference to those passages in Scripture that apply attributes of one nature of Christ to the other – for example, when Paul writes that in Christ, "God purchased the Church with his blood," or when John writes: "No one has ascended into heaven but the Son of man who was in heaven."[82] God does not have blood, and Christ, as a man, was not then in heaven, "[b]ut because the selfsame one was both God and man, for the sake of the union of both natures [the author] gave to the one what belonged to the other."[83] It is not that either nature of Christ possesses the attributes of the other essentially or actually; Calvin says that these attributes are applied to the other nature "improperly" – but not without reason. For the writers of Scripture desired "earnestly to express this union of the two natures that is in Christ." The *communicatio idiomata*, in other words, is a means to express Christ's unity, not to explain it. In holding this opinion, Calvin is obviously diverging from his Lutheran critics who held that these passages point us to an actual ontological change in Christ's natures – a change on which the unity of Christ's person could be founded. As the natures share attributes and are intertwined, so is Christ in his person bound together. Calvin rejects this as an intermingling of the natures and prefers to read the *communicatio idiomata* more in the manner of theologians like Aquinas – it is a hermeneutical term that expresses Christ's unity without defining the

---

[82] *Inst.* II.xiv.2, p. 484 (*OS* 3:460).   [83] Ibid.

mechanics of that unity or threatening the integrity of the natures in that unity.[84]

This does not mean that Calvin has nothing to say of the how of this union, for, in his battle with Servetus, Calvin was forced to defend his claim that the distinction of Christ's natures was not incompatible with their unity. In raising this defense, he offers a glimpse of an explanation of the foundation for this unity. Again, the heart of Calvin's battle with Servetus lies in Calvin's insistence on the eternal and divine existence of Christ as the second person of the Trinity before Christ's incarnation. Servetus rejected this claim for the eternal, personal existence of Christ in his divinity, and argued that Calvin's claim that both the *Logos* and the incarnate Christ were God's Son was Nestorian since it implied two Sons. Calvin responded that Servetus had entirely misunderstood his point. He was not arguing that there were two Sons, but that the one, Eternal Son of God took on a human nature, not creating a second Son but manifesting himself therein. Christ was none other that God's eternal Son hypostatically united with his humanity – one person in two natures.[85] Here Calvin definitively separates himself from any charge of Nestorianism. He is clear that there is no human person of Christ apart from the person of the Word – Christ is the one person of the Word made flesh – and that likewise the person of the Word, God's eternal Son, is the One who has taken a human nature in Christ. Admittedly, Calvin does at times attribute a certain independence of activity or feeling to Christ in his human nature – Christ in his humanity may pray to God for those souls whom he in his divinity has predestined for damnation, but this is an independence of will necessary to the integrity of his human nature and which in no way impinges on the unity of that nature with the divine. Though Christ's human will is independent, it never stands opposed to his divine will, thereby introducing division into Christ.[86] There is, then, no second person of Christ apart from the person of the Word and no human nature of Christ apart from its assumption by and existence in the Word. Moreover, Calvin establishes the foundation of the union of natures in Christ in the Word's assumption of his human nature. As Calvin

---

[84] Willis explains Calvin's hermeneutical, rather than ontological, interest in the *communicatio idiomata*, but he accepts Witte's suggestion (Witte, *Die Christologie Calvins*, p. 500) that the whole of *Institutes* II.xiv in some way relates to the *communicatio*. This notion for Calvin occupies only a brief space within Calvin's broader exposition of the hermeneutical rules for reading Christological texts, and it plays a very minor role in his Christology overall. See Willis, *Catholic Christology*, pp. 65–67. Aquinas understands the *communicatio* in a manner similar to Calvin (*ST* III.16.4).

[85] *Inst.* II.xiv.5, p. 488 (*OS* 3:465).

[86] Again, Aquinas offers a beautiful defense of Calvin's position. See *ST* III.18, esp. III.18.5.

states at the beginning of the chapter: "The Word chose for himself the virgin's womb as a Temple in which to dwell."[87] Christ's unity rests not in the intertwining of natures in his one person, but on the activity of God, whereby the Son of God put on our nature and made himself also Son of man. And, given that this is the central point of Calvin's understanding of Christ's human nature, that through it Christ became our brother and identified with us, we can see as well that Christ did not simply clothe himself with this human nature, as a garment to be put on and taken off again, rather, he became human: God's Son is our brother. That is how, in and through Christ, we become children of God. Thus, the unity between the Word and its assumed human nature is not only guaranteed by the activity of the Word, but it is also substantial, for only in that way is the Word truly our brother.

Indeed, Calvin's emphasis on both the distinction and the unity of natures in Christ is most evident in his doctrine of our adoption as children of God. On the one hand, this adoption is possible only as each of the natures in Christ is distinct in its own integrity. We become Christ's brothers and sisters only because he is like us in every way except for sin, while we become God's children only because he is God's Eternal Son. Through his human nature, we are bound to Christ; through his divine nature, Christ is bound to God. On the other hand, this adoption is, in fact, enacted only through the true and complete unity of these natures. It is only because of this unity that God's Son is our brother and our brother, Christ, is God's Son. Our union with God is dependent on the union of humanity and divinity in Christ. Calvin, thus, is mindful that, though he distinguish Christ's natures, he not pull them apart, in the manner of Nestorius, for Christ's work as Mediator depends upon their conjunction.

Again, as I noted at the outset of this exploration of Calvin's notion of Christ's identity, Calvin believes that certain scriptural passages speak to Christ's humanity and others to his divinity. Those that set forth Christ's "true substance" most clearly, however, refer to neither nature apart from the other – they would, in fact, speak improperly if they were applied only to one nature or the other – but only to Christ in his whole person and office as the Mediator. Just as he unites us to God as God's children only through the union of natures in his one person, so, too, does he forgive sins, defeat death, teach us God's truth, and pour out God's Spirit through this union. Returning to Oberman's comment, mentioned in the Introduction

---

[87] *Inst.* II.xiv.I, p. 482 (*OS* 3:458).

above, that in Calvin there is a shift of accent "from a natures-Christology to an offices-Christology, converging toward a Mediator theology," Calvin's Christological focus is finally not on the distinction of natures, nor on their union; rather, he focuses on the activity of Christ in his *persona* as Mediator. What he says of Christ's identity, then, is directed to this activity as its foundation, even as that activity is directed to his identity, which is its goal, that God might be with us.

Conclusion

In this book, I have suggested that we best understand Calvin's Christological thinking if we pursue it under the rubric of Christ as Mediator, the rubric that Calvin himself repeatedly offers. Moreover, I have argued that we go to the heart of this Christology when we locate Christ's mediation within the context of the covenant history, even as Calvin does in his introduction to Christology in the *Institutes* (II.vi). This has allowed me to explicate Calvin's Christology expansively, under the threefold office of priest, prophet, and king, and to situate Calvin's understanding of Christ's person in relation to his office.

What, finally, can I say about the character of Calvin's Christology on this basis, and what might such a Christology contribute to contemporary Christological thinking? A first characteristic of Calvin's Christology is its eclecticism – that it embraces a variety of biblical themes and addresses a multitude of existential situations in the breadth of its exposition. But this eclecticism does not leave us with a doctrine that is scattered and unfocused.[1] Rather, the approach that I have taken suggests that the rich diversity in Calvin's thinking emerges from and revolves around a Christology that is historical and relational in character. That is what it means to locate Christology in Christ's office as Mediator of the covenant. Lest this seem like a trivial observation, let me expand on the significance of these additional characteristics, turning first to Calvin's concern for history and then to his attention to relationality. When we have understood each of these in their interaction, we will uncover two additional qualities of Calvin's project, its dynamism and its personalism.

In chapter 2 of this book, I introduced Calvin's understanding of history in relation to his Christology. The import of history for Calvin was suggested by his attention both to the broader history of the covenant, that

---

[1] A conclusion that Gerrish reaches about Robert Peterson's monograph of Calvin's Christology (*Calvin's Doctrine of Atonement*). See Gerrish, *Grace and Gratitude*, p. 56, fn. 16.

forms the context for the content and form of his Christological discussion in the *Institutes*, and to the Gospel history that clothes Christ, in which we are to seek "every kind of good." But we grasp the significance of Calvin's attention to history only when we take into account his understanding of the category of history – its matter and purpose. For Calvin, an interest in history is an interest in both its actuality and its rhetorical shape and intent. In this conclusion, let me recall these two ideas to our attention and add a third, the narrativity of history, on which I have traded without naming to this point.

Calvin continually emphasizes the actuality of the history that Christ accomplishes, an actuality on which our renewed relationship with God is based. Christ appeases God's wrath, serving as a sacrifice and substitution to cover our sin. Christ wrestles with and defeats our enemies – sin, death, and the devil. Christ pours out his Spirit upon us, filling us with all manner of God's grace. Christ teaches us the perfect understanding of God's Law and the true significance of his work among us. For Calvin, there is a covenant between God and humanity only insofar as Christ has enacted that covenant in his threefold office. God's merciful will is realized in human history only as Christ has concretized and fulfilled that will, incarnating God's love in the world. When Calvin focuses readers' attention on Christ's Gospel history, he is focusing their attention on what Christ has done and established in history to make God's grace present and active among them and within them.

History, in this sense, is what Christ does to redeem us.[2] Calvin's emphasis on this point, while not surprising (though some fifteenth- and sixteenth-century humanists would have neglected it), is notable. For Calvin, the world is altered, and we in our relation with God are altered through what Christ has done.[3] This is the foundation for everything else that Calvin writes. In particular, Calvin asks us to attend closely to Christ's history because we are to draw confidence from that history – confidence in God's love and in the blessing and protection that accrues to us from that love. Such confidence, Calvin would surely argue, is firmly founded only in

---

[2] I have explored Calvin's understanding of creation little in this book, but I do not mean here to limit Calvin's understanding of history to the history of redemption. Calvin will also speak of the history of creation, and here, again, it concerns both what God has done and how this work should shape us in its rhetorical power. See the *Argumentum* to his commentary on Genesis (1.57–64 [*CO* 23:5–11]).

[3] As Hesselink points out, only the world-altering reality of what Christ accomplishes can make sense of Calvin's view of the proleptic grace present to the people of God of the Old Testament (I. John Hesselink, "Calvin und Heilsgeschichte," *Oikonomia: Heilsgeschichte als Thema der Theologie*, Felix Christ, ed. (Hamburg-Bergstedt: Herbert Reich Evang. Verlag GmbH, 1967), pp. 168–170).

events that are actual and concrete. There is little of the ideal – what he would term the "fabulous" – in his thinking.[4]

The term "history," for Calvin, also refers to texts and events (insofar as they have been orchestrated by the divine historian) that have been authored so to shape the character and actions of history's readers and observers. Implicit in Calvin's notion of history, in other words, is the presentation of the events of history in a manner that is intentionally subjectively effective. Thus, he in his theological and exegetical writing, following the lead of the Gospels, presents Christ's history with an eye to this rhetorical effectiveness. We saw an example of this rhetorical intentionality behind the events of history and their textual presentation in the discussion of Christ's judgment and death in our place. There Calvin argued for the necessity of Christ's death as a criminal and not at the hands of an angry mob, so that we might see that he, the innocent one, was judged in the place of the guilty. God, therefore, dictated the shape of these events to present on the stage of history God's mercy, active in Christ, whereby we were relieved of our guilt. It was to no purpose for Christ to bear away this guilt if we were not grasped by this actuality so that we turned to God in Christ in faith and love. This concern for rhetorical shaping was likewise evident in the discussion of the relative meaning of God's "hatred" for humanity before Christ's advent (*Inst.* II.xvi.2), as Calvin argued that the story was told in this way to impress upon us the direness of our situation and the magnitude of God's mercy, that we, again, might be moved to the proper attitude of piety.

I should be clear that by "rhetorical shaping" I refer not to "mere rhetoric," but to the power of word and event in the meanings they enact and convey to mold human lives in their depths. Serene Jones has written persuasively on Calvin's rhetorical purposes. My point is that Calvin found history – or, more specifically, the biblical history – to be the most powerful rhetorical tool of which God has availed Godself, precisely because its rhetorical force is bound up with its actuality. The rhetoric of God's history is never mere rhetoric, inasmuch as the presence and activity of God in Christ are the motive forces at work within it. (We might say that here God practices what God preaches.) And, indeed, if we pushed this consideration further, I would argue that, for Calvin, the primary *locus* of God's rhetoric is in this history as event – here God's love is communicated most powerfully – while history as the text of Scripture serves as clothing

---

[4] Hence his emphasis on the truth of narratives of this history in Scripture. See Millet, *Calvin et la dynamique*, p. 263.

for these events or, to borrow another of Calvin's metaphors, as spectacles to focus our understanding of them.

Yet we have no access to the rhetorical power of these events except as they are clothed; hence the significance of narrativity in Calvin's Christology. We have contact with God's saving work in Christ principally in the stories that we have been told about that work, the histories that have been written, and the narrative shape of these stories is essential to Calvin's Christological work. Calvin himself never reflects self-consciously on the narrative element in his theology, but it pervades the Christological writings that I have discussed. In his commentaries, Calvin continually returns us to the narrative in the biblical histories, while at the same time locating and explaining nonhistorical books (like the Psalms) in the broader historical narrative. This close relation that he maintains with the historical narrative is what, in many ways, separates his commentaries both from some allegorizing efforts that preceded him (for example the work of Bernard or Richard of St. Victor) and the dogmatic interests of some more contemporary to him (Bucer, for example).[5] We see this interest in narrative confirmed if we accept my argument at the beginning of chapter 2 that the first two books of the *Institutes* are organized around the narrative that Calvin found in Scripture, culminating (II.xvi) with an exposition of the creedal synopsis of the Gospel narrative.

Please note, I am not interested in making grand claims for narrative here – I believe that Calvin turned to narrative not out of any commitment to be a narrative theologian (whatever we might think that to be), but rather because narrative plainly recommends itself in making an account of a history.[6] As Wayne Booth explains, we turn instinctively to stories when we

---

[5] The fruit of Muller's work on Calvin's method in his commentaries and the *Institutes* supports this notion. By reserving the bulk of his theological discussion of the *loci* that emerge from his commentaries for the *Institutes*, he is able to maintain a *brevitas* that allows him to stay close to the text (Muller, *The Unaccommodated Calvin*, pp. 101–117). This *brevitas* contrasts, as well, with the expansive nature of his sermons, which explains, to some degree, Dawn DeVries' difficulty in locating an attention to the narrative in Calvin (DeVries, *Jesus Christ in the Teaching of Calvin*, pp. 41–43). Although DeVries will argue that, for Calvin, "there is little or no difference between the task of the preacher and the task of the commentator" (p. 8), I would follow Muller's understanding that Calvin's sermons are distinct from his commentaries in their willingness to move beyond the text for the sake of doctrinal development or hortatory application (Muller, *The Unaccommodated Calvin*, p. 143). I also believe that DeVries' work evinces the presence of a narrative concern in Calvin's sermons, if we understand narrativity at the low level that I work with here and not in late twentieth- or early twenty-first-century terms (see DeVries, *Jesus Christ in the Teaching of Calvin*, pp. 32, 45 fn. 47).

[6] This fundamental connection of Scripture's narrative to its history explains why Calvin reads the narrative expansively, given his understanding of the nature and purpose of history, rather than tightly, staying always between the lines of the narrative, as some twentieth-century theologians would request. See George Stroup, "Narrative in Calvin's Hermeneutic," in *John Calvin and The Church: A Prism of Reform*, Timothy George, ed. (Louisville: Westminster/John Knox, 1990), pp. 158–171.

wish to tell the stuff of our lives.[7] But the use of and attention to narrative on Calvin's part does bear significant implications for his Christology, related to his commitment to the actuality and rhetorical form of the Christological history.

I noted above the eclecticism of Calvin's Christological thought while arguing, at the same time, for its coherence. It is Calvin's use of narrative that allows him to integrate this diversity of material within his Christology into a harmonious whole by providing a framework for this material that is open to and congruent with its diversity. Insofar as Calvin seeks to capture in his theology all that Christ did, seen through the lens of the wide-ranging history of Israel as that history is constituted by the ministries of priests, prophets, and kings, he is committed to cobbling together a kaleidoscopic Christological mosaic from stones not necessarily cut to fit. He wants to depict Christ as fountain, brother, criminal, and king as Christ exhibited these realities in the varied details of his life. This eclecticism is essential to Calvin's thinking, for it represents simply the fullness of Christ's history, and he can make good on this eclecticism only as he grounds it thoroughly in that history. To commit oneself to a history in its actuality is to commit oneself to a broad, diverse, detailed reality that threatens at all times to exceed one's grasp.

By tying his theological appropriation of this history to the narrative in which it is instantiated, Calvin has significantly extended his analytical and synthetic reach. Narrative, in its mimetic relation to the events it presents, can conform itself to the diversity of those events, allowing them each to shine forth with integrity even in their juxtaposition with one another. Hence, Christ can appear at one moment as the criminal, bereft of God, thrown into the abyss of human guilt and despair, while in the next he triumphs as the warrior-king over Satan's hordes who beset us. Narrative also conforms events to a unity of perspective (which counts as a strength if you are looking for coherence), but this unity need not imply univocity. It is sufficient for narrative that perspectives resolve within the narrative's logic, so that Christ's story can be simultaneously the story of the wrath of God poured out on the innocent Christ, the justice of God pronouncing an unimpeached verdict over all sinfulness, and the mercy of God superintending the whole process.[8] The trick in reading complex

---

[7] Wayne Booth, *The Company We Keep: An Ethics of Fiction* (Berkeley: University of California Press, 1988), pp. 13–15.

[8] Indeed, this capacity of narrative coherently to render multiple metaphors and to reflect the multi-faceted nature of reality resolves, I would argue, DeVries' concern over the incompatibility of Calvin's Christology and soteriology (DeVries, *Jesus Christ in the Teaching of Calvin*, p. 96).

narratives is to find the categories or storylines from which one can follow the variety of narrative threads. Calvin found these in Israel's covenant history with God, and a methodological assumption of this book is that we can best understand Calvin's own Christological narrative, offered in II.xiv of the *Institutes*, by reading it through precisely these categories of the threefold office, offered in II.xv.

Calvin's Christology, then, is tied to history's narrativity first through the capacity of narrative to represent the complex diversity of a life – in this case Christ's life – in its actuality. (I will turn at the end of this conclusion to the corollary of this capacity – that narrative can also constrain and distort such a life in its presentation.) But history's narrativity serves Calvin in a second way, insofar as it is particularly conducive to his rhetorical project. As Calvin has argued, a central aim of Christ's history is to present God as a loving parent so that we, recognizing God's love, might draw near to God in faith and obedience. The presentation and formation of character (God's and ours, respectively) are central to Calvin's theological task, and Calvin is quite deliberate in turning narrative to these ends, though he never names it as such.

Hans Frei has written on the power of narrative to depict character, a claim grounded, at least in part, in his study of Calvin. In realistic narrative, or narrative that is "history-like," Frei explains, the identities of the characters within the narrative are rendered through the interplay of subjectivity and action within external circumstances fit to the characters.[9] Such narratives are not meant to refer primarily to a more truly real "beyond," but locate their meaning precisely in this rendering of subject and social setting. Frei's understanding of this capacity of narrative is apt to Calvin's Christological work, even more so when it is married to Frei's earlier observations that, in the Gospels, Christ's identity is constituted by the intersection of intention and action over the course of his history.[10] The interplay of these two notions – that narratives render character and that human identities are grounded in the relation of intention and action, which is precisely the relation that narratives convey – is vital to Calvin's use of narrative to depict persons in his claim that God has rendered God's own character through history in its narrativity and its actuality (not in its mere "history-likeness").

We saw Calvin's perception of the effectiveness of this mode of personal depiction in the preceding chapter in his argument that Christ drew his disciples near through his humanity while gradually rendering his divinity

[9] Frei, *The Eclipse of Biblical Narrative*, pp. 13ff.
[10] Hans Frei, *The Identity of Jesus Christ* (Philadelphia: Fortress Press, 1967), pp. 91–94.

plain over the course of his history – the narrative of his enacted intention. Thus, after his resurrection he was recognized as both Lord and God.[11] More significant for Calvin's theology, however, is the claim that God reveals Godself as Father through the course of Christ's history; note that here we encounter the uniquely Trinitarian marriage of God's eternal intention with Christ's temporal action through which God's identity is depicted to the world.

The flip side of this capacity of narrative to depict character is Calvin's intent that the Christological narrative render our character, not merely as we are, telling the truth of our sinfulness, but as we should be, working to effect our sanctification. This capacity of narrative to shape and form the character of its readers is evident broadly throughout Calvin's work. It was illustrated above in Calvin's understanding of Christ's judgment before Pilate and comes through even more powerfully in his discussion of Christ's descent into hell. In many ways, these passages function as corollaries to God's revelation as Father; through them we find ourselves conformed into children of God whose lives are shaped by a repentant gratitude. But Calvin's explicit interest in the narrative shaping of the lives of Christians is most evident in his specific discussion of sanctification in the *Institutes* (III.iii, vii–xi), that he organizes under the categories of mortification and vivification. Through this process of mortification and vivification, we are to become more Christ-like as we participate in Christ's narrative – in his crucifixion and resurrection. Our participation in Christ is, for Calvin, an engagement in Christ's history mediated through the narrative of the triduum. My interest here, then, begins with Wayne Booth's notion of the capacity of narrative to shape character;[12] but Calvin's use of narrative moves beyond its imaginative power insofar as the narrative in question seeks not merely to shape us, but to induce our participation in it through a community of activity with Christ in his history.

Here we are led to the second aspect of Calvin's Christology as I have defined it, its fundamentally relational character. In some sense, to pronounce his Christology relational is to rely on a truism – all Christologies, to some degree, revolve around the renewal of our relationship with God in and through our relationship with Christ. This is why the rubric of mediation is a commonplace across Christologies. But, nonetheless, it is useful to highlight this as a mark of Calvin's Christology for, in its connection to

---

[11] Ch. 6, pp. 198–201 above.
[12] Booth, *The Company We Keep*, pp. 227–373. Note particularly his discussion of narrative and the determination of patterns of desire (p. 272) in relation to Calvin's discussion of sanctification in the *Institutes*.

the historical concern within his thinking, it reveals two essential aspects of his theological project overall.

Calvin's emphasis on relationship is obvious in his choice of the covenant history to provide the context for his Christological work. Christology is hereby defined by its place in the broader story of God's desire for relationship with God's chosen.[13] Equally, we must say that the covenant history defines the type of Christological relationship with which Calvin deals – it is the kind of relationship that is formed and consummated within a history. Hence, in chapter 4, I was led to construe the communion we have with Christ primarily as a fellowship, as a relationship in a social context, or a relationship among persons, rather than a relationship in a mystical or metaphysical context. This means, among other things, that I believe Calvin to rely more on the metaphor of the parenthood of God and brotherhood of Christ, such that we are God's children through our fraternity with Christ, than the metaphor of God or Christ as the fountain of all good from which we draw through our mystical participation in Christ.

Most significantly for my project, however, the covenantal relationship at the heart of Calvin's Christology is a relationship both shaped and consummated by a history. Indeed, it has been the burden of this book as a whole to indicate the manner in which Calvin defines this relationship through Christ's activity as Mediator. Thus, throughout my argument, the subjective and objective dimensions of Christ's work as Mediator have been reiterated – that Christ mediates God's covenant with God's Church both as he effects that covenant in his history and as he draws God's chosen into that covenant in faith through his history. This theme was reflected in my discussion of the Old Testament covenant history where, for example, we saw that the priestly office was effective in the Church both as it enacted God's forgiveness in the midst of God's people, Israel, and as it led the people, through that effective forgiveness, to look in hope for the Christ. In chapter 3, on Christ's priesthood, I discussed the manner in which Christ reconciles the Church to God by addressing not only God's wrath toward the Church, but also the Church's fear of and alienation from God. And, in chapter 5, I considered the manner in which Christ's history, through its rich depiction of God's grace, directs God's chosen to place their faith in

---

[13] Here Calvin distinguishes himself from the approach of Duns Scotus, in which God's desire for relationship with the human nature of Christ serves as the formal context for God's broader relationship with Christ's brothers and sisters (see Allen Wolter, "John Duns Scotus on the Primacy of the Personality of Christ," in *Franciscan Christology*, Damian McElrath, ed. [St. Bonaventure, NY: Franciscan Institute Publications, 1980], pp. 139–145), or that of Bonaventure, where Christology is defined as much by God's desire to complete God's Creation in its perfection as by God's need to repair an already broken relationship (see Hayes, *The Hidden Center*, pp. 161–182).

Christ, accepting as the foundation for this faith "the rich store of goods," the forgiveness, strength, wisdom, security, and mercy established by Christ in his history.

To some degree, every theology includes both of these elements in their doctrines of the redemption found in Christ. On the one hand, it is difficult to speak of Christ's redemption without a sense of the foundation of this redemption in Christ's objective work, apart from any subjective appropriation on the part of humanity, while, on the other hand, it is hard to imagine a theology that does not assume and seek faith and love as the appropriate response of the believer when confronted by Christ's redemptive work. What is noteworthy about Calvin's theology, then, is not simply the inclusion of both of these dimensions within his Christology, but the methodological orientation of his Christology around them. As I have just discussed, this is endemic to Calvin's choice of history as a vehicle for Christology, with its stress on both actuality and rhetorical effect.

Thus, Calvin maintains coordinate emphases on the grace established by Christ in his history and on the fruition of this grace only as it is appropriated by believers through a faith elicited by Christ's history. Because God in Christ has drawn near and touched us and borne the Father's wrath for us, we believe that God might love us. Because Christ has wrestled with death in the face of abandonment by God, we take heart in our own struggles with despair. Because Christ has defeated our enemies, we find security in him. Because Christ has filled us with all manner of good things, we seek salvation in him. Insofar, then, as he has enacted God's covenant with us, he has drawn us to participation in the covenant through faith. When Calvin narrates Christ's Gospel history, he is not simply reciting a list of Christ's accomplishments so that we might know what Christ has done apart from us; he is representing Christ to us, that we might be united to Christ by the faith that Christ's Gospel clothing evokes. Christ's mission, in other words, is not simply to "save" humanity, nor to cover our sins; rather, it is to effect a relationship between humanity and God – this is what God desires – and this relationship necessitates both enaction and elicitation.

The understanding of this interplay of the subjective and objective as the effect of Christ's mediating work has implications for the long debate over Calvin and the bilateral covenant. It suggests that recent discussions of the covenant in Calvin that wish to balance an emphasis on God's sovereignty in the determination of the covenant with a recognition of Calvin's profound sense of the mutuality of the covenant are on the mark;[14] but notable in all

---

[14] See Anthony Hoekema, "The Covenant of Grace in Calvin's Teaching"; Lyle Bierma, "Federal Theology in the Sixteenth Century: Two Traditions"; and Peter Lillback, *The Binding of God*.

of these discussions is a relative absence of Christological discourse, leaving the field to the contrast or tension between divine election and human responsibility. One wonders if Calvin's complex thinking on this matter would not resolve more cleanly with the recognition of both the Christological instantiation of God's establishing grace and the Christological foundation and source – with the activities of redemption and the gift of the Spirit – of the human response in return. Without an understanding of his Christology, you cannot understand covenant in Calvin, in any dimension.

These two characteristics of Calvin's thinking about Christ – its concern for history and relationality – capture in some ways the flow of this book, as I have moved from the office of Christ, enacted in his history, to the person of Christ, with whom we are called to transforming relationship. My exposition, I hope, has depicted a history that opens out on a relationship and a relationship defined by its history. Indeed, it is the interaction of these two characteristics that suffuses Calvin's Christology with the dynamic and personal qualities inherent in it.

The dynamism of Calvin's Christology has often been noted,[15] and I have striven to illustrate precisely this dynamism as it is embodied in the salvation worked out by Christ in his Gospel history. There are any number of Christological rubrics under which this dynamism could be explained. Calvin's Christology is dynamic insofar as it is undergirded by Christ's three-fold office, which is the foundation of Christ's reality for Calvin. Likewise, Calvin's penchant for describing Christ as "God manifest in the flesh" points us to an understanding of who Christ is – the God–human – in terms of what Christ does – reveal God through his incarnation. The static reality of hypostatic union, that in Christ divinity and humanity are united, is subordinated to the dynamic function of God's revelation in Christ, that in Christ his divinity is revealed through his humanity. But I prefer to understand this dynamism in relation to the broader historical orientation of Calvin's Christology because it not only catches up these other understandings, but also directs us to the overarching purpose of Christ's dynamic work for Calvin, the renewal of covenant fellowship between humanity and God insofar as we are united to Christ in his history.[16]

The dynamism of Calvin's Christology is evident in Christ's history in the first place because this history is the *locus* and medium of the grace of

---

[15] See Barth, *Church Dogmatics* I.2, p. 168; Raitt, "Calvin's Use of Persona," p. 280; and Witte, *Die Christologie Calvins*, p. 505.

[16] E. H. Harbison writes helpfully about the nexus of dynamism, history and Christology in Calvin. See "Calvin's Sense of History," in *Christianity and History* (Princeton: Princeton University Press, 1964), pp. 283–285.

God that Christ enacts. The focus of Calvin's theology is on all that Christ has done, from his birth to his ascension, through which he has reconciled us to God, overcome death and the devil, poured out upon us God's Spirit, and united us into one body in him; out of this history, Calvin has told us, Christ has given to us "a rich store of every good." But the dynamism of this history is significant in relation to the manifestation of this grace, as well as its enactment. As Christ's history was originally presented in Christ's activity and is now represented through the proclamation of the Gospel, its dynamism works out beyond itself, drawing the faithful into its vortex; we are drawn into the flow of Christ's history, as our lives are shaped by the Christological movement of mortification and vivification, and thereby into the flow of God's history with God's Church, as we are brought into covenant relationship with God. Christ's history, for Calvin, is dynamic not only as it is enacted, but as it is engaging, and this engagement is fundamental to his notion of salvation as the realization of the Church's fellowship with God through faith.

Witte criticizes Calvin for his overemphasis on this dynamism, arguing that Calvin undervalues the salvific significance of the hypostatic union in and of itself – that simply as Christ has taken on human nature and united it to the divine, so he has, in some sense, divinized all human nature and given believers a share in the divine life. As a case in point, he criticizes Calvin for the appropriation of the patristic notion that Christ took what is ours to give us what is his (in II.xii.2) without drawing the same conclusions as would the patristic and medieval authors before him – that Christ united himself to human nature so that human nature in Christ and in all believers could in some metaphysical way be united to and have a share in the divine.[17]

Witte's critique boils down to a concern that Calvin, in his emphasis on Christ's office, has neglected Christ's person; but, in making this critique, he unfortunately does not follow what Calvin will say about the significance of this Christological exchange, and so he loses Calvin's point. However, we will pursue Calvin's argument since it illustrates beautifully not only the dynamic quality of Calvin's Christological thinking, but also the personal quality tied to this dynamism, which capitalizes on Christ's hypostatic union in a different way.

Calvin expresses Christ's exchange in terms of sonship – that he who is the Son of God became the Son of Man that we may with him become children of God. The medium of this exchange is Christ's brotherhood with us. He took on our human nature and shared all that was ours so that

---

[17] See Witte, *Die Christologie Calvins*, pp. 495–496.

he might become our brother and, through this shared brotherhood, adopt us into the family of God. Calvin writes:

Ungrudgingly he took our nature upon himself to impart to us what was his, and to become both Son of God and Son of man in common with us. Hence that holy brotherhood which he commends with his own lips when he says: "I am ascending to my Father and your Father, to my God and your God" (John 20:17). In this way we are assured of the inheritance of the Heavenly Kingdom; for the only Son of God, to whom it wholly belongs has adopted us as his brothers.[18]

For Calvin, Christ through this glorious exchange gives us a share in the divine life; but, he gives us a share in this life through an interpersonal relationship of brotherhood, sealed by our faith in Christ through the work of the Spirit, not through a union of natures. It is this share of the divine life through our relationship with Christ our brother that I have labeled our covenant fellowship with God, realized through Christ's work as Mediator.

Calvin's notion of exchange illustrates the dynamic character of his Christology insofar as it is clear that this fellowship is dynamic in and of itself, consisting in the give and take of mercy and faith, and is also realized through the dynamics of Christ's history. Christ truly becomes our brother and unites himself to us not simply by taking on a human nature, but by sharing all that is ours in his history. He is hungry, he is anxious, he is, at times, ignorant of God's ways, he laments the fate of the reprobate, he suffers, he dies, he is faced with despair over the prospect of abandonment by God. It is through this participation in our experience that he is able to draw near and touch us, to reach out a brotherly hand to us so that we might grasp his hand and be lifted into fellowship with him. Again, Calvin is attempting to describe the interpersonal relationship of faith and love that is realized through Christ's work as Mediator, and such a relationship comes about dynamically, insofar as it is worked out in the histories of the persons involved.

Equally, we must recognize that such dynamics are both achieved personally and call us to respond personally. It is the person of Christ, not in his metaphysical definition but in his personal experience, who comes to the fore in the above description of his union with us. The union he establishes through this shared experience is a personal union with himself – a fellowship – and this union opens out into our personal union with God – not through a union of our natures with God, but through our union as children with their Father.

---

[18] *Inst.* II.xii.2, pp. 465–466 (*OS* 3:439).

Indeed, in this last union, we see that the personal quality of Calvin's Christology rather than excluding the significance of the hypostatic union, serves to emphasize it in a different way. It is critical that Christ is God manifest in the flesh, not only that God in Christ might draw near, but that God through Christ's history might be revealed, and be revealed personally, as Father. With all that has been written about Calvin's intuition of the hiddenness of God, we must recognize that it is only God's nature – that whatness of God – that is hidden. Who God is manifests itself clearly for those who have joined themselves in faith to Christ. God is a loving parent who has turned Godself in love toward God's elect.[19] Thus, there is a deeply personal quality to Calvin's theology that emerges in his understanding of the person and work of Christ.

What I have found, then, in Calvin's work is a Christology that is historical, richly diverse, relational, dynamic, and personal. I hope as I have made this case that all of these characteristics have recommended themselves on their own merit. Surely each of these attributes can be critiqued for what it is not. For example, however much the personal dimension of Calvin's Christology might both capture the quality of Christ's ministry found in the Gospel accounts and speak to the hearts of those who live in a numbingly impersonal world, it misses the majesty of John's prologue and the metaphysical mysticism that can ecstatically lift us out of this world. Of course, Calvin in his eclecticism embraces this second vision as well, at least to a degree – hence the section on Christ as the fountain of life – but this cosmic quality is clearly subordinated to the personal throughout his work.

This is only to point out that, in saying many things, Calvin has not said everything, and this is less a critique of Calvin than a suggestion for the necessity of diversity among theologians as well as within a theology. Yet, if Calvin's Christological work is to prove useful to contemporary discussion, the first of the characteristics above, its concern for history, must be addressed in relation to at least two concerns. The first relates to Calvin's tendency to read the many narratives of Scripture as the one narrative of God's history, while the second asks, conversely, if there is anything of what we would call history in the narrative with which Calvin leaves us.

Although there is the possibility of exaggeration in my emphasis on Calvin's unification of the biblical narratives, the picture that I have presented is entirely coherent with Calvin's work across his commentaries and

---

[19] Of course, we can ask what kind of parent only turns in love to his chosen, and not to all his children, but that is a question for another time.

in the *Institutes*. Calvin recognizes only one consistent history of Israel that in all of its parts depends on and points to Jesus of Nazareth as its Mediator; and, although he recognizes the divergent voices of the four Gospels, he nonetheless is comfortable compiling a harmony of the Synoptic Gospels and of assuming that all these three together with John's Gospel tell precisely the same history, only with different ends in mind.[20] This unifying program springs, at least in part, from Calvin's conviction of the one Author behind the whole of the biblical text, but it also serves to quell any intra-biblical dissent from the theological vision that Calvin articulates from the text.

There is a loss, however, in such a program, as voices are silenced that could open us to the varied communities woven into Scripture and to an even more immense diversity of theological currents that would flow from Scripture. Taking these each in turn, it would be obvious to the modern reader that Calvin has utterly effaced one community in his reading of the Hebrew Scriptures, the Jewish community, who would find it difficult to recognize their faith in the texts as Calvin reads them (and this would neither surprise nor dismay Calvin). Calvin does validate the people of Israel in the Hebrew Scriptures as God's people who, when they respond in faith, live fully, even if only in the shadows, within God's promise; but Calvin is clear that, in doing so, they are living the life of the Church, not the synagogue. In Calvin's narrative, the Jewish people are entirely dispossessed of their narrative as they were their land. This displacement is emblematic of a number of communities that lose their voice in Calvin's somewhat monolithic narrative, the distinctive communities of each of the four Gospels, for example; and I wonder if it would be possible to work within a biblical narrative that maintains multiple narratives, each rendering the particular identities of their communities in response to God's activities in their midst, even as they are interwoven to create a more complex tapestry. The advantage of attending to these multiple narratives, beyond a faithfulness to the communities that produced them, is that they are more adequate to capturing that complex and multifaceted truth of a person's life, especially a life as profound as that of Jesus.

Likewise, we must note that Calvin's own history intrudes on his reading of Scripture's history so that themes that might emerge from the text are displaced or muted by concerns more contemporary to a sixteenth-century

---

[20] In his introduction to the Synoptic harmony, he claims to arrange the three Gospels into "one unbro-ken chain" or "a single picture." The result attends to the differences in each Gospel, but the broader context of each history is lost. See Dieter Schellong, *Calvins Auslegung der synoptischen Evangelien* (Munich: Chr. Kaiser Verlag, 1969), pp. 58–60; Stroup, "Narrative in Calvin's Hermeneutic," p. 167; and Millet, *Calvin et la dynamique*, pp. 265–266).

pastor and civic leader.[21] Hence, for Calvin, Christ's prophetic office is tied more to the teaching of right doctrine than to the denunciation of injustice, especially injustice toward the powerless, though this latter theme is not absent from Calvin's work (see his commentary on Amos 2:6, for example). A contemporary historical Christology would want to recover themes intrinsic to the biblical text – Christ as liberator from oppressive political and social forces, not just spiritual forces – that are backgrounded in Calvin's narrative. Of course, in doing so, we must recognize that we are no closer to the simple history of Scripture than was Calvin; rather, we are allowing our histories to aid us in recovering truths of the biblical history, even as Calvin did. This, again, opens us to a Christological narrative that is more complex as it now must recognize the depths within a scriptural narrative sounded by the multiple narratives of Scripture's readers as well.

Through a reading of Scripture that is informed by this greater diversity, recognizing both the multiple narratives within Scripture and the multiple narratives of Scripture's readers, we gain access to a greater diversity of detail within the text than even Calvin grants us. Some modern readers of the text, for example, have brought into sharp focus details that in the past were often lost – Christ's solidarity with the poor, his inclusion of women in his circle, or the place of table fellowship at the center of his ministry.[22] The challenge for these efforts is to not lose the breadth of Calvin's picture by excluding formerly dominant details in the process of highlighting those that have been neglected.

Whatever we say of the scriptural narrative or narratives, for them to be helpful in a Christology in conversation with Calvin, they need to be able to make claims of historicity, claims that Calvin treasured but that he would no longer be able to make with the same intellectual assurance. We are interested in stories that make sense of our lives – hence the interest in which narratives we have available; but essential to Scripture's narrative(s), which claims that God acts and that God is present, is the actuality of the narrative. It is not enough that it be history-like. This is the appeal of the Jesus Seminar and the plethora of Christologies that have emerged from it. Their claims for actuality are compelling for many in the face of a general skepticism about the historical accuracy of the Gospel accounts.

---

[21] Calvin would have recognized this. Given his concern that a narration of history be rhetorically useful, it must always be shaped by the social situation of the narrator.

[22] John Sobrino, *Jesus the Liberator: A Historical–Theological Reading of Jesus of Nazareth*, trans. Paul Burns and Francis McDonagh (Maryknoll, NY: Orbis Books, 1999), pp. 67–104; Elisabeth Schüessler Fiorenza, *In Memory of Her: A Feminist Theological Reconstruction of Christian Origins* (New York: Crossroad, 1983), pp. 105–159; John Dominic Crossan, *The Historical Jesus: The Life of a Mediterranean Peasant* (San Francisco: HarperSanFrancisco, 1991), pp. 265–353.

On the basis of these claims for actuality, then, these authors can present a rhetorically powerful case for what Jesus, in fact, enacted and accomplished. There are, however, problems with this approach.[23]

First, the scriptural narratives of Christ's history quickly recede into the background in many modern historical approaches. This leads to a loss of meaning, as Frei has documented,[24] and to the displacement, yet again, of the multiple narratives testifying to Christ's life by the monolithic narrative of the historian. Often modern historians claim to be recovering the voices of lost communities; but, in fact, the product of their efforts seldom sounds like the voice of any community that responded to Christ's ministry, unless there existed, miraculously, an unrecorded group of twentieth- and twenty-first-century academics in Galilee some two thousand years ago.

Second, it is not clear that we are any closer to the events of Christ's history through all of our modern efforts. I am persuaded by Schweitzer's original claim that historical Jesuses too often look more like the historian than like Jesus. Indeed, perhaps the most damning fact for contemporary claims to historical accuracy on this matter is the booming cottage industry that has arisen to produce history after history. One would think that, if we had gotten it right, we could stop. This opens the question of whether the category of history is useful in Christology and, hence, whether Calvin has anything to say to us, given our difficulties of getting back to anything that we can call history.[25] This development would be ironic with respect to Calvin, given that our deep interest in history in relation to Christology is rooted, I would argue, in his work.

I believe that Calvin does have something to say to us, and this is evident in the path he opens for us out of the dilemma of obscured historicity. Calvin's assumption of history's two edges – that it both narrates God's activity in Christ and shapes communal response through that narration – clears

---

[23] Luke Timothy Johnson has done an excellent job arguing the fallacy behind the claims of the Jesus Seminar to get at the truth of the Jesus of history (*The Real Jesus: The Misguided Quest for the Historical Jesus and the Truth of the Traditional Gospels* [San Francisco: Harper Collins, 1996]). His book also notes their broad popular reception, an indication of rhetorical effectiveness, in spite of their problems. What follows largely agrees with his work, I believe, though Calvin would place far more emphasis on the importance of the facts of Jesus' ministry if it is the case that in the whole of Jesus' life we have God made manifest to us and salvation enacted.

[24] Frei, *The Eclipse of Biblical Narrative*.

[25] Johnson documents the difficulty of getting back to the details of Christ's history through the canons of modern historiography quite ably (*The Real Jesus*, pp. 105ff.), and on this basis seems at times to dismiss the usefulness of history as a category for understanding the meaning of Christ (pp. 133–134). In fact, he is directing his attack against reconstructions of Christ's history on the basis of modern canons of historiography as the basis of faith. We need to distinguish this reconstructive approach from the claim that an understanding of what Christ did in his history is vital to understanding the identity of the Resurrected one. The question, then, is how we might come to such an understanding.

a way to Christ's activity through that communal response. Christ's history is only complete when it is set in relation to the community that responds in faith and obedience, and in the Gospels we have accounts of communities who, whatever their record on obedience, have responded in faith.[26] In the Gospels, then, we have complete histories of Christ that capture the actuality of his history in and through the reality of a community determined by that actuality. Christ's history is inscribed on these communities so that we hear what is truly his history in their subjective echoes of his objective work.[27] Here subjective and objective are interwoven in our apprehension of the real, such that, though we may be clear on their differences (a Christian's receptive faith is distinct from Christ's atoning death), we must, in practice, treat them as a whole. Here, also, we see the importance of recognizing the diversity of narratives involved in the transmission of Christ's history, insofar as acknowledging this diversity of communities that stand behind the narratives is essential for communicating the fullness of his history.[28]

---

[26] By "gospels," I mean the four Gospels included in the biblical canon. In these documents we have a response and relationship to Jesus that was recognized and shared across the broad Christian community. My suggestion, however, is open to a more expansive understanding of "gospel."
[27] Johnson, *The Real Jesus*, pp. 133, 152.   [28] Ibid., p. 149.

Bibliography

PRIMARY SOURCES

CALVIN

Ioannis Calvini Opera quae supersunt Omnia. Edited by Wilhelm Baum, Edward
Cunitz, and Edward Reuss. 59 vols. *Corpus Reformatorum*: vols. 29–87.
Brunswick: C. A. Schwetchke and Son. 1863–1900.
Ioannis Calvini Opera Selecta. Edited by Peter Barth, Wilhelm Niesel, and Doris
Scheuner. 5 vols. Munich: Chr. Kaiser Verlag. 1926–52.

TRANSLATIONS

The Commentaries of John Calvin. 46 vols. Edinburgh: Calvin Translation Society.
1843–55. Reprint, Grand Rapids: Eerdmans, 1948–50.
The Deity of Christ and Other Sermons. Translated by Leroy Nixon. Grand Rapids:
Eerdmans, 1950.
Institutes of the Christian Religion. Edited by J. T. McNeill. Translated by Ford Lewis
Battles. 2 vols. Library of Christian Classics, vols. 20 and 21. Philadelphia:
Westminster Press, 1960. All quotations from the *Institutes* will be from this
text.

OTHER EARLY WORKS

Aquinas, Thomas. *Summa Theologica.* Blackfriars edition. New York: McGraw-Hill
Book Company, 1964–.
"The Incarnate Word," in *Summa Theologica*, vol. 48. Translated by R. J.
Hennessey, OP, 1976.
"The Grace of Christ," in *Summa Theologica*, vol. 49. Translated by Liam Walsh,
OP, 1974.
"The One Mediator," in *Summa Theologica*, vol. 50. Translated by Colman
O'Neill, OP, 1965.
Athanasius. *Orationes contra Arianos*, in *Athanasius.* A Select Library of Nicene and
Post-Nicene Fathers of the Christian Church, Second Series, vol. IV. Edited
and translated by Philip Schaff and Henry Wace. Edinburgh: T. & T. Clark.
1987.

On the Incarnation of the Word, in *Christology of the Later Fathers*. The Library of Christian Classics, Edward Rochie Hardy, ed. Philadelphia: The Westminster Press. 1954.

Augustine. *Confessions*. Translated by R. S. Pine-Coffin. New York: Penguin Books, 1961.

Bonaventure. *Hexaemeron*, in *Opera omnia*, vol. 5. Quaracchi: Collegium S. Bonaventurae, 1882–1902.

Commentarius in IV libros sententiarum, in *Opera omnia*, vol. 5. Quaracchi: Collegium S. Bonaventurae, 1882–1902.

Gregory of Nyssa. *Answer to Ablabius*, in *Christology of the Later Fathers*. The Library of Christian Classics, Edward Rochie Hardy, ed. Philadelphia: The Westminster Press, 1954.

Irenaeus. *Against Heresies*, in *The Apostolic Fathers with Justin Martyr and Irenaeus*. The Ante-Nicene Fathers, Alexander Roberts and James Donaldson, eds. Grand Rapids: Eerdmans, reprinted 1996.

John de la Rochelle. "Introduction to the Four Gospels," in *Franciscan Christology*. Damian McElrath, ed. St. Bonaventure, NY: Franciscan Institute Publications. 1980.

Justin. *Dialogue with Trypho*, in *The Apostolic Fathers with Justin Martyr and Irenaeus*, The Ante-Nicene Fathers, Alexander Roberts and James Donaldson, eds. Grand Rapids: Eerdmans, reprinted 1996.

First Apology, in *The Apostolic Fathers with Justin Martyr and Irenaeus*, The Ante-Nicene Fathers, Alexander Roberts and James Donaldson, eds. Grand Rapids: Eerdmans, reprinted 1996.

Second Apology, in *The Apostolic Fathers with Justin Martyr and Irenaeus*, The Ante-Nicene Fathers, Alexander Roberts and James Donaldson, eds. Grand Rapids: Eerdmans, reprinted 1996.

Origen. *Contra Celsus*, in *Fathers of the Third Century: Tertullian, Part Fourth; Minucius Fleix; Commodian; Origen, Parts First and Second*, The Ante-Nicene Fathers, Alexander Roberts and James Donaldson, eds. Buffalo: The Christian Literature Publishing Company, 1885.

Simons, Menno. *On the Incarnation of Our Lord*, in *Complete Works of Menno Simons*. J. C. Wenger, ed., L. Verduin, trans. Scottsdale, PA: Herald Press, 1956, 783–943.

Zwingli, Huldrych. *Writings*, vol. 1. Translated by E. J. Furcha. Allison Park, PA: Pickwick Publications, 1984.

SECONDARY SOURCES

Armstrong, Brian. "The Nature and Structure of Calvin's Thought According to the *Institutes*: Another Look," in *John Calvin's Institutes: His Opus Magnum*. Proceedings of the Second South African Congress for Calvin Research. Potchefstroom: Potchefstroom University for Christian Higher Education, 1986, 55–81.

Armstrong, Brian and Elsie Anne McKie, eds. *Probing the Reformed Tradition: Historical Studies in Honor of Edward A. Dowey, Jr.*, Louisville: Westminster/ John Knox. 1989.

Auer, Alfons. *Die Frommigkeit des Christen: Nach dem Enchiridion militis Chistiani des Erasmus von Rotterdam.* Dusseldorf: Patmos Verlag, 1954.

Auerbach, Erich. *Mimesis: The Representation of Reality in Western Literature.* Translated by Willard Trask. Princeton: Princeton University Press, 1968.

"Figura," in *Scenes from the Drama of European Literature.* New York: Meridian Books, 1959.

Baron, Hans. *The Crisis of the Early Italian Renaissance: Civic Humanism and Republican Liberty in an Age of Classicism and Tyranny.* Princeton, NJ: Princeton University Press. 1966.

Barth, Karl. *Church Dogmatics*, 1.2. Edited by G. W. Bromiley and T. F. Torrance. Translated by G. T. Thompson and Harold Knight. Edinburgh: T. & T. Clark. 1956.

Battles, Ford Lewis. *Interpreting John Calvin.* Edited by Robert Benedetto. Grand Rapids: Eerdman's, 1996.

"Calvin's Humanist Education," in *Interpreting John Calvin.* Robert Benedetto, ed. Grand Rapids: Baker Books, 1996.

"God was Accomodating Himself to Human Capacity." *Interpretation* 31 (1977): 19–38.

Bauke, H. *Die Probleme der Theologie Calvins.* Leipsig, 1922.

Benoit, Jean Daniel. *Calvin, Directeur d'ames.* Strasburg: Oberlin Press, 1947.

Bierma, Lyle D. "Federal Theology in the Sixteenth Century: Two Traditions?" *Westminster Theological Journal* 45 (1983): 304–321.

Bohatec, Josef. *Bude und Calvin: Studien sur Gedankenwelt des franzosischen Frühhumanismus.* Graz: Bohlaus, 1950.

Booth, Wayne. *The Company We Keep: An Ethics of Fiction.* Berkeley: University of California Press. 1988.

Bouwsma, William. *John Calvin: A Sixteenth-Century Portrait.* New York: Oxford University Press. 1988.

Breisach, Ernst. *Historiography: Ancient, Medieval, and Modern.* Chicago: University of Chicago Press. 1983

Brunner, Emil. *The Mediator: A Study of the Central Doctrine of the Christian Faith.* Olive Wyon, trans. Philadelphia: The Westminster Press. 1947.

Burke, Peter. *The Renaissance Sense of the Past.* London: Edward Arnold. 1969.

Butin, Philip Walker. *Revelation, Redemption, and Response: Calvin's Trinitarian Understanding of the Divine–Human Relationship.* New York: Oxford University Press. 1995.

Calvin, Jean. *Commentary on the Gospel according to John*, vol. 1. William Pringle, trans. Grand Rapids: Eerdmans, 1949.

Childs, Brevard. *Biblical Theology of the Old and New Testaments: Theological Reflection on the Christian Bible.* Minneapolis: Fortress Press, 1992.

Christ, Felix, ed. *Oikonomia: Heilsgeschichte als Thema der Theologie.* Hamburg-Bergstedt: Herbert Reich Evang. Verlag GmbH, 1967.

Church, F. *The Italian Reformers*. New York, 1932.

DeVries, Dawn. *Jesus Christ in the Preaching of Calvin*. Louiseville: Westminster/ John Knox, 1996.

Dominice, M. *L'humanité de Jésus d'après Calvin*. Paris: Je Sers, 1933.

Dorner, I. A. *History of the Development of the Doctrine of the Person of Christ*. D. W. Simon, trans. II, 2. Edinburgh: T. & T. Clark, 1866.

Dowey, Edward. *The Knowledge of God in Calvin's Theology*. New York: Columbia University Press, 1952.

"The Structure of Calvin's Thought as Influenced by the Twofold Knowledge of God," in *Calvinus Ecclesiae Genevensis Custos*.W. Neusr, ed. Frankfurt: Peter Lang, 1984.

Ferguson, Wallace, ed. *Facets of the Renaissance*. New York: Harper Torchbooks, 1963.

Fiorenza, Elisabeth Schüessler. *In Memory of Her: A Feminist Theological Reconstruction of Christian Origins*. New York: Crossroad, 1983.

Frei, Hans. *The Eclipse of Biblical Narrative*. New Haven: Yale University Press, 1974.

The Identity of Jesus Christ. Philadelphia: Fortress Press, 1967.

George, Timothy, ed. *John Calvin and The Church: A Prism of Reform*. Louisville: Westminster/John Knox, 1990.

Gerrish, B. A. *Grace and Gratitude: The Eucharistic Theology of John Calvin*. Minneapolis: Fortress Press, 1993.

"Atonement and Saving Faith." *Theology Today* 17 (July 1960): 181–191.

"'To the Unknown God': Luther and Calvin on the Hiddenness of God." *The Journal of Religion* 533 (July 1973): 263–292.

Gilmore, Myron. "The Renaissance Conception of the Lessons of History," in *Facets of the Renaissance*. Wallace Ferguson, ed. New York: Harper Torchbooks, 1963.

Giradin, B. *Rhétorique et théologie*. Geneva. Editions Beauchesne, 1979.

Greer, Rowan. *The Captain of Our Salvation: A Study in the Patristic Exegesis of Hebrews*. Tubingen: J. C. B. Mohr. 1973.

Grillmeier, Aloys, SJ. *Christ in the Christian Tradition*. Pauline Allen and John Cawte, trans. London: Mowbray, 1987.

Harbison, E. H. "Calvin's Sense of History," in *Christianity and History*. Princeton University Press, 1964.

Hayes, Zachary, O. F. M. *The Hidden Center: Spirituality and Speculative Christology in St. Bonaventure*. St Bonaventure, New York: The Franciscan Institute, 1992.

Hesselink, I. John. "Calvin und Heilsgeschichte," in *Oikonomia: Heilsgeschichte als Thema der Theologie*. Felix Christ, ed. Hamburg-Bergstedt: Herbert Reich Evang. Verlag GmbH, 1967.

Hoekema, Anthony. "Calvin's Doctrine of the Covenant of Grace." *Reformed Review* 15 (1962): 1–12.

"The Covenant of Grace in Calvin's Teaching." *Calvin Theological Journal* 2 (1967): 133–161.

Huizinga, J. *The Waning of the Middle Ages.* New York: St. Martin's Press, 1924.

Huppert, George. *The Idea of Perfect History: Historical Erudition and Historical Philosophy in Renaissance France.* Chicago: University of Illinois Press, 1970.

Jacobs, Paul. *Prädestination und Verantwortlichkeit bei Calvin.* Darmstadt: Wissenschaftliche Buchgesellschaft, 1968.

Jansen, John F. *Calvin's Doctrine of the Work of Christ.* London: James Clarke and Co., Ltd., 1956.

Johnson, Luke Timothy. *The Real Jesus: The Misguided Quest for the Historical Jesus and the Truth of the Traditional Gospels.* San Francisco: HarperCollins, 1996.

Jones, Serene. *Calvin and the Rhetoric of Piety.* Columbia Series in Reformed Theology. Louisville, KY: Westminster/John Knox Press, 1995.

Kelly, J. N. D. *Early Christian Doctrines.* New York: Harper and Row, 1960.

Krause, H.-J. "Calvin's Exegetical Principles," *Interpretation* 31: 1 (January 1977): 8–18.

Kugel, James and Rowan Greer. *Early Biblical Interpretation.* Philadelphia: The Westminster Press, 1986.

Lacugna, Catherine. *God For Us.* San Francisco: HarperSanFrancisco, 1991.

Landgraf, A. M. *Dogmengeschichte der Frühscholastik,* II.2. Regensburg: Friedrich Pustet, 1952–56.

Lillback, Peter A. *The Binding of God: Calvin's Role in the Development of Covenant Theology.* Grand Rapids: Baker Academic, 2001.

Martines, Lauro. *Power and Imagination: City-States in Renaissance Italy.* New York: Vintage Books, 1979.

McElrath, Damian, ed. *Franciscan Christology.* St. Bonaventure, NY: Franciscan Institute Publications, 1980.

McKie, Elsie Anne. "Exegesis, Theology, And Development," in *Probing the Reformed Tradition: Historical Studies in Honor of Edward A. Dowey, Jr.* Brian Armstrong and Elsie Anne McKie, eds. Louisville: Westminster/John Knox, 1989, 154–172.

Millet, Olivier. *Calvin et la dynamique de la parole: Etude de rhétorique réformée.* Paris: Librairie Honoré Champion, Editeur, 1992.

Momigliano, Arnaldo. *The Classical Foundations of Modern Historiography.* Berkeley: University of California Press, 1990.

Muller, Richard A. *Christ and the Decree: Christology and Predestination in Reformed Theology from Calvin to Perkins.* Durham, NC: The Labyrinth Press, 1986.

The Unaccommodated Calvin: Studies in the Foundation of a Theological Tradition. New York: Oxford University Press, 2000.

Neuser, Wilhelm. "Calvins Verständnis der Heiligen Schrift," in *Calvinus Sacrae Scripturae Professor: Calvin as Confessor of Holy Scripture.* Wilhelm Neuser, ed. Grand Rapids: Eerdmans, 1994, 41–71.

Calvinus ecclesiae Genevensis custos: International Congress for Calvin Research. Edited by Wilhelm Neuser. New York: Lang, 1984, 273–287.

Calvinus Sacrae Scripturae Professor: Calvin as Confessor of Holy Scripture. Grand Rapids: Eerdmans, 1994.

Niesel, Wilhelm. *The Theology of John Calvin*. Harold Knight, trans. Philadelphia: The Westminster Press, 1956.

Oakley, Francis. *The Western Church in the Later Middle Ages*. Ithaca: Cornell University Press, 1979.

Oberman, Heiko. "The 'Extra' Dimension in the Theology of John Calvin." *Journal of Ecclesiastical History* 21:1 (Jan. 1970): 43–64.

Parker, T. H. L. *Calvin's Doctrine of the Knowledge of God*. Edinburgh: Oliver and Boyd, 1969.

    Calvin's New Testament Commentaries. Louisville: Westminster/John Knox Press, 1971.

    Calvin's Old Testament Commentaries. Edinburgh: T. & T. Clark, Ltd., 1986.

Peterson, Robert. *Calvin's Doctrine of the Atonement*. Phillipsburg, New Jersey: Presbyterian and Reformed Publishing Company, 1983.

Puckett, David. *John Calvin's Exegesis of the Old Testament*. Louisville: Westminster/John Knox, 1995.

Raitt, Jill. "Calvin's Use of *Persona*," in *Calvinus ecclesiae Genevensis custos: International Congress for Calvin Research*. Wilhelm Neuser, ed. New York: Lang, 1984, 273–287.

Schellong, Dieter. *Calvins Auslegung der synoptischen Evangelien*. Munich: Chr. Kaiser Verlag, 1969.

Schreiner, Susan. *The Theater of His Glory: Nature and Natural Order in the Thought of John Calvin*. Grand Rapids: Baker Academic, 1991.

    Where Shall Wisdom be Found? Chicago: University of Chicago Press, 1994.

Sobrino, John. *Jesus the Liberator: A Historical–Theological Reading of Jesus of Nazareth*. Paul Burns and Francis McDonagh, trans. Maryknoll, NY: Orbis Books, 1999.

Stephens, W. P. *The Theology of Huldrych Zwingli*. Oxford: Clarendon Press, 1986.

Stroup, George. "Narrative in Calvin's Hermeneutic." *John Calvin and The Church: A Prism of Reform*. Timothy George, ed. Louisville: Westminster/John Knox, 1990.

Torrance, J. B. "The Concept of Federal Theology – Was Calvin a Federal Theologian?" in *Calvinus Sacrae Scripturae Professor: Calvin as Confessor of Holy Scripture*. Wilhelm Neuser, ed. Grand Rapids: Eerdmans, 1994, 15–40.

Torrance, T. F. *The Hermeneutics of John Calvin*. Edinburgh: Scottish Academic Press, 1988.

Tylanda, Joseph. "Christ the Mediator: Calvin versus Stancaro." *Calvin Theological Journal* 7 (1972): 5–16.

    "The Controversy on Christ the Mediator: Calvin's Second Reply to Stancaro." *Calvin Theological Journal* 8 (1972): 131–157.

Van Asselt, Willem J. *The Federal Theology of Johannes Cocceius (1603–1669)*. Raymond Blacketer, trans. Leiden: Brill, 2001.

Van Buren, Paul. *Christ in Our Place: The Substitutionary Character of Calvin's Doctrine of Reconciliation*. Edinburgh: Oliver and Boyd, 1957.

Weir, David. *The Origins of Federal Theology in Sixteenth Century Reformation Thought*. Oxford University Press, 1990.

Wendel, François. *Calvin: The Origins and Development of His Religious Thought.* Philip Mairet, trans. New York: Harper and Row, Publishers, 1950.

Widdicombe, Peter. *The Fatherhood of God from Origen to Athanasius.* Oxford University Press, 1994.

Williams, Rowan. *Arius: Heresy and Tradition.* London: Darton, Longman, and Todd, 1987.

Willis, E. David. *Calvin's Catholic Christology: The Function of the So-called "Extra Calvinisticum."* Studies in Medieval and Reformation Thought, vol. 2. Leiden: E. J. Brill, 1966.

'Rhetoric and Responsibility in Calvin's Theology," in *The Context of Contemporary Theology: Essays in Honor of Paul Lehmann* (Atlanta: John Krox, 1974), 43–64.

Witte, Johannes. *"Die Christologie Calvins." Das Konzil von Chalkedon: Geschichte und Gegenwart,* vol. 3. Edited by Aloys Grillmeier and Heinrich Bacht. Wurzburg: Echter-Verlag, 1954.

Wolter, Allen. "John Duns Scotus on the Primacy of the Personality of Christ," in *Franciscan Christology.* Damian McElrath, ed. St. Bonaventure, NY: Franciscan Institute Publications, 1980.

Zachman, Randall. *The Assurance of Faith.* Minneapolis: Fortress Press. 1993.

"Jesus Christ as the Image of God in Calvin's Theology." *Calvin Theological Journal* 25: 1 (April 1990): 46–52.

Index